TOO CLOSE TO THE SUN

THIS BOOK is about and belongs to BUZZIE

At the White
House
Feb. 20, 1935

TOO CLOSE
TO THE SUN

Growing Up in the Shadow of My
Grandparents, Franklin and Eleanor

CURTIS ROOSEVELT

PublicAffairs
New York

Published in the United States by PublicAffairs™, a member of the Perseus Books Group.

All efforts have been made to contact the copyright holder of each image in this book.
Picture Editor: Vincent Virga

Credits for photos on pages ii–iii:
Top left, Sistie and Buzzie sliding on the White House lawn: Franklin Delano Roosevelt
    Library, Hyde Park (FDRL)
Middle left, boarding the bus: Author's collection
Bottom left, snowball fight on the White House lawn: FDRL
Top right, riding in the car with FDR: FDRL
Middle right, playing with the fort: Author's collection
Bottom right, Buzzie with Eleanor Roosevelt, Sistie, and Johnny: FDRL

PublicAffairs books are available at special discounts for bulk purchases in the U.S. by
corporations, institutions, and other organizations. For more information, please contact
the Special Markets Department at the Perseus Books Group, 2300 Chestnut Street,
Suite 200, Philadelphia, PA 19103, call (800) 810-4145, ext. 5000, or e-mail
special.markets@perseusbooks.com.

Designed by Brent Wilcox
Text set in 12.25 Fairfield Light

Library of Congress Cataloging-in-Publication Data
Roosevelt, Curtis, 1930-
    Too close to the sun : growing up in the shadow of my grandparents, Franklin and
Eleanor / Curtis Roosevelt. — 1st ed.
        p.   cm.
    Includes bibliographical references and index.
    ISBN 978-1-58648-554-2 (hardcover : alk. paper)
    1. Roosevelt, Curtis, 1930–Childhood and youth.   2. Roosevelt, Franklin D. (Franklin
Delano), 1882–1945.   3. Roosevelt, Eleanor, 1884–1962.   4. Grandchildren of
presidents—United States—Biography.   5. Grandparent and child—United States—Case
studies.   6. Presidents—United States—Family.   7. Presidents—United States—
Biography.   8. Presidents' spouses—United States—Biography.   I. Title.
E807.1.R345A3 2008
973.917092—dc22
[B]
                                                                                        2008033994

10 9 8 7 6 5 4 3 2 1

To my sister, with whom I shared
my strange and wonderful childhood

PREFACE

I was born five and half months after Black Tuesday, when the crash of the New York Stock Exchange in October 1929 paved the way not only for the Great Depression but also for the election of my grandfather as president of the United States. My mother, Anna Roosevelt Dall, my sister (also named Eleanor but known as "Sis"), and I soon joined my grandparents in their new residence, the White House, in the wake of my parents' separation. We needed a roof over our heads, my mother explained. History had my family in its grip, and I had no choice but to go along for the ride.

When he took office in 1933, replacing the far-from-charismatic Herbert Hoover, Franklin Delano Roosevelt instantly claimed center stage, as he always had. At home in the White House as no other president before him, he projected a natural, seductive radiance that no one could resist. Everyone around him, from the most distinguished members of his circle to his young grandchildren, became supporting players. We were all more than willing to bask in his limelight.

For our part, my sister and I instantly turned into the country's "First Grandchildren." Though we were used to the intrusions of waving newspaper reporters and the flare of flashbulbs, moving from New York to the White House family quarters was something else altogether. The press milked the phenomenon of the towheaded Roosevelt moppets, and we became a full-blown, pint-sized double act. My family called me Buzzie, and our tabloid moniker became "Sistie and Buzzie"— pronounced as one word, Sistie-and-Buzzie. Soon we were as familiar as five-year-old movie star Shirley Temple to a nation hungry for distraction from breadlines and boxcars.

During the twelve years of my grandfather's tenure as president, Sis and I bounced from coast to coast, following our mother's criss-crossing path. She had remarried in 1935, and in 1937 we moved to Seattle so that she and my stepfather could work for William Randolph Hearst's *Post-Intelligencer*. Throughout this time, we returned regularly to the White House and to the Roosevelt family home at Hyde Park, New York. Any sense I had of routine and stability was rooted in those two places. The Big House in Hyde Park and the White House were, I felt, my real homes. As a teenager they were more than that; they were my school. I received my real education by listening closely to my grandparents and their friends conversing over the dining room table.

Franklin and Eleanor Roosevelt were my Papa and Grandmère, and they were the most influential figures in my life. Both of my maternal grandparents possessed complicated natures; they were difficult to penetrate. Still, for me they were human beings, not mythological figures. Moreover, they became, for me, surrogate parents, as was my great-grandmother, Sara Delano Roosevelt. I can still clearly recall my grandmother's meaningful glances when I became too enthralled with some White House ceremony—such attention was for the president, I was reminded. And I can hear my grandfather's comical readings of the "funnies" as we sat on his bed while he ate breakfast each morning, his aides standing around laughing at FDR's hamming it up.

I inhabited my grandparents' world from the time I was three until I was fifteen. It was an immense and wonderful privilege. Yet the experience, as one might expect, had a double edge. All of the people important to me during my childhood, indeed everyone in the orbit, were strongly affected by living and working so close to the magnetic personalities of my grandfather and grandmother. I was no exception. Life outside the protective—and isolated—White

House cocoon became hugely distorted, especially for an impressionable youngster like me. My early surroundings provided not only excitement and comfort but also a reality-rejecting sense of specialness, which did not stand me in good stead as I grew older.

Intoxicated by the exhilarating environments of Washington and Hyde Park, I created a dream world that protected me—and became a form of addiction. In fact, as I grew older, I found it easier to inhabit this fantasy world than to develop and nurture my own strengths and talents in the real one. It has taken me a lifetime to understand my role as a tiny planet circling the dual suns of my grandparents and to accept and adjust to a world devoid of their reflected glory. Change has come only rather recently—and it continues.

While writing this memoir, it has been a godsend to have all of my family's correspondence gathered in one place: the Roosevelt Library at Hyde Park. As I sort through photographs and letters from the early, formative period of my life, I can still feel the force of my grandparents, their irresistible allure—and its disabling effects.

I remember the thrill of standing next to my grandfather as he reviewed the 1937 inaugural parade, taking off my cap whenever he did to greet the color guards of soldiers, sailors, and marines. I also remember the sorrow of leaving the White House after that inauguration, and the long train ride across the country, which felt like being exiled. It is hard, even from this distance, to break free entirely from the perspective I had at the time, or the feelings. So I am taking readers along with me, stepping through the gates of time into the distant world that formed me.

My family just after FDR's election (1933).

My family near the end of FDR's life (1945).

In our new home—My sister stands with our grandfather and our mother on the White House South Portico. I am in my grandmother's arms.

ranklin Roosevelt took the oath of office on March 4, 1933, becoming the thirty-second president of the United States. He was fifty-one years old and had been active in politics since 1910, when he'd won a seat in the New York State Senate. My grandfather had made his first visit to the Executive Mansion when he was just a little boy—about the same age that I was when I moved into the White House. He was accompanying his parents, James and Sara Delano Roosevelt, to see President Grover Cleveland. Family lore has it that when he was introduced to the president, the president responded with one of those pleasantries called for in such circumstances. Looking down at young Franklin, Cleveland said, "And perhaps you might one day become president."

Apparently FDR, a doted-upon only child, took the avuncular prediction to heart. Twenty years later, as a law clerk in New York City, he confided to his colleagues at Carter, Ledyard & Millburn that he hoped one day to be elected president of the United States.

By 1920, that goal appeared to have a chance of being realized, the irony being that it followed a resounding defeat. After campaigning across America with Ohio governor James M. Cox, the Democratic presidential nominee who'd made him his running mate, FDR was now a truly national figure. It didn't matter that the Cox-Roosevelt ticket had been defeated in a landslide, with almost double the number of voters preferring Republican Warren Harding, also of Ohio. What counted was that my grandfather's goal of returning to Washington—where he'd earlier served eight years as assistant secretary of the navy in the Woodrow Wilson administration—was potentially in his grasp. He had only to channel his political ambitions and take advantage of the political opportunities that now would present themselves. He was still a young man, just thirty-eight years old. He could run for president in 1932; 1936, even 1940, was hardly out of the question.

But tragically, within ten months my grandfather's glorious career plan slammed against the seemingly impenetrable wall of cruel fate. In August 1921, while vacationing with his family in Canada on Campobello Island in the Bay of Fundy, he began to complain of stiffness and chills after a swim in the bay's frigid waters. The next day, one leg weakened, and then the other. Within three days he could not stand; he had been stricken with polio.

My grandfather's political peers, Democrats and Republicans, allies and enemies alike, considered him finished, their fixed belief being that a cripple could never be elected to office. The physical tragedy seemed immutable, and the political consequences devastating.

For the next six years, FDR tried, in vain, to surmount the obstacles created by paraplegia, desperately willing himself to feel the least sensation in his withered legs—to just wiggle a toe! During this period, anyone watching him couldn't help but note his enduring courage and consistently upbeat attitude. But admired as he was, there was all too often a shade of condescension. This must have been especially hard for him to take from his political friends.

My grandfather was a realist. The limitations arising from the fact of his paralysis were obvious to everyone, most of all to him. But something—I see it as just plain stubbornness—kept him from ever seeing himself as a has-been. To serve his country as president remained a private goal from which he never truly wavered. All through those discouraging years, as he strove ceaselessly, valiantly, to regain the use of his legs, he was also making what efforts

FDR on crutches greeting Governor Al Smith (far right) on Hyde Park's front terrace in 1924, three years after my grandfather had been seized with polio. George Lynn and John W. Davis are on either side of FDR.

he could to keep himself alive politically. To accomplish this, he enlisted the help of his wife, Eleanor Roosevelt, to carry his message. At first, she hesitated, uncomfortable in front of audiences, but then she gradually came to embrace the challenge, and shortly became a political figure in her own right.

My grandparents, who were fifth cousins, had had their first adult encounter at a reception given at the White House in 1902 by President Theodore Roosevelt, who was my grandmother's uncle and also a fifth cousin to my grandfather. As FDR resolutely navigated the long passage of a political career that would culminate in the presidency, my grandmother went gamely along, proving to be more than equal to the challenge.

Eleanor Roosevelt was also a realist. While she did not believe her husband would ever be able to return to active politics, she was determined to help him stay engaged in a world that meant so much to him—and, indirectly, to her. The idea of Franklin as a semi-retired invalid was impossible to countenance.

Nor could my grandmother imagine herself trapped in the role of dutiful wife, living with her disabled husband and his mother on the family's country estate, Springwood, at Hyde Park. Having borne six children—five surviving—before the age of thirty-one, she was more than ready to move beyond the wholly domestic sphere.

FDR's braces are clearly visible as he poses with his wife and mother after his election as governor of New York State in 1928. My grandfather had found that the voters ignored his being a cripple.

As a result of the hundreds of meetings Eleanor attended and the many, many speeches she gave in her husband's stead, FDR's views on important matters were "out there," and with his intensive correspondence, my grandfather's name remained before the public. Her work on behalf of her disabled husband, of course, soon propelled Eleanor Roosevelt onto her own very public path. Within five years, she would become a political pro, chairwoman of the women's committee at the 1924 Democrat's national convention, well before my grandfather reentered politics. Soon she was making more money than he was, mostly from writing magazine articles.

Undoubtedly convinced it was now or never, my grandfather agreed to join the fray in 1928, and to everyone's surprise, including FDR's, he won the governorship of New York State. That he could not walk seemed not to have bothered most voters. However, to men like the outgoing governor, Al Smith, he was still just a cripple. Recognizing this, FDR pushed aside the help Smith pressed on him—a rejection that his predecessor much resented—and entered the governor's mansion in Albany with his own agenda and his own staff. Reelected two years later with

My family, all dressed up for church, standing under the south portico of the White House in 1933.

a substantial plurality, my grandfather had regained, amazingly, a position within shouting distance of the 1932 Democratic presidential nomination.

The nomination fight was a closely fought battle at the convention in Chicago, but FDR managed to fend off fierce challenges from other Democratic contenders (including Al Smith) and went on to claim his party's top prize. As the Democratic candidate for president, he then proceeded to defeat the Republican incumbent, Herbert Hoover, at the polls in November.

Inauguration Day, 1933, was cold and blustery. Standing on the south portico of the Capitol in Washington, Franklin Delano Roosevelt raised his right hand to take the oath of office. It must have been a day of triumph. FDR's personality, radiant and exuberant, came across in his inaugural address. I think that the hope he instilled in people had its source in his ability to overcome the despair he felt when faced with the paralysis he could not surmount. FDR had spent years passing through the fires of frustration and had survived. His faith and confidence, given the devastating circumstances and the barriers aligned against him, were seen by the American people as a sort of supraconfidence that was beyond depletion—or so it seemed.

⸻

From the first moment in residence, our grandfather felt totally at home in the White House. It was more complicated for my mother, my older sister, and me. We arrived in 1933, when I was three years old, leaving my father behind in New York. Our mother, Anna, was Franklin and Eleanor's eldest child and their only daughter. She had four younger brothers—my uncles James, Elliott, Franklin Delano Jr., and John. At twenty-seven, she had been married for six years, a wife and mother no longer used to living under her parents' roof. Yet all through her marriage she had clung to her Roosevelt identity—as she continued to do all her life.

My mother may have been delighted at the thought of living in the White House, but I was not without anxiety. Neither "Washington" nor the "Executive Mansion" had any clear location in the geography I understood as a three-year-old. Since my birth in Manhattan, I had regularly moved up and down the Hudson River, alternating between the family's estate at Hyde Park, under the supervision of my great-grandmother, Sara Delano Roosevelt (whom we called Granny), and our family house in the city on East 65th Street, with my mother and grandmother. When we traveled from one home to the other, my nurse—our anchor—accompanied my sister and me.

My father lived at the 65th Street house too, though it was plain to the family that my parents were already well into the process of separating. He and my mother had owned a handsome place in Tarrytown, but they had been forced to sell it when the stock market crashed. For financial reasons, they were now compelled to share our family house in New York City.

The push for "separation," I'm told, was instigated by my mother. After the loss of the Tarrytown house, things continued downhill. My father, Curtis Dall, lost nearly everything during the Great Depression, even his seat on Wall Street's stock exchange, and he was without any real leverage. Moving in with his mother-in-law was not to my father's liking—he and my grandmother didn't get along well—but he had no choice if he wanted to hold his family together, and he very much did.

While my father wasn't alone in his financial difficulties—many Wall Street brokers found themselves in the same position—his consistently poor judgment in financial matters meant he never really got back on his feet.

My mother had moved to the White House with her parents after the inauguration, but my sister—and thus I, too—had stayed in New York so she could complete the academic year at her school. (My grandmother was a co-owner of Todhunter School and taught there as well.) In early September of 1933, after spending the summer with Granny at Hyde Park, Sis and I took a train from Poughkeepsie to New York City with my nurse, Beebee, then a taxi from Grand Central Station to Pennsylvania Station, and finally a train to Washington. Accompanied by Secret Service men the entire way, I was relieved when we finally arrived. My mother would meet us, we'd been told—and there she was, waiting at Union Station.

A White House limousine awaited us too. Mummy, Sis, and I lolled in the nice leather backseat as we made our way toward the White House. Beebee was so far away in the front seat with the chauffeur that I had to shout to her through the glass partition separating us. The Secret Service officers went ahead of us in their own car, one that had a flashing red light. We headed up Pennsylvania Avenue and turned left into the circular drive of the White House, stopping under the north portico.

My grandmother was there waiting for us, along with a number of ushers and White House staff. At six feet tall, Grandmère, as we called her, seemed like a colossus to a little boy. All the adults in my family seemed to be very big people. Still, I felt better for seeing her there.

Impressive as the White House was, at three years old I found nothing out of the ordinary about an imposing house with a large, gracious staff. We'd always lived in such places, and there had always been a staff—nursemaids and cooks, chauffeurs and gardeners—to see to the household's needs. I was quite accustomed to my life of privilege.

The Big House, home to all of the Roosevelt family.

Yet, for me, a dark cloud lingered behind all the excitement that accompanied the move to Washington. Increasingly over the previous couple of years, the time my sister and I had spent with our father was separate from time spent with our mother. I remembered little else, so I didn't take it amiss. And time spent with our parents was not unlike "visitations," always scheduled. But when we came to Washington without Dad—and it had been made plain to me that he wasn't included—it made me uneasy.

CHAPTER 2

AUTHOR'S COLLECTION/FDRL

Traditionally, the third floor of the White House was reserved for children and servants. Our quarters there were very like our nursery at Hyde Park, although a big difference for me was that there was less light; the windows in my bedroom were small and placed high on the wall, so I could see only the sky and a bit of the balcony. When people walked out on the balcony—which they did every morning and evening to raise and lower the American flag—I could see only their legs.

We have arrived—Sis and I on the South Lawn of the White House with my mother's dog, Chief.

That's because the third floor was set back and lower than the decorative balcony that surrounds the top of the White House.

My sister and I quickly became acquainted with all the rooms in the White House. Our floor on top was fairly simple. The second, reserved for the family, was grander, with some lovely large rooms, such as my grandfather's beautifully proportioned oval study with its portrait of my grandmother, dressed in a light blue evening gown, hanging over the entranceway. The second floor's furnishings—some of which were pieces my grandmother had requisitioned from a government warehouse— echoed the comfortable but rather dowdy style we were used to in the Big House at Hyde Park or in the family's house in New York City.

Sis and I were very impressed by the White House first floor, which boasted a large reception area leading to the red-carpeted hall hung with immense portraits of previous presidents. Each painting seemed four or five times my height! There was the majestic ballroom, called the East Room, with an enchanting chandelier, and at the other end of the hall, the wood-paneled State Dining Room next to the private family dining room. In between were the Green Room, the Blue Room, and the Red Room—furnished accordingly, of course. We were impressed.

More exciting to me was the basement, which in those days consisted of a hodgepodge of rooms, some rarely used. With Beebee in tow, I kept discovering new ones. Next to the infirmary, where FDR's personal physician, Dr. Ross McIntyre, eased the president's congested sinuses at the end of every day, was a little room without windows. Turning on the light, I discovered my grandfather's collection of model ships. I couldn't wait to tell my mother about my find! But when I shared my wonderful news with her, she forbade me to enter the room again. When I told Papa (our name for our grandfather), his response was to laugh, saying I could visit the room whenever I wanted. If I was very careful, I could pick up some of the models of the more modern navy ships—but not the sailing ships with their intricate rigging.

At the beginning of World War II, this small room would be converted into the president's Map Room, and the model ships would be removed to the just-completed Roosevelt Library at Hyde Park. Before they were dispatched in late 1939, my grandfather selected two navy cruisers, the *Houston* and the *Indianapolis,* vessels he'd actually traveled on, and asked the White House carpenter to mount them in a two-foot-long glass case for my Christmas present. I was over the top!

Next to my bedroom on the third floor, the male servants, married or not, had their own quarters, behind a louvered door that was always closed. It was off-limits to me, but I could smell the tobacco and aftershave lotion and could hear their laughter and "carrying on," as the women servants called it. The women were at the other end of the floor, always quiet among themselves. Marguerite "Missy" LeHand, my grandfather's secretary, also had her rooms on the third floor.

Both the men and women had a gentility of manner, formal but easy. It seemed to me a happy atmosphere, full of life, much jollier than anything I'd experienced before. The staff on our family's estate at Hyde Park, kind as they were, expected us always to know our place, just as they did. Children were at the bottom of the pecking order, and armed with this instinctive awareness, Sis and I were well schooled in politeness and understood perfectly how to behave. One knocked and waited, for example, at the entrance to the pantry for Ward, Granny's English butler, to open the door. But the atmosphere was different at the White House. The openly expressed affection of the butlers, maids, and all the people who worked there was quite beyond anything I was accustomed to. With Sis and me, the servants would banter, tease, and laugh, making ordinary things, such as serving our meals or overseeing my eating, into an enjoyable game.

Ever since I could remember, I'd been in the care of a black nurse. Christened Betty, she was known to us all as Beebee. I loved her dearly. I remember her by the starched white uniform she wore—an expanse of which was always at my eye level. I also remember that the hairs from a mole on her face tickled my cheek as she held me close. At the White House, she seemed to have a world of her own, now that there were other people like her. She seemed more at ease than she had in New York City or at Hyde Park, and this set a comfortable tone for me in my new home.

Whenever my mother or grandmother appeared on our third floor, or whenever Sis and I descended to their second-floor domain, a mantle of "propriety" seemed to drop into place. Beebee and the other black servants did so automatically, gracefully shifting into higher gear. I intuitively grasped that more formal behavior was called for in the company of adults. Form and style, rituals of behavior, had always dominated—and always would—my relationships with mother, father, uncles and aunts, grandmother, grandfather, and great-grandmother—literally *all* adults. It was easy to adapt to, not oppressive, simply what we were used to.

There in the White House, Sis and I found two old friends. One had worked as a butler for my mother and father in New York. His name was James Mingo, though we always called him Gogo. (Fifty years later I met him again in Washington to reminisce. He had become a well-respected figure in the African American community in the city and was directing a large charitable organization.) We also knew well the wife of my grandfather's valet. Her name was Elizabeth McDuffie, but everyone, including our grandparents, called her Duffie. She usually stayed with me when Beebee went on vacation.

We all referred to Duffie's husband as *Mister* McDuffie, because that's what my grandmother called him. I later realized that she chose this unusual formality as a way of indicating her disapproval of his drinking. His fondness for the bottle eventually caused his dismissal after he was unable to pull himself together one night in time to help my grandfather get ready for bed, forcing my grandmother to do it. It was not an easy chore, even for a six-foot woman, assisting a cripple who can't walk, or take off his shoes and socks, or get to the bathroom on his own.

In many ways, the members of the White House staff were the only friends Sis and I had. We had very little contact with other children, and I had almost no idea how boys and girls actually played and got to know each other. My sister was pretty much my exclusive playmate, and I hers. She resented it—rightfully—since the difference between a three-year-old and a six-year-old matters to the six-year-old. And she let her impatience with me show by acting the bully. Fortunately, Beebee was always around to intervene, and Sis would be told to "be nice."

On special occasions, other children were imported into the White House. The *New York Times* would reliably report the names of "guests" attending our birthday parties—along with their nannies—to share cake and table favors. Of course, under the eagle eyes of all the nurses and governesses, decorum mostly ruled. Not much spontaneous fun was to be had. Even so, I remember my excitement when hide-and-seek or blindman's bluff was scheduled at our rare social events. I truly was like someone released for a few hours from a highly controlled institution. I also remember my mother's nervous observation to Beebee that "Buzzie's getting overexcited." She made such remarks often enough that I learned to control my enthusiasm, lest I be withdrawn to watch from the sidelines.

⸻

At the White House our days were organized into a routine that most children today would find utterly foreign. Yet, for us, it was comforting and completely secure. We knew what we were to be doing nearly every moment from morning till night—and who was to be in charge.

Beebee and I shared my bedroom. Every morning around 7:30 A.M., she got me out of bed and took me into the bathroom. There she washed me, dressed me, and combed my hair. (She was, herself, already impeccable in her starched uniform.) My sister got herself washed and dressed alone, although Beebee brushed her hair. Breakfast arrived at 8:15, encased in a large, wheeled cart that had hot water compartments for warming our scrambled eggs, bacon, and toast. The White House kitchen was in the basement, and we would hear the creaky old elevator, installed in President Cleveland's time, wheezing up its shaft to the third floor, and then the door very slowly clanking open. Pushing it out of the elevator was invariably a familiar smiling face whom we would greet loudly.

Even today I can remember the fascination that the rolling cart held for me and still feel its allure. It measured about 2 feet by 3 feet and must have been 5 feet high, standing on its large wheels. That is to say, it was nearly twice my height. I loved studying its numerous compartments with lids that slid up or down or sideways to reveal yet more storage space. Endless possibilities! I imagined it would make a great playhouse, one you could push around from place to place. To get me to eat my breakfast, Beebee had to tear me away from my exploration of this wondrous contraption.

It wasn't only our schedules that had a clockwork aspect. Life at the White House, in general, was all about routines. There was the president's schedule, the First Lady's schedule, the housekeeper's schedule, the servants' schedules, mealtimes, menus, and the schedules of guests, as well as the comings and goings of the other residents. The one keeping track of all this was the usher on duty. He could tell you where anyone was at any given time, who was coming to which meal, the hour any event was scheduled, who was out and who was in. Naturally, having such serious duties to perform, he was white.

There was no joshing with the usher. I remember one man in particular, a Mr. Crim, formal and aloof, with a detached air befitting his position. He and the housekeeper, Mrs. Nesbitt, were the only White House staff of whom I was in awe. I don't remember either of them ever smiling, other than politely. When one of them did "smile," it resembled more a gesture like a nod, say, than an expression of pleasure.

After breakfast, still on schedule, we'd be taken down to my grandfather's bedroom on the second floor, the "family floor." FDR regularly began the working day by convening his close aides in his bedroom, even before he'd finished with his breakfast tray. In this casual setting the work of that day was discussed, the schedule reviewed, persons to be seen would have their ration of time allotted, and lists were drawn of urgent telephone calls Papa was expected to make. It was a serious work session, but it was peppered with flip remarks and easy laughter. My grandfather loved conviviality and surrounded himself, whenever possible, with people who could share his innate sense of amusement about life. Following his lead, they would tease among themselves.

My sister and I were familiar with most of the people around the bed from earlier encounters at Hyde Park or Albany. They'd known us since we were born, and we'd become almost mascots. They were like extended family, and they were treated that way by my grandmother and grandfather.

Missy, FDR's personal secretary, was even closer than "extended" family—she was more like actual family. She had been my grandfather's secretary during his 1920s campaign for the vice presidency and resumed this role during the years he was trying to recover from polio and keep himself in the game politically—which meant streams of letters to write, FDR's method of keeping in touch with politicians around the country. She always had a room in the house when work-

And they teased him, too!—For FDR's birthday party his coterie, family and staff, dressed in Roman togas, paying obeisance, I suppose, to the emperor.

ing with my grandfather, and one in the governor's mansion in Albany, just as she now did on the third floor of the White House. Grandmère called her "Missy," but she always called my grandmother "Mrs. Roosevelt."

This "court" of people attending my grandfather in the mornings sounds more like a *levée* of Louis XIV than a twentieth-century staff briefing, but it was the style of work that best suited my vibrant, inquisitive grandfather. It reinforced a sense of intimacy and belonging for the immediate staff and made the loyalty they felt more like that of family than employees. In this setting, he was never aloof or distant—not with us, nor with them.

The arrival of "Sistie-and-Buzzie" was always expected. We entered boisterously, to be greeted with equal noise by our grandfather and the group standing around his simple, double bed. There he lay, propped up with lots of pillows, usually wearing an old, nondescript pullover sweater. When Sis and I entered, the work stopped. It was our turn with "the Boss." We hopped up onto Papa's bed, one of us on either side of him. My grandfather seemed to savor the few minutes of silliness with my sister and me as much as we did, and the staff were free to join in the fun. The fact that the occasional morning visitors—like Dean Acheson, then assistant secretary of the treasury, who had to set the price of gold every day with the president's approval—were not equally amused by such playful goings-on didn't trouble FDR. Papa often read "the funnies" aloud, an entertainment enjoyed by us children and the adults alike. His comic intonations and emphases often made for sly allusions that went over our heads, but I loved the guffaws of laughter all around me.

After chatting with Papa on his bed, we'd be fetched by Beebee, who was standing in attendance outside his bedroom. She would enter, bob to my grandfather, and whisk us out. She then shepherded us next door to my grandmother's quarters to say good morning. Grandmère used the large room as a study and sitting room, and the corner dressing room as her bedroom.

Despite the fact that she was a lot less jolly than Papa, we wouldn't have missed the opportunity of seeing Grandmère every morning. Even as children we could feel her own brand of magnetism, and we saw plainly how other people responded to her. I couldn't help but be aware that my grandmother was someone "important," for my own mother behaved as if this were so and, indeed, seemed often in awe of her.

My grandmother was charming, gracious, and always sincerely concerned, yet understanding how to entertain a three-year-old and a six-year-old—how to enter their world and enjoy their pleasures—didn't come as easily to her as it did to Papa. There remained a reserve within her—even when she obviously cared for and loved someone—that kept her from ever releasing herself totally with another human being. It was a wall that was always there.

After the more subdued audience with my grandmother, Sis and I went off to see our mother in the rose-colored suite—in size, a duplicate of my grandmother's—at the opposite end of the family floor of the White House.

(Queen Elizabeth occupied this room with her lady-in-waiting when she and George VI visited America in 1939. Winston Churchill also used it—his bodyguard replacing the lady-in-waiting—during his wartime visits.)

With Mummy we could be easier. Sometimes she would read to us from a book she was working on about a rabbit named Scamper who lived in the White House. *Scamper: The Bunny Who Went to the White House,* which was published in 1934, and its 1935 sequel, *Scamper's Christmas,* were both illustrated by noted children's book artist Marjorie Flack. In these books, my mother, whose previous writing career included contributions to such magazines as *Liberty* and *Cosmopolitan,* made Scamper the pet of two White House grandchildren called Babs and Dave. Everyone knew who they were meant to be. Dave was the older and Babs the younger, but the trick of reversing the children's ages was so transparent that I made the connection without a thought. When Grandmère wrote a book a few years later titled *Bobby and Betty Come to Washington,* the same subterfuge was attempted, though again with little success!

A water color—a little damaged after all these years. A Walt Disney artist painted this and presented it to my mother after she published her books about Scamper, the White House rabbit. Disney has Mickey Mouse introducing Scamper to Minnie, Pluto, and the Three Little Pigs.

Mummy and my sister had a particularly strong rapport, and I felt—indeed I knew—they shared confidences that excluded me. The three years difference in age between me and Sis inevitably made for difficulties as I sought my own place in both the small family structure that was the three of us and the larger one that was my grandparents' household. The fact that I was a boy, too, put me outside the intimacy my sister had with our mother.

After spending a short time talking or reading to us, Mummy would turn to Beebee to review the day's plans. She mostly offered instructions about what we should wear and what would be expected of us. My mother usually spoke *about* us but not *to* us, over our heads, as if we were not there. Sis and I were quite accustomed to her speaking about "the children" in the third person. Children raised as we were had, in effect, two mothers: one, our nurse, accompanying us through our daily life, and the other, our mother, the higher authority, with whom we had intermittent and usually scheduled contact.

Sometimes as a very special treat our grandfather might join Sis and me for lunch. On these occasions we usually ate on the sun porch, weather permitting; it was a room built to take advantage of the occasional bright days of Washington's winter. As Sis and I normally used it as a playroom, Papa's coming to lunch meant we had to put everything tidily away. He would arrive on the elevator just ahead of the food trolley and would be wheeled onto the third floor and then up the ramp—installed to accommodate his wheelchair—to the table.

Sis and I had been raised in the tradition of not speaking to adults unless spoken to, but during these special times with Papa, we could be silly and spontaneously rattle on as we wished. Like no other adult in the family, he let us enjoy with him something more like the teasing, laughing relationship we had with "our gang," the butlers and maids of the White House.

FDR had a particular fondness for Duffie, who always found a reason to bring us something special, usually a treat she'd baked herself, when Papa was our noontime companion. They gleefully competed for our laughter—for each was a talented storyteller—and they adored heaping on the outlandish details, often about Sis and me, making rich capital of the simplest of incidents. A decade later, Duffie would be tending to FDR at Warm Springs when he died in April of 1945.

Everything proceeded like clockwork for the rest of the day, from teatime to supper to bedtime, which came very soon after we ate. If I dawdled too long over my food, there'd be no time for playing. Saying good night was another family ritual. When I'd been tucked in, Beebee would "send word." This message was passed to Papa's study on the second floor, where the cocktail hour was underway, then to Grandmère in her study. My grandmother picked up my mother and Missy from FDR's study, and they proceeded upstairs. Gathered around my bed, each intoned her wish that I should sleep well, kissed me, and then returned downstairs.

My first memory of putting my foot in my mouth occurred in front of this little delegation. I'd noticed that Missy had a little dark fuzz on her upper lip, and when she bent over to kiss me good night, I took it into my head to announce, "Missy has a mustache!" Nobody knew quite what to say, and there was embarrassment all around.

If anyone read to me before bed, it was Beebee. Some nurses possess the quality of love that comes naturally, and Beebee was one of them. My mother, as a child, had had an unfortunate experience with a nurse, an experience she never forgot, and her sense of the episode's unfairness still resonated whenever she recounted it to us. The problem had been that the nurse repeatedly combed her hair so roughly that it hurt. Yet when she finally complained to her mother, Grandmère didn't know how to respond, except to consider carefully her daughter's story.

There were many considerations to weigh. Was the woman actually cruel, or was my mother just trying to get attention? And how might this episode be handled without undermining the nurse's authority? Rather than show instinctive concern, my grandmother chose instead to reflect thoughtfully on her daughter's professed victimhood. As it turned out, the nurse was later dismissed for what was considered a valid reason—liquor was found in her bureau drawer—but she was never confronted about her tyrannical attitude. In the meantime, my mother continued to learn about endurance.

My grandmother wrote candidly, and with regret, about having been afraid of her own children's nurses, of feeling that they knew so much more than she did about raising children. In situations where expressions of maternal sympathy might have come naturally, she fell back upon the rationalization of "not knowing how to do it." She saw caring for children as something one had to learn how to do—not a matter of instinct but as if it were something one needed to learn from books written by experts. In fact, she consulted the physician L. Emmett Holt, whom she proclaimed "the greatest baby doctor of that period." Dr. Holt's best-selling book, *The Care and Feeding of Children*, published in 1894, was full of discipline and regularity, all very reassuring to mothers like my grandmother who were trying to maintain some control over their lives.*

An only child, FDR was very close to his mother, Sara Delano Roosevelt.

For my mother, discipline began when she was still in her crib. She had to have her hands tied to its sides because it was suspected she might be "touching herself." And such discipline was also applied to me. When I was a baby, I sucked my thumb. To solve the problem, my mother got little metal cages for my thumbs from the pediatrician, and they were put on when I was settled in my crib. Stubbornly, I sucked my thumbs through the cages.

My grandmother's arm's-length relationship with her children was not unusual in families where mothers could afford to hire surrogates to carry the daily burdens of child care. In contrast, Sara Delano Roosevelt, known as

---

*Geoffrey Ward, *A First-Class Temperament: The Emergence of Franklin Roosevelt, 1882–1905* (New York: Harper & Row, 1989), p. 50.

Granny to all of us, had a natural, confident relationship with her only child. She picked up my grandfather all the time, and she bathed him herself, while the nurse stood by, her role limited to passing a towel and making appreciative noises about the little boy.

My mother did try to bridge the gap between herself and my nurse. She would surprise us and appear at mealtimes or sometimes join Beebee giving us our baths before supper. She was concerned with our habits, our routine, and our welfare. But following her mother's lead, she focused primarily on the "things" in our lives, the happenings, the details of our schedule, the checklist she reviewed with Beebee during our morning visit as the two of us stood by, impatiently waiting to be dismissed.

My mother understood, in principle, that to give her children love was important, and she did attempt to do so. But it's difficult when one has had little experience oneself of both giving and receiving love. Mummy's love emerged "thoughtfully," as her own mother's had been. Reflecting back, I recognize that both of them were put off by easy spontaneity. Perhaps it was threatening. (My mother admitted that watching people performing on the stage sometimes caused her embarrassment.)

My grandmother had well-formulated ideals for raising children, most likely a reaction to the rigid, confining upbringing she'd endured, a childhood typical of her class and era. Grandmère felt children should be allowed to think for themselves and, as much as possible, to make decisions for themselves. Her aim was to see them develop as individuals and not necessarily as their elders might dictate. At least, that was the desired objective. Yet, this seems to me a veneer, an intellectual cover for my grandmother's difficulty in being close to others.

More viscerally, my grandmother seemed to have felt strongly that too much loving attention could actually *inhibit* a child from achieving the independence needed as he or she matured. A boy or girl who received too much attention might fail to develop the fortitude, discipline, and self-sufficiency needed to become a successful person.

In practice, pursuing such an ideology requires a mindfulness, and a managing, of the amount of love that might be good for a child. It insists that a parent maintain a careful observation of a child, continually adjusting the kind and quality of attention required. For example, if Sis or I, or any child, seemed unhappy, my grandmother would carefully ask what the problem was, listen, and then offer advice, expressing a level of caring and love that would be, she felt, appropriate.

I remember well her reaction when, one morning not long after our arrival at the White House, Grandmère found me on the second floor, whimpering and, she thought, causing a nuisance. Unable to get any response about what was causing me to make such a fuss, she informed me that if I wanted to cry I should find a bathtub to do it in. It was undoubtedly a pat maternal phrase she'd heard long ago, but I must have looked at her with bewilderment. Later that day, as she was showing some visitors the Lincoln Bedroom, my grandmother heard sorrowful noises coming from the adjacent bathroom. With guests in tow, she marched in to find me sitting in the bathtub and, as she told the story, "crying his heart out." It became an oft-repeated tale used to put her guests at their ease, a useful icebreaker.

When she told the story, her sympathy was obvious. But there was no sign of actual empathy, no identification with my very real misery at the time. What she offered as a response in no way resembled the comfort I was seeking. Most likely I was sent back to my nurse.

As she reports in her memoirs, my grandmother had found her own childhood devastating. Over the years, I listened to her tell story after story about herself as a young girl. Timorous and fearful, she was plagued by inhibitions, patterns of behavior, she said, that she carried throughout her life. There was no question about her receiving proper care in her household, but this attention was not accompanied by her mother's love.

The paradox is that my grandmother's lasting reputation rests upon the broad concern she evinced for others, those expressions of perceived empathy and her genuine desire to be of service. She was loving and yet detached at the same time. Empathy eluded my grandmother when it came to family members, or anyone else for whom she felt responsibility. She was much more at ease with people who were simply her friends, and she was even less inhibited with strangers. I remember my mother and uncles making sotto

In this strange and unusual picture Eleanor Roosevelt formally poses as Whistler's Mother. One Christmas she gave each of her children, my mother and her four brothers, this photograph, beautifully framed—with absolutely no explanation. When asked about it Grandmère would only smile enigmatically.

voce remarks about this contradiction. In books my uncles James and Elliott later wrote—*My Parents: A Differing View* (1976) and *Mother R: Eleanor Roosevelt's Untold Story* (1977), respectively—both complained that they never felt really cared for, loved, in the way they yearned for.

My grandmother wrote with keen insight about herself: "There is something locked up within me." I know the pattern all too well. It is my inheritance. Only recently have I been able to let go of this canned variety of behavior. Indeed, I might never have known the difference—the merits of being spontaneous or, occasionally, downright silly—had it not been for those relationships that were the exceptions in my young life, the ones I enjoyed with my nurse, my grandfather, and his mother, my Granny.

My father was officially part of the president's family for FDR's first Inauguration on March 4, 1933. He poses with my sister in front of the White House, but, at my grandmother's direction, he wasn't allowed inside. Note my sister's inauguration medal.

CHAPTER 3

Just when my parents first separated is unknown to me. Being compelled to sell their fine house in Tarrytown may have initiated their separation. But my father still joined in the family pictures taken during Papa's presidential campaign in 1932 and through his first year of office, when I was two and three years old. There was a period when the Dall family had no choice but to live in the red brick house my grandparents owned at 49 East 65th Street. It was a double house and adjoined the city residence of Papa's mother. My room was in her part of the house, so I did not even know whether my mother and father shared a bedroom. In a letter to FDR dated November 29, 1932, my great-grandmother refers to "keeping my fourth floor room for Anna and Curtis" (my parents; not me and Sis), but this may have been wishful thinking on Granny's part.

At some point, probably after my grandfather was elected president, Dad moved out, and the separation became public. But, as Dad was still in the city, Sis and I saw him frequently, and even when we were at Hyde Park, he visited us.

He remained on good terms with both Papa and my Granny. My great-grandmother sympathized with my father, writing to FDR that "everything seems to have gone against him."* Indeed my father had become her executor at some point and remained so until she died. She loaned him money with no expectation that he would pay it back. Even after my mother had been separated from Dad for a couple of years, FDR wrote to him in a warm tone, inviting him to Hyde Park "for a leisurely chat."

The supposed case against my father—beads on a thread strung together by my mother and grandmother—I find impossible to interpret. According to my mother, she'd married Dad to get away from a stressful and complicated home life. She reported to my sister and me that "she wanted to get out of the house," and our father was the first person "to come along."

Decades later, my half brother, John R. Boettiger, researched our mother's early life for a book he wrote about the relationship between her and his father, my stepfather, John Boettiger.** By his account—and I trust it—our mother, a young debutante, had plenty of suitors, a whole host of young men to choose from. Mummy always emphasized to me and Sis that she detested "the whole debutante thing." She *had* been something of a tomboy, but the evidence also shows that she eagerly made the social rounds, attended the house parties and dances, typical of her set—the social activities our grandmother felt were so frivolous.

Curtis Bean Dall, my father, was born in New York City and grew up in New Jersey. He served in the U.S. Navy during the First World War and then attended college at Princeton. He graduated in 1920, after which he took a job in a Wall Street bank.

My parents met at a charity ball in 1925, an encounter that obviously made enough of an impression on my mother for her to invite him to her family's house at Hyde Park for the upcoming New Year's weekend. She was a lanky blonde who'd been nicknamed "Anna Banana" by her boarding school chums. Twelve years her senior, Curtis Dall must have seemed to her attractively mature. He was then working for Lehman Brothers and had an air of established security.

---

*Letter to FDR, October 15, 1934.
**John R. Boettiger, *A Love in Shadow: The Story of Anna Roosevelt and John Boettiger* (New York: Norton, 1978).

Had her eyes been fully open, my mother might have been able to see that, quite soon, she'd be expected to be just like the other wives in the set to which they belonged, a comfortable upper-middle-class world of lawyers, bankers, and brokers. But she was young, and there was the excitement of being engaged; suddenly she felt very grown up.

They married in a ceremony at St. James Church, our church in the town of Hyde Park, in June 1926, two years before FDR was elected governor of New York. My parents settled into suburban respectability in Tarrytown, a Westchester County village that every weekday morning saw a good portion of its male citizens depart on the train south to Manhattan's financial precincts. My parents' life together was heavily weighted in favor of all the things Dad loved to do—Princeton football games and hunting trips among them.

Happier days—our mother and father skiing at St. Moritz.

But after four years, something in my mother's sense of herself shifted. Her acceptance of the new role she'd been playing as the young commuter's wife fell away. Along with this vanished her rebellion against her mother. Making a 180-degree turn, my mother now wanted to be engaged in "the issues of the day," the very things that had made her mother a well-known figure.

I imagine that my grandmother fully approved, applauding her daughter's new attitude. Indeed, by this time, she was fully launched on the path that made her not just a national figure but a role model for women.

Typical of his generation, my father's unthinking paternalism had turned into fresh cause for rebellion. Their orderly, predictable life had become just as confining in its own way as the parent-dominated existence that my mother had rejected.

My mother soon found she had even more cause for disenchantment with my father and their marriage. Humiliatingly, my father lost his seat on the New York Stock Exchange, while owing a great deal of money to a cousin, Henry Parish (my godfather), with only a slightly smaller debt to my grandfather. Not all of Dad's financial debacle could be blamed on the country's economic woes, either. Although risk-taking *is* what stockbrokers do, in my mother's and grandmother's view, his behavior had been reckless, and there was no debate. Throughout my childhood, Mummy often spoke of my father as being "irresponsible."

Long afterward, Dad himself would be able to laugh at an incident that had occurred when he was flat broke and living at the Roosevelt family house in New York City. At the time there wasn't anything funny about it. As Dad told it, his much younger brother-in-law, James, whom I knew as Uncle Jimmy, had been given $1,000 by Granny for a summer vacation in Europe. Jimmy asked my father if he couldn't quickly double his money on the stock exchange. Dad cautioned him that such a move would be like gambling, more like roulette than investing. Fine, said Jimmy, assuring my father he was quite willing to risk it.

The money was lost. The next morning, over breakfast, my grandmother confronted Dad. "Curt, I hear you've lost Jimmy's money for his summer trip. Don't you think you should pay it back to him?" My father understood that this was, in fact, not a question but a command. "Yes, Mama," answered Dad, only hesitating briefly. He knew he had no choice in the matter and that excuses or explanations were not wanted, just the money—which my father then had to borrow. I'm glad my father eventually could laugh at this story, but the fact was that my grandmother and mother chose to see Dad's financial downfall as a moral shortcoming, one that helped justify their hostile attitude toward him.

My own emotions regarding Dad were always inhibited by the way my mother and grandmother had closed ranks against him. As early as I can re-member, I knew Dad was out of favor. Sis sided with my mother and grand-mother, adopting their attitude toward him. Their hostility was opaque, but it permeated the air when they spoke of my father. Since their approval was of paramount importance, I had to learn at an early age to curtail or hide my af-fection for him.

Although Dad made persistent efforts to spend time with Sis and me, they were usually met with rebuff and procrastination. Visits were granted only grudgingly. Despite this, he took the two of us nearly every summer during the 1930s to Plum Lake, Wisconsin, to a private island retreat owned by the family of his friend Willis Wilmont, which we adored. Once, when Mummy mentioned that Dad wanted to spend time with us, I clapped my hands in glee at the thought of visiting Plum Lake. No one said a word. My sister and mother looked at me as if I'd just spilled my milk all over the table.

Canoeing at Plum Lake with Dad.

Fantastic! Owning a whole island. The Wilmot's place, Plum Lake, Wisconsin, where Sis and I spent many lovely visits with our father.

The warnings about my father, the constant hints that I must avoid becoming anything like him, must have been upsetting, but they were so much a regular part of my diet that I wasn't aware of any grinding in my stomach. Playing to her audience, my sister would grimace and groan whenever he was mentioned. I once overheard my mother remark, as she nodded toward me, "Well, he does carry his father's genes!" I instinctively understood the implications. And so did my sister. Out of Beebee's earshot, Sis would cap our frequent disputes with her most potent barb, "You're just like Dad!" Not knowing what to reply—not *really* knowing what it meant—I'd begin to cry.

Even my nickname was a way to create distance from Dad. Nicknames for children are ordinary enough, but in my case, my own name was also that of my father. Once Granny was visiting us and wrote to Papa, "I got here yesterday about 5 and was glad to find little Eleanor and Curtis (he says he does not wish to be called "Buzzie" or "Sonny" as I called him *once*, but prefers *Curtis*)." But this preference was short-lived. My first name was rarely acknowledged by any of them. "You wouldn't want to be called Curtis, would you?" my mother once asked me. (Things weren't complicated for Sis. She was another Anna Eleanor Roosevelt, the third in line, with each generation alternating in the use of Eleanor or Anna.)

So I was Buzzie Dall, and when we began using my stepfather's name, I turned into Buzz Boettiger. I had been christened Curtis Roosevelt Dall, but as a child, I never used the middle name of Roosevelt, only my initial "R." When I first began attending public school, the name that went at the top of the page for my written work in class was Curtis Dall, but all the teachers were instructed by my mother to call me Buzzie. They were told that we didn't use my first name at home and that I didn't like it.

I was a teenager, close to eighteen, before I understood why my nickname was so important to everyone—why "Curtis" was so persistently sidelined and "Buzzie" so firmly established. And it was not until the end of 1948, when my mother's divorce from John Boettiger was pending, that I, at the suggestion of my grandmother, stopped using both my father's and stepfather's names and legally took the name Curtis Roosevelt.

<hr />

While Dad was the father I was expected *not* to care for, and certainly *never* to emulate, his four rambunctious younger brothers-in-law exhibited such perpetually boyish charms that they'd always be forgiven, whatever their missteps. Dad was more stolid than my uncles, dull in comparison—not a playboy, not a heavy drinker.* When Mummy's brothers spent money irresponsibly, the most they'd ever suffer was a mild slap on the wrist.

During my first year at the White House I saw my two youngest uncles, Franklin Roosevelt Jr. and John Aspinwall Roosevelt, whenever they came home from college and prep school for holidays. Nineteen-year-old Franklin was in his second year at Harvard, and John was a seventeen-year-old senior at Groton when we first moved to Washington. Both of these uncles had spent their very early years in Washington when FDR was assistant secretary of the navy during the eight years of Woodrow Wilson's presidency. They'd always divided their time among several places: the family houses in New York City, Hyde Park, Campobello, and when they were old enough, their boarding school, Groton. So "home" was where their parents were, and the White House was no exception.

Franklin Jr. and John were rowdy and full of themselves, and they brought a raucous energy to the normally sedate Executive Mansion. Living such an unsettled life in an ever-shifting landscape, they must have found it necessary to make their presence felt, laying their tracks firmly in whatever turf was beneath their feet.

<hr />

*At their wedding, among my father's written instructions to his ushers was one titled DRINKING: "Ushers will please carry out my feelings in this matter, which are pretty well known, namely, that if any drinking is to be done at all at the dance Friday night or at any other time during the wedding festivities, it is to be of the most conservative nature."

Papa was often amused by the stories of their antics. During the 1933 inauguration festivities, for example, Franklin Jr. "borrowed" a motorcycle policeman's bike to tour Washington, an episode that became part of family lore, much embellished by my mother. My grandmother, however, was less amused, particularly when it came to her sons' drinking and all-night partying. After we'd moved into the White House, Grandmère made the Monroe Room on the second floor the family sitting room and had its antiques replaced by more sturdy furniture. "What was there looked to me too fragile for my husky sons, and I had visions of its being broken," she wrote.

If I was thought to be "too big for my britches," I was only following my uncles' model—Franklin and John on holiday in Hawaii, 1934.

Eleanor later acknowledged her inability to control the boys' early teenage aggression, describing scenes that obviously alarmed her. This was especially true of Franklin and John, who hit puberty when their father was often absent, with my grandmother left to tend the household. Eleanor's own schedule of meetings and speeches took her, too, away from home. Given to speeding, often after too much partying, the Roosevelt boys amassed more than their share of tickets and didn't take kindly to police reminders that, as the sons of the president, they should be setting a better example. My uncles had gotten to the point where they expected instant recognition—and special treatment. Woe to the White House guard who didn't recognize them returning to the fold from their carousing just as the sun was coming up and demanded identification at the front gate.

My two elder uncles, Jimmy and Elliott, who were twenty-six and twenty-three respectively, visited less often. They were much less boisterous but equally loud. For all four brothers, chasing girls and drinking were their favorite pastimes, and as my mother noted in later years, the alcohol they consumed made them more crude than charming. My mother, seeking her mother's approval—and already cast in the role of staid mother of two, despite being just twenty-seven years old—weighed in with exasperated criticism. As both women were concerned about "things getting out of hand," my own behavior was closely monitored. "Buzzie's getting overexcited" constantly hung over my head.

Though confused by what I heard about my uncles and their excesses, I found my mother's brothers fascinating and made them my idols. And the truth was, so did my mother and grandmother. My uncles' high spirits triggered a double standard in my matriarchy. Speaking out of both sides of their mouths, they voiced sharp criticism while at the same time exhibiting tolerance for, and even a riveted fascination with, what "the boys" got up to.

I'd hear my mother repeating their latest scrapes—often belligerent encounters with intrusive photographers or strangers who recognized them—voicing a disapproval that then turned into giggles and an exchange of amused glances. Once I heard Grandmère regale guests with an anecdote in which teenaged Franklin Jr. held John by the ankles out of a fourth-story hotel window during a European tour. It had so horrified the spectators below that they had called the police. My grandmother's response to her sons' antics was always a mixture of amusement and fear. Both she and my mother shrank from any overt expression of conflict, and even avoided using any tone of voice that might offend someone.

Nevertheless, I instinctively took in their ambivalence. And from as early as I can remember, I took their attitude to be indirectly aimed at me. All of their eye rolling, clucking, and tsk-tsking, their little barbs about male behavior, were meant for my edification, as well as their own amusement.

I grew up afraid of anything resembling violence. My mother instructed Beebee to keep me well clear of Franklin and John when they were roughhousing. I didn't mind; their shouts and wrestling bewildered and frightened me. I had never encountered anything like it. Everyone else in my life was gentle, rarely raising their voices, and I had no experience of the normal scrappy way that kids sort things out when left to themselves. More important was the message that I was supposed to develop differently. I wasn't to be like my uncles (nor like my father). So I took seriously being "a good boy." I knew on which side my bread was buttered. I wanted my ladies' approval.

Though I constantly struggled to control myself in order to please my mother, my grandmother, and even Sis, in the end, the one I really admired the most was my grandfather. He was my ultimate father figure, the male image I couldn't help but want to emulate. But I knew enough not to reveal this!

CHAPTER 4

AP IMAGES

I first saw this picture of us a few years ago, on the front page of Barcelona's *La Vanguardia*, published in 1933. The fame of "Sistie and Buzzie" had spread across the Atlantic. I like the vintage automobiles.

Being allowed to join our grandfather on any outing was always the biggest and best treat for Sis and me, even going to church. What excitement there'd be on a Saturday when my mother announced we'd be going with Papa and Grandmère the next morning! It meant dressing in my best, which in winter was a heavy coat and leggings, gloves, plus a beret on my head. No matter how cold the weather was, underneath I wore short trousers. I wasn't allowed my first pair of long ones until I was ten. My outfit was invariably all navy blue, from head to toe, even my mittens, the monochromatic effect relieved only by gold buttons. Bundled up, my sister and I looked like two Humpty Dumptys reporting for Arctic duty. We were always too warm.

More often than not, we drove in the open car with my grandfather, his vehicle leading the cavalcade. The drive from the White House to the Episcopal Church on Lafayette Square took only a few minutes, but if we were going to the National Cathedral, the ride was longer. Even though we were just going to Sunday services, people we passed waved and cheered. FDR waved back, doffing his hat. We children, however, were most decidedly not to wave back, on our mother's orders. The cheering, she said, was for my grandfather and didn't include us. It seemed to me that it did include us—I could hear my name shouted—but her damper detracted very little from my pleasure.

We were escorted by four motorcycle outriders, and their deep rumble was exciting. If we slowed down for a major road crossing, a couple of the Secret Service men from the car immediately behind us would jump forward to lope along beside the president's car, at which moment my grandfather would exchange a smiling "Good morning!" with the men trotting beside us. As we again sped up, they'd fall back to their own car, jumping in as it gathered speed. The whole performance took less than a quarter of a minute. Mummy, who was often anxious that things might somehow go wrong, always worried that one of the men would fall when getting into their moving car on the run and be hurt.

Often when we were returning from our excursion, Papa would order the car to slow down to twenty miles per hour. He wanted to be able to look around at the people on the streets and sidewalks. He loved commenting on the passing scene and pointing out to Sis and me pedestrians he found especially interesting, including ladies in funny hats. Sis and I also loved the rare opportunity to stare; so much of our lives were spent being polite and *not* staring. Staring, we'd been instructed, was rude.

My grandfather's personal bodyguard, Gus Gennerich, would've been sitting on the front seat next to Monty Snyder, the chauffeur. A former New York City cop, Gus was big and husky but agile, and he would be the first one out when we arrived at the church. Upon arrival, as there was usually no one in the jump seat in front of him, Papa could hitch himself forward, stretching to push out his legs and snapping their steel braces in place. Gus then opened the rear car door, which was hinged from the back rather than the front, making it much easier for my grandfather to get in or out.

Gus would step partway into the car, putting his arm under his charge's outstretched arm. Together they lifted up and then turned, and—hey presto!—my grandfather was on his feet, a smile on his face, his hand reaching out, making greetings all around. Simultaneously, Gus would put FDR's cane into his right hand and then take my grandfa-

Nobody could imagine the fifteen seconds of precise drill that enabled FDR to be on his feet, appearing as he wanted to appear. Grandmère, Granny, Papa, and Gus.

ther's left arm—never for a moment letting go of him. My grandfather's balance was so precarious that a strong gust of wind or a too-enthusiastic handshake could topple him.

If one of my uncles was home, he'd substitute for Gus, having familiarized himself with the necessary maneuvers. Papa moved himself forward in such a way that it appeared he was walking, yet there was always a robotic quality that was unmistakably the gait of a cripple. He lurched forward, steadied himself, and lurched forward again. Going up steps was more than even his hard-won skills could manage. He had to be carried or else have a ramp in place for his wheelchair. Within the church, FDR, with Gus at his side, would silently inch his way up the long center aisle to the first pew. The march was tedious for everyone, not least for the strong-willed man making it. Walking on steel braces that put your entire weight on your bones—ankles, knees, and hips— is painful. But since I'd seen him do no other sort of walking, it all seemed quite normal to me.

None of the arrangements devised to accommodate his useless legs, particularly when he was in public, were foolproof. There was always the chance of a misstep. Just imagine smiling, confident, in-control FDR spilling to the floor, unable to get up without several people helping. It was the scenario Papa most dreaded, and it happened only once that I know of. He knew he was continually vulnerable.

What amazes me now is that even though my grandmother and her children frequently assisted FDR, none of them—indeed none of us watching— understood that FDR was, in fact, *not* walking. Technically, he always required tripartite support: his own legs encased in braces, a cane, and someone on his arm. (Sometimes he would put his hand out, supporting himself on some solid immovable object such as a tree or, if he was addressing an audience, a podium.) When FDR had scheduled public appearances, my grandmother would discuss arrangements with the Secret Service. Yet my family's assumption was that their patriarch *could* walk, albeit in a very wooden way.

In the 1994 television documentary *The American Experience: FDR,* Geoffrey Ward revealed that my grandfather had learned from his Warm Springs physical therapist how to propel himself forward. Papa practiced this slow, swinging gait, but we now know that he wasn't actually walking but rather mimicking what walking looks like. In the end, it seems that not only my family but the public simply chose not to dwell on a much loved and respected figure's disability.

Often when my grandfather made public appearances, Sis and I served as a distraction. When we arrived at church, getting FDR out and standing erect took about fifteen seconds from the time Monty stopped the car until the president was fully upright for the hellos. They were, however, long seconds, and during that time the receiving delegation—clergy and other dignitaries—

would try not to look too closely at their handicapped president. Averting their eyes, they'd wave at my grandmother, or perhaps make a bland remark to someone else in the group, or watch and comment on Sis and me. As we made our way down the aisle, people around us were probably torn between watching the president's jerking progress, with the obvious risk of his falling at every step, and the domestic spectacle that my sister and I presented as we struggled with our nurse's help to get out of all those warm clothes.

Whether in public or in private, people seemed to understand instinctively that my grandfather wanted his physical condition ignored and that he wished to be treated as if everything were quite normal. In all the years I was around him, I never heard a soul make a comment about this handicap, at least, not within his earshot. The subject was considered private, and not just because he was president. It would have been the same if he'd never left Hyde Park. I feel it was a matter of pride, his attitude toward his crippled legs. My grandfather, like my grandmother, disdained self-pity.

FDR wore his braces only when he absolutely had to. Most often we saw him with his lifeless legs crossed, their thinness plainly visible through the drape of his trousers. Sis and I knew never to sit on his lap. The wheelchair was used only when Papa had to be moved from one place to another. He never sat in it; it was too uncomfortable. He simply used it as a vehicle. Sis and I might surreptitiously watch Papa's careful shift, a flip really, from chair to wheelchair and back again, but for the two of us, it was a routine we witnessed daily. We never talked about it, not even to each other.

I revered my grandfather. And I was in a position to watch a coterie of others trying out for the acolyte role, always jockeying to be close to him. The adulation in which Papa basked looked wonderful to me. I couldn't help wanting to be like him, and since I lived in the White House, opportunities to bask in his glow abounded. On Sundays after church, for example, Sis and I would be called outside to pose for the newspaper photographers. "Just one more!" was

FDR, after his election as president in 1932, leaving for vacation on Vincent Astor's yacht. The owner (a distant cousin) is holding my hand aloft, something I resented greatly—as if I didn't know how to wave to the photographers! Raymond Moley, a principal member of FDR's "Brain Trust," is on the far left.

the repeated cry. Most often, Sis and I stood next to Papa. We were, of course, well behaved, proper, not calling attention to ourselves, though I couldn't help but grin.

While my grandmother, my mother, and my sister professed to find little enjoyment in the spotlight, I had to "mind my manners." In contrast to my sister, who was going through an awkward stage of childhood, I was a sweet-faced, outgoing blond toddler. I was continually being petted and fussed over—and I loved every minute. I grinned, jumped up and down, and liked to chatter. Sis resented the adult smiles that I seemed to get more than my fair share of, and I was an easy target for her bullying.

Like my uncles, I thought it was fun to be pursued by press photographers! And Papa seemed to enjoy all the excitement. The trouble was that I had a different part to play, one more suited to a little boy. If I seemed to enjoy the public attention—if I ever smiled or waved—the ruling matriarchy that ran my life was swift to notice. I was told that I should take my sister's modesty and reticence for my model instead. This didn't make very much sense to me. I enviously observed the way my uncles were allowed to puff themselves up as they gathered around their father, sharing his aura and getting away with it. But the family party line—at least where I was concerned—was that "we" didn't like photographers and that "we" went to endless trouble to avoid them. Newspaper reporters were included in this category, too. "The goldfish bowl"—my family's term for that glare of public scrutiny to which all presidential households must submit—was a reality of my childhood. For example, if Sis and I were playing together, a small crowd might gather outside the gates to watch us on the White House South Lawn. Someone might shout "Sistie!" or "Buzzie!" Embarrassed, we would retreat to a secluded area where we had a swing and a jungle gym.

Our grandmother had gone to great trouble to install a swing there for us. She wanted it hung from a branch of one of the big trees, just like our swing at Hyde Park. When she broached the matter, making what she thought was a simple request of the White House garden staff, she was informed that permission would have to be sought from the government agency responsible for the grounds surrounding all official buildings. In the end, permission was denied. To put spikes in a tree trunk to hold the ropes of a swing, came the reply, would deface the tree. Grandmère was appalled. To her it seemed the height of bureaucracy-run-amok, and so she mentioned it to Papa one night at dinner. He thought it pretty funny. In the end, we got our swing, but it hung from a metal stand.

Sis and I weren't always protected from public solicitations in our outdoor play area, though. When we reported these to our grandmother, she made us understand that the White House was government property and that we lived there only because Papa had been elected president. What she implied was that the public had every right to watch us. Or that's the message I got. To make her point she would invite press photographers to snap pictures of Sis and me playing together. She or my mother would escort them to us personally, and Sis and I would obediently perform. I'd get in the swing and my sister

"For the next picture, Sistie, you push Buzzie."

would push it, or Grandmère would push. Not very exciting—but it probably looked "cute" if you were seeing it in the newspaper. Beebee, my nurse, stood off to one side, where she wasn't visible. In the background, my mother and grandmother replied guardedly to reporters' questions about us.

My grandmother rationalized these public "snapshots" by explaining that people needed some distraction from the hardships they were suffering in the Great Depression. Besides, we were living in the White House; being available to the press was a matter of obligation—our family duty. I came to know that obligations, even ones I couldn't grasp, were very important to my grandmother.

Sis and I never saw our press clippings. The family line was that it was better for us to be kept in the dark about our popularity and the constant exposure "Sistie-and-Buzzie" received. The guarded and fenced-in White House was essentially our cocoon. Yet, despite being sheltered, Sis and I knew the score. Our early fame coincided with the era of the Dionne quintuplets and with America's little sweetheart, Shirley Temple. Though our backgrounds couldn't have been more different, and though we were told that *they* were celebrities and *we* were not, to the world at large we were just a different variety. There'd always be that moment when we'd be spotted in a railway station or in a hotel lobby. "There's Sistie and Buzzie" would be the shout.

We were also clued in to our burgeoning popularity by the White House guards and Secret Service. To them it was only to be expected that the president's grandchildren, living in the White House, were sought after by the media. My nurse and all the other servants also took for granted my eagerness for recognition, my pleasure at people's interest in me, treating my youthful enthusiasm with amused tolerance. In fact, *anyone* working in the Executive Mansion gained distinction, since a position there was much more than an "ordinary" job.

Living at the White House seemed full of compromised pleasures, delights given with one hand and denied with the other. The nuanced, sometimes hypocritical stance that my mother and grandmother adopted toward the press quite confused me. Papa didn't have to apologize for enjoying the attention. But my father's similar pleasure in his status was one of

"*There's Sistie-and-Buzzie!*"

the charges against him, and sometimes it seemed as if his outstanding sin might have been the enjoyment he had felt at being the president's son-in-law. It stung to overhear whispers that Buzzie's untoward behavior "had been inherited from his father."

Thus, I was painfully aware that the enormous joy any proximity to my grandfather gave me was ultimately considered "not good for Buzzie." I tried to watch my step, to quell my vulgar desire to be a part of it all. I learned to mask my real feelings. I lived with a kind of duality—how I felt *and* how I knew I must appear to feel.

AW, GEE, GRAN'POP, YOU'RE RUNNIN' OVER INTO ED WYNN'S PROGRAM!

My sister's and my behavior, as presented in *Esquire*, is rubbish. If we'd said anything like that, we'd have been sent immediately to our rooms!

CHAPTER 5

Whatever our schedule, no matter how occupied with another activity, one thing Sis and I did every day was change for teatime. Until I was about five, I usually put on a sailor's suit, which was the standard dress-up outfit for boys, the same outfit my grandfather had worn at that age.

This late afternoon occasion was always a very important part of any Roosevelt household's schedule. Tea at Val Kill with Grandmère, tea at Hyde Park with Granny, tea at our 65th Street house in New York, or being taken "to tea" at the home of some family friend or relative—no matter where we were, teatime was an *event,* and its place was well established in our lives.

Sis and I dressed to be presentable.

Our grandfather dressed to be presentable.

My grandmother's tea at the White House took place in the West Hall, between her rooms and the Lincoln Bedroom suite on the other side. Although it was only late afternoon, the evening shift of waiters was on duty in their starched fronts with white ties and tails. (The daytime shift wore dinner jackets and black tie.) They served from behind a large screen at the entrance to the West Hall, keeping everything moving at the proper pace. When the guests first arrived, they ushered them in and announced each one's name. The atmosphere was a mixture of formality and informality, with Grandmère setting the tone. She definitely presided, but her overriding concern was making sure people felt at ease.

What mattered most to us, aside from the pleasures of such staple treats as the delicious pound cake and—my own favorite—cinnamon toast, was the opportunity for Sis and me to join the adults. Otherwise, we rarely ate with our family. Our grandfather wasn't often present at tea, as he stayed in his office until about 6:00 P.M. Perhaps on a Sunday, when he didn't go to his office, he'd join us.

Grandmère's teatime ritual was used as an occasion for her to entertain people she might not wish to ask to dinner, which was a different sort of social occasion with FDR the center of attention. My grandmother selected her teatime guests for many reasons. They might be people to whom she felt an obligation, experts who had information she wanted to hear, or maybe just strangers she'd run into on her many journeys and simply told, "If you're ever in Washington . . ."

My grandmother was not undiscriminating when it came to extending invitations, yet she paid no attention to class or educational background. She responded spontaneously to those she felt drawn to, anyone who struck her as "interesting." Her style as hostess was her own, and it came off as a unique graciousness—a melding of her personal values and interests, which were wide-ranging, overlaid with her innate courtesy, a reflection of the manner in which she'd been brought up.

There could be ten or more people at tea or, just as likely, only a few. Sometimes it was an odd mix. One afternoon it was just Sistie, age eight, Buzz, age five, and the Polish ambassador. As Grandmère later reported to her friend Joseph Lash, she "read poetry to the assembled." Among her selections, which can only be called eclectic, were Noyes's "The Highwayman," Keats's "Ode on a Grecian Urn," Milton's sonnet "On His Blindness," and Kipling's "Danny Deever."

When we made our entrance into the West Hall, following Beebee, everyone stopped talking and introductions were made all around. It often was a mixture of familiar faces and new ones. Sis and I, well trained, said "how-do-you-do" to each guest and then sat down in our proper places. My grandmother poured weak cambric tea for us, with not too much in the cup, as it had to be balanced on a rather small and unsteady high-legged table next to the chair. These "tea tables" came in sets of three or four, one fitting under the other, like a nest. That seemed very clever to me. We sipped our tea carefully, and I tried to eat the cake I'd been given without appearing greedy. Once I disgraced myself by spilling in my lap the small cup of very hot tea I'd been given—quite painful but not serious. It was a few weeks before I was again allowed to sit in at my grandmother's teas.

Grandmère sometimes took my sister and me with her on her visits. These were not trips to the zoo or other traditional places one goes to amuse children—that was left to Beebee—but, rather, official appointments. As First Lady, she was invited to open new buildings, launch ships, and cut ribbons for various occasions. From her perspective, the excursions to housing programs—reviewing new community centers or slum projects for poor people—were most valuable for us. She took us to see awful shacks put together from debris, and I learned from the Secret Service men that these shantytowns were rudely referred to as "Hoovervilles."

It was the beginning of a very special education. My grandmother was a keen observer and a good teacher, and we liked going with her. She saw underneath and through things, and she explained all that we were seeing. Modestly, she would say, "Pa taught me to be a good observer." I wanted to be like that, too. I watched my grandmother's shrewdness, observed how she balanced distance with intimacy, gleaning what was valuable.

Once, probably when I was no more than four years old, Grandmère took Sis and me to christen a U.S. Navy ship at Newport News.* Flying from Washington to Virginia in the admiral's plane, I was given a privileged seat behind his felt-covered desk. We taxied to the end of the runway, then, with the engines roaring loudly, gathered speed and took off. We flew low over the city. I liked flying. Someone pointed out to me the Washington Monument, the Capitol, and the White House, where I lived. Suddenly, without warning, I was airsick—all over the lovely desk.

I cried not from any discomfort but from embarrassment—and the expression on my grandmother's face. "Perhaps Buzzie is a bit too young to be flying," she commented gravely. I shook my head, stifled my tears, fearing I'd be sent home. How I'd ever get there didn't enter my head. For the rest of the flight, perhaps a half an hour, I remained in a state of controlled queasiness.

Once on the ground, I was fine, feeling more like myself, distracted by the excitement of seeing the sailors and the marine honor guard drawn up on the runway. Sis and I were close behind Grandmère as she stepped out of the plane to greet the navy entourage, resplendent in gold braid, wearing starched white "summers," their swords at their sides. "Always stay close to me or you might get lost" was one of her standing instructions, and we always did. I laugh when I remember that refrain; I can't imagine getting lost in a situation where, next to the First Lady, we were at the center of all the attention.

As First Lady, Eleanor Roosevelt's practice of "seeing for myself"—which is how she described going out on her fact-finding missions around America—made for a steady stream of news features and photo opportunities. Curious and

---

*This was the USS *Yorktown*, which would be sunk in World War II in the Battle of Midway.

courageous, she used her position to visit places where past presidents' wives had not ventured. (The famous cartoon of her surprising two miners deep in the earth—"For gosh sakes, here comes Mrs. Roosevelt"—was on the mark.)

While often at the edge of some political controversy, and drawing steady criticism from opposition members in Congress, my grandmother was loved by the vast majority of the public. They didn't doubt her concern for their personal welfare and enjoyed catching glimpses of her, whether in the flesh or, more likely, in newsreel footage. Even her opposition had to acknowledge that with her daily newspaper column and regular magazine articles backing her up, the president's wife was a power to be reckoned with.

Those who've lived long enough remember "Mrs. Roosevelt" with extraordinary detail—what she said, how she was dressed, her kind eyes, her smile, her unflagging interest. If they did, in fact, meet her, they recall her unfailing warmth and individual greeting. Yet how she kept it up over her twelve years in the White House—and after—I can't imagine. It wasn't just her ingrained formal politeness. She projected, somehow, a warmth that shone through and made every man, woman, and child she met feel recognized. And their responses in turn helped her transcend what remained of her childhood shyness and reticence.

Sis and I enjoyed attending receptions as a way of varying our all-too-familiar routine. The First Lady was responsible for the receiving-line duties, and only when the occasion was extra-important would FDR join her, as it was much too tiring for him to stand on his braces for more than a short time. Often, several hundred guests would have been invited. The time allotted to the event was little more than an hour, so it was necessary to keep the line moving. A certain number of visitors had to pass through the receiving line every minute, moving on to their coffee or tea in the next room, in order for the occasion to finish on time.

That meant Grandmère had to shake hands at a steady rate, not always easy when someone stopped with something they urgently wished to say. She would have one of the White House military or naval aides standing immediately to her left to carefully pronounce each person's name (and title if they had one) while introducing the person to my grandmother. This activity went forward with a rhythm you could nearly keep time to. However, a voluble person in the line would inevitably have a long-winded story to tell Mrs. Roosevelt, breaking the steady pace. If it went on too long, the aide stepped in to assist Grandmère by taking the storyteller's arm and urging him on to the refreshments. Some guests were amazingly stubborn, ignoring the plight of all those lined up behind them. But the lure of gaining the ear of Mrs. Roosevelt was more than many people, given the opportunity, could resist.

Sometimes Sis and I joined my grandmother in the receiving line, holding out our hands to be shaken by each visitor in turn. "This is Sistie and Buzzie," Grandmère would say. My sister and I maintained our modest profiles, smiling up at the guests. I enjoyed these occasions, and probably showed it, while Sis feigned indifference to the visitors' attentions.

My uncle Elliott, I remember being told, once joined the reception line, knowing that his mother had been shaking hands for at least an hour. Moving slowly forward until he got to her, he gave the aide announcing guests a fictitious name, wondering if she, never expecting to see him, would be too crowd-weary to notice who it was. She recognized her son, of course, and made a big joke of his prank.

My grandmother's keen, almost sacred, sense of fulfilling obligations—public ones in particular—meant that she had to endure unending public occasions and the fulsomeness of strangers, all the while seeming to welcome every syllable. She remained unfailingly gracious. It's not a skill that can be faked well; it has to come from inside—and it positively emanated from my grandmother.

As a little boy, watching her, I grasped that my grandmother was *for* real. Looking back I can see that this may not have been what she wanted to do, or where she wanted to be—not all the time anyway—but it was where she was, being "Mrs. Roosevelt." And it was the White House that provided that identity. She had turned the role of First Lady into a never-to-be-repeated phenomenon—because she was always "for real."

Within a couple of years after moving into the White House, my grandmother had become simply "Mrs. Roosevelt." In fact, almost no one ever called my grandmother "Eleanor" in conversation or otherwise. Her friend Lorena Hickok did, but she intentionally made herself the exception, signaling to Grandmère's other friends that she was the closest friend.

Grandmère's actual name was Anna Eleanor, but she never used Anna. FDR called his wife by the nickname "Babs," her children called her Mummy, and we grandchildren called her Grandmère. Close friends who had known her since the twenties, such as Nancy Cook and Marion Dickerman, called her Eleanor. To the rest of the world, including the people who worked most closely with her, she was always "Mrs. Roosevelt."

But "Mrs. Roosevelt" was much more than a name that identified her. Rather, it soon signified her distinct personality, one that she had instinctively fashioned for herself through her use of the platform provided by living at 1600 Pennsylvania Avenue. It turned out to be a personality that perfectly suited her, one in which she felt comfortable.

I understood from my mother that Grandmère wielded a lot of influence and that she, like my grandfather, was a public figure—even though she didn't have an official position. No matter where we accompanied her, there'd be the same reporters and photographers and the same eager crowds that surrounded FDR. I watched the way guests treated her when visiting the White House: even Cabinet members and Supreme Court judges deferred to her, often asking her opinion about serious subjects. Plainly, Grandmère was more than just my mother's mother, more than simply my grandmother. And she was obviously not just the wife of the president, the First Lady. She was "Mrs. Roosevelt" in the same way Papa was FDR.

All of us in the family—and my grandmother's friends, too—soon understood that their mother, grandmother, or old friend was no longer just Mummy or Grandmère or Eleanor. She was now a larger-than-life figure and, in a sense, a grandmother for all Americans. It added a kind of strange echo to her relationship with all of us, and undoubtedly picking it up from my mother, I was very conscious of it.

My mother and uncles tried hard to treat their mother as just that—their mother. But my grandmother's new public persona was becoming immutable, beyond anything they could effect, and they felt it. Although Sis and I knew Grandmère as Mrs. Roosevelt—our time with her in the White House was essentially our sole experience with her—Mummy and her brothers could remember a time when their mother had not been a public figure. They couldn't help but be conflicted, and this led to resentment.

Later, I could feel their frustration at this transformation. Perhaps it was a sense of deprivation, of no longer having their mother available to be their Mummy. My grandmother's innate reserve did little to remedy the problem. My uncles, for instance, were annoyed at having to make an appointment for a private visit with their mother. The ground rules were the same as they were for FDR. Grandmère moved without stopping from one appointment to the next, so my uncles, or my mother, would have to ask my grandmother's secretary, Tommy, to fit them into a break in the schedule. When and if they managed to secure a few minutes of their mother's time, it was often a maddeningly rationed encounter, with the next person on the schedule waiting outside. My mother and her brothers were forced to recognize "who she was." It was a situation ripe for ambivalence.

CHAPTER 6

From the moment she made the decision to leave him, my mother froze up whenever she had to talk to Dad. After she moved to Washington and the time came to speak directly to him about her wishes regarding the divorce, she asked her father to do it for her. So Papa was the one to inform his son-in-law that his wife, Anna, was planning soon to leave for Nevada, where she would establish residency, as was the practice then, and then petition for divorce.

My father was shocked by the call from FDR, and he called my mother to try to convince her to delay the trip west, still hoping for a rapprochement. Dad later explained to me that he felt he was getting back on his feet and just needed a bit more time. My mother's version of their conversation pegged Dad as a social

AUTHOR'S COLLECTION

Our mother dressed for horseback riding, which she and my sister both loved. With my wandering mind, I tended to fall off my horse.

climber; she claimed that he was after her money. (In fact, he knew just how little she received from her small annual stipend.)

Whatever my parents said, or didn't say, to one another, the exchange was acrimonious. And it was made worse by the fact that my father didn't know that my mother wanted a quick divorce in order to marry again. The man waiting for her was John Boettiger, a reporter she'd met when he was covering the presidential campaign in the fall of 1932 for the *Chicago Tribune.* But my mother's plans for proceeding straight to Reno had to be postponed. Her brother Elliott was in the midst of his own divorce proceedings, about to shed his first wife, Betty Donner, so he could immediately marry Ruth Goggins. Grandmère felt, and Papa concurred, that it would "look better" if there were not two divorces in the president's family during the first year of his administration. Uncle Elliott refused to be deterred, so it was my mother who agreed to wait.

So, in the summer of 1934, after we had been living at the White House for about a year, my mother set off for Nevada to seek an official divorce. Sis and I, along with a nurse named Katie, accompanied her. My guess is that we were included on the trip so that there could be no question about the legitimacy of my mother's residency. Nevada law required that we stay for six weeks. Sis and I were not keen, missing our horseback riding, swimming, and all the activities that we normally would have enjoyed at Hyde Park.

Mummy was understandably nervous about the trip. It was to be a long train ride across the country, and she expected that the press would have a field day covering her journey to America's divorce capital. Getting a divorce in those days was a scandal—sufficient cause for being dropped from the Social Register!—and the fact that she was the president's only daughter made the stakes enormous, her every move a potential scoop. Her biggest concern was to avoid causing her parents any more embarrassment.

It was mid-June when we left Chicago aboard the *Pacific Limited* bound for Reno. Although every effort was made to keep the travel arrangements under wraps, the press had gotten wind of them. Once en route, my mother stayed in seclusion in our compartment, asking that our meals be brought to us. After a day's travel beyond Chicago, she agreed to talk to an Associated Press reporter. Perhaps she yearned for some adult company. "I see I made the papers again" was the first thing she said upon greeting him. She went on to explain that she was exhausted from looking after her children. I was fretful with a cold, and Sis was restless from boredom. She did not attempt to hide her journey's ultimate agenda, but the interview produced nothing in the press.

Our six weeks in Nevada did not begin well. In a letter to my grandmother, my mother offered an account of our first forty-eight hours in the little California town of Truckee, which lies on the border about twenty-five miles southwest of Reno:

> . . . our arrival at Truckee was gosh awful. A terrific battery of cameras—stills, movies, sound apparatus—getting in our way—Buzzy, in my arms—weeping and coughing all at once—Sisty walking ahead obviously weak as a cat, and getting a whooping spell just as we reached the car. The drive, eighteen miles, followed by fifteen or twenty cars, two bad accidents taking place along the winding, narrow roads, one newspaper man or photographer so badly injured that he died the next day—and all this because the photographers wanted to get ahead of us and get pictures [of us] in the car and as we arrived, and the Nevada State Police wouldn't let them by. I wouldn't have a motor cycle escort, but now I think I was wrong. The house here is a terrible disappointment— worst of all one highway runs in front of it about 25 feet away and another one runs along side about one hundred feet away. That afternoon we couldn't move out of the house because news hounds of every description stayed around until dark. The next morning I just couldn't keep the kids in a moment longer and a Paramount man took movies of all of us with a long range lens. . . . Right now and all day and every day there are three or four movie and still men and three newspaper men sitting in a shack two hundred feet away!

My mother finished by adding, "there was nothing I could even do about the injured people as no one told me of the accident until the next day."[*]

---

*Letter in JAR papers, AR to ER, dated 19 June [1934], Lake Tahoe.

My mother's lack of sensitivity over the injured member of the press was mirrored by my grandmother's. "Anna darling," Grandmère wrote in reply, "What a dreadful time you had, it seems too dreadful & must have seemed unbearable. There is one consolation, however, that all the photographers & news hounds seem to have had no luck in disseminating their news for you've been out of the papers except for the small notice Friday that you'd gone to the ranch."

The letters that my grandmother sent to my mother during this period show her focused, as usual, on the continual presence of journalists and her ambivalent attitude toward appeasing them. Here are excerpts, written over the course of a single week, as my grandmother was herself traveling:

July 6 ". . . I've tried to stay out of the papers but fear it has not been very successful . . ."

July 9 ". . . I am a bit weary from dodging news photographers (quite unsuccessfully) . . ."

July 12 "Gee! What a time I've had with reporters in Chicago & on the way but this a.m. when I found I was followed I pulled up on the side of the road & told them I'd wait till they phoned their editors but if I had to be followed I'd leave any state I was in and go home & I wouldn't meet Pa who might be a bit annoyed! We invited them to breakfast in a coffee shop in the nearest town* & there I waited till their editors got up & they were told they could go home."

July 13 "The trip coming out was horrid, papers had it tho' I wouldn't be photographed or interviewed it seemed so ungracious not to go out & say 'hello' . . . I felt if people were there at that hour I must go out . . ."

Of course, today the idea of a First Lady casually touring the countryside without a phalanx of advance persons and Secret Service agents, along with

---

*Her companion was Lorena Hickok, another of my grandmother's close friends and a second grandmother to Sis and me. We never called her "aunt," just Hick, as did my mother and everyone else.

aides galore, cannot even be imagined. But it was something my grandmother insisted upon. After FDR had been elected president, one reporter wrote that Mrs. Roosevelt "refuses to allow the new honor that has come to her husband to interfere with the varied interests of her own life."

In spite of a Secret Service man, a Mr. Rich, being assigned to us, the house on Lake Tahoe was deemed too vulnerable to reporters and news photographers. Sis and I had to stay indoors all day. Soon we moved to a large ranch belonging to Mummy's friends Mr. and Mrs. William Dana. There, we were surrounded by flat, empty Nevada desert. In the center of the Danas' grand but rustic house was a large enclosed patio with a garden, which meant plenty of space for Sis and me to run around in.

Eventually, my grandmother arrived to spend a few days with us. After settling in, she reported back to John Boettiger, my mother's fiancé, with whom she was in regular touch. Telling him his bride-to-be was sunburned, she noted how rested her daughter looked. "The real people around here have been good to her," she added. In another letter, to her friend Nancy Cook, Grandmère echoed the same sentiments, observing Sis and me. "The kids have gained a lot in other ways, it is good to be where human beings count on their own worth & not for what they have. . . . " This was directed at her mother-in-law and our life with Granny at Hyde Park.

Especially fascinating to me was our hosts' Rolls Royce touring car, the same size as Papa's limousine, in which they roared over the landscape without regard for the roads, the difference between any road and the surrounding desert being minimal in those days. It was exhilarating riding at high speed in the huge open car, and it reminded me of careening around the back roads of Hyde Park with Papa. We were given to understand that the Danas and their friends would fire their shotguns from the car at anything that moved, aiming without slowing down. Greater sport! But they refrained from this pastime while Sis and I were in the car. I think my mother had made it clear the noise made by the guns was too much for our delicate nervous systems.

With Dad at a San Francisco Fair in 1934.

After our mother's divorce proceedings were completed, Sis and I went with our nurse to meet our father in California for our annual summer visit. Because of his Wall Street debts, Dad was undoubtedly short of money, but it never stopped him from dressing well. He was always stylish in a conservative sort of way, and he always stayed in the right sorts of places. Although now the *ex*-son-in-law of the president, he remained very conscious of appearances, making sure his place in society was not just secured but also recognized. He looked the part: tall, athletic, not handsome but attractive, his baldness providing a dignified air.

Dad laughed readily, and he liked to have fun. At one elegant house where we were visiting friends of his, the atmosphere was light, and he carried me around the room on his shoulders. I was a bit afraid of this elevated position and had only allowed myself to be hoisted there—Dad being adamant—after first tearily protesting. Bobbing in the air on top of his six-foot frame made me nervous. So, fearful of swallowing the chewing gum I had in my mouth, and with no other place to put the gum, I stuck it on top of his bald head. Down from his shoulders I was quickly brought and fixed with a terrible look. Of course, Dad's anger soon evaporated when his friends all howled with laughter at what they assumed was a stunt of mine. No one realized how completely guileless I was.

At the end of our visit, after an emotional good-bye (for me, at least), Sis and I boarded the train for the trip back across the country, from Los Angeles to New York, making it a summer of 6,000 miles traveling the rails. She and I shared a compartment with Katie. A Secret Service man was nearby to keep a discreet eye on us throughout the journey.

Ever since FDR had been governor of New York, we'd been regularly guarded, and so we were used to it. Although instructed never to talk to strangers in the usual way, we'd never had anyone sit down with us and explain why. The terrible Lindbergh kidnapping, which had happened only the year before, was on the minds of my mother and grandmother—and of concern to the Secret Service's White House detail—so the two of us were kept on a short leash.

Because we traveled the country by train a dozen times in the following few years, the many long days and restless nights of each trip are a muddle in my head. The mountains, even the deserts, in the far west were magnificent, but the Midwest was marked by tedious hours and seemingly endless fields of grain and corn that filled the train windows for days. What a relief it was to see green again as we approached the eastern states.

The tedium of the train would be broken up by stops several times a day. If there was time, we'd get off, stand around, and gawk back at the people gawking at us. Sis and I were dressed in traveling clothes, things as light as we could manage. (Air conditioning on trains didn't exist, though our compartment had a small fan. Although the windows could be opened, we didn't dare, as the coal-fired engine would have filled the compartment with soot in a minute.) While we didn't look odd to each other, we must have seemed a strange species to the townspeople. But we were not recognized as Sistie and Buzzie.

I learned to play simple card games with my sister. She could also read books, and though I couldn't yet, I had my picture books. The most welcome interruptions were the three meals a day, plus tea in the afternoon. The sound of the gong announcing the opening of the dining car was a thrilling summons, and we always proceeded excitedly, on the run, to the first sitting. We would watch in awe as the waiters dexterously delivered our food, trays held high above their heads, while the car heaved back and forth.

Home, and everything as it should be.

The experience of making this cross-country trip by train became my personal yardstick for extreme journeys. As a child, the ride from New York City to Hyde Park, two and a half hours winding north along the Hudson River, had always seemed quite slow. But the trip across America—hour after hour, day after day, with great patches of unending sameness—felt like it might never end. I think it actually took about five days and six nights.

In early August 1934, when Sis and I arrived back in New York from Los Angeles, my mother and grandmother met our train. Their familiar faces were wonderful to see. Beebee joined us, and we had one night at the 65th Street house. The next day, Sis, Beebee, and I went to Hyde Park, where we were to spend the rest of the summer. Grandmère said she'd see us there the following weekend, and Mummy, too, reassured us that she'd be visiting soon. Home with Granny, settled into the Big House, I felt life was returning to normal.

CHAPTER 7

Springwood, which we referred to as the Big House (center), a typical nineteenth century Hudson Valley estate. (Rose garden, stables, and carriage house on right.)

B ecause of our trip out west, Sis and I were very late arriving for our usual stay in the Hudson Valley home of our great-grandmother. Granny's estate at Hyde Park was called Springwood, a name my grandfather didn't like. We all referred to it as "the Big House"; it was the magnetic north of our entire family. Sara Delano Roosevelt had inherited the 1,500-acre property from her husband, James Roosevelt, who'd died in 1900 at the age of seventy-two. Much younger than he—by twenty-six years—she was his second wife and Franklin

FDR was born and buried at Springwood. Here he poses with his mother and father.

their only child together. She had raised him with a maternal concentration that Papa enjoyed and prospered under. In the summer of 1934, she was eighty years old, and I, her oldest great-grandson, was four. Sis and I had spent a lot of time at Hyde Park and would continue to do so. Granny was special, like a surrogate mother to me.

Like my great-grandmother, the Big House, where she lived, was a survivor from another era. The farms were the fiefdom over which she reigned. I loved the way I knew everyone there and everyone knew me. "My, how you've grown!" people from every corner of the estate would greet me. Or they'd ask after my mother, Anna. The Big House was home to her and to her brothers, just as now, along with the White House, it was home to Sis and me. Springwood, with its unchangingness, was a special bond among all of us.

My strongest recollections of my early years there are of the third-floor nursery, which was the center of my universe. My crib, later exchanged for a bed, stood on one side of the room, Beebee's bed on the other. A Victorian bureau with a large mirror was placed against the opposite wall. The room was light and airy with big windows at either end. On one side was a fireplace; on the other, up a few steps, glass doors opened onto the roof built out over the library.

In the center of the room were a little round table and a small chair, both child-sized. Some of my first memories are of my meals being brought up to me there on a tray. The food would be placed in the tray's three hollowed recepta-cles. Contained underneath was hot water, which kept my food warm as it trav-eled to the third floor from the kitchen and while I dawdled over eating it. Dessert and my cup of milk were also included on the tray. Beebee tried to teach me to eat on my own, but I was content to let her feed me most of the time.

Not until about the age of three was I judged sufficiently able to feed myself—and not the surrounding floor—and so was allowed to join my sister at the side table in the bay of the dining room. We ate there for many years—until, finally, we were permitted, at age nine and twelve, respectively, to sit with the grownups at the big table.

The nursery fireplace was painted white and black. Over the mantelpiece hung a large picture of a formidable-looking man who, I was informed, was President Roosevelt. I found this very confusing since the man in the paint-ing didn't look at all like my grandfather, whom I knew very well was presi-dent. It was explained to me that this was President *Theodore* Roosevelt, my great great-uncle. I nodded, uncomprehendingly, and continued to stare in disbelief. Were there two President Roosevelts? Since *we* lived in the White House, where did that *other* president live?

All this I learned from my mother, but she rather labored over the telling. That she was withholding part of the story was obvious. The rest would grad-ually emerge over the next few years, when I was deemed "old enough to understand." When I finally learned that another significant Roosevelt family existed, rooted in Oyster Bay, not Hyde Park, I also discovered that there was friction, largely owing to jealousies over my grandfather's rise in politics. Some of my relatives never spoke to one another across this divide.

In fact, I was nearly a teenager before I came to know that my grand-mother, Eleanor Roosevelt, was from the Oyster Bay branch of the family and that her maiden name was Roosevelt when she married her fifth cousin once removed, Franklin Delano Roosevelt. (Early in her marriage, she signed her personal checks "Eleanor Roosevelt Roosevelt.") My grandmother loved to ex-plain the intricacies of our family tree, who was related to whom, and how, often leaving my sister and me even more perplexed.

Sara Delano Roosevelt was proud of her Delano heritage. An extraordinary figure, one minute in her presence left you no doubt that she knew very well who she was. She was self-assured, confident in what she was doing. At the same time, she projected an air of serenity, which might have deceived the unwary into thinking she was passive. Like her son, my Papa, Granny had a broad smile, which befitted her regal bearing. She carried a bit of weight when I knew her, but she still was erect and walked gracefully, and always dressed tastefully—in silk chiffons most of the summer. Whenever Sis and I appeared, her face lit up with welcome.

What was true of my great-grandmother—who, famously, has been a figure much debated and considerably vilified by writers of the Roosevelt history—was simply that she understood her place in the world and maintained it. As perhaps the most celebrated, and scrutinized, of all presidential mothers, she has too often been depicted as an opinionated and unpleasant person who presided dictatorially over her household and its inhabitants. One of my cousins once referred to her as the "bossy one." All I could think when I heard this was that this cousin was too young to have known her! She never seemed domineering or aggressive to me.

Her responsibilities were certainly great. The whole estate, 1,500 acres, had been left to her by her husband. So although my grandfather considered Springwood his home, he didn't actually inherit the estate until 1941, upon his mother's death, which was only four years before he himself died. James Roosevelt had left his son a modest income, with the duty of overseeing the estate going to Granny. He'd charged her with the financial management of the property and instructed her to maintain it as it had always been. For forty-one years, Granny carried out his wishes devotedly. Efforts to introduce innovations on the estate were not well received, not even those initiated by her beloved Franklin. "This is the way 'Mr. James' wanted it done," Sara would reply, and that was that.

My great-grandmother was in every sense a good employer, "taking care of the people on the estate" to an exemplary degree, which was not always the case with the proprietors of mansions along the Hudson valley. She was paternalistic in her approach; it would be unreasonable to expect otherwise. She was born in 1854, the heart of the Victorian era, and her class background determined her outlook and her behavior. In addition, she had "Mr. James's" example to follow when it came to the many daily decisions that confronted her.

Our summer days at Hyde Park were pretty much the same year after year, right through 1938. Life at the Big House was less organized than at the White House, but my sister and I still were kept to a regular routine. After we were awakened and dressed, two long flights of stairs took us down to the dining room where we were served a large breakfast of eggs, bacon, toast, milk, butter, and honey, all from the estate's farm. Then we went back upstairs "to do our duty," all supervised.

Following this ritual would be a visit to Granny. Thundering down from the floor above, barely slowing to round the corner, we'd run pell-mell along the second-floor corridor, with Sis in the lead, of course. By the time we arrived at our great-grandmother's door, she had been alerted by the pounding of feet. "Good morning Granny," we loudly chimed.

Propped up in her bed, wearing something silk and lacy around her shoulders and smelling of lavender, as she always did, she'd be having her breakfast on a tray just like Papa did. Our arrival was greeted warmly. Usually she'd offer us a little tidbit to taste, for which we competed with the two yappy Pekinese dogs, who also occupied her bed. I loved dogs, but not these two. If it was a Sunday, Sis and I would prop ourselves on either side of Granny, and she would then read "the funnies" to us from the Poughkeepsie newspaper. (The *New York Times*, which she read regularly, never had comics.) When we visited Granny in the mornings, I was never impatient to get on with the day.

I liked Granny's bedroom with its panoramic view of the Hudson. There was an armoire with a big mirror in the door and a large marble-top dressing table covered with silver combs and brushes and a hand mirror, all polished brightly. A small jar with a silver lid caught my attention and fascinated me. One day I finally succumbed to the temptation to see what it contained, opened it, and discovered what looked like chocolate candy. After helping myself, I was immediately sick, hardly managing to find the bathroom in time. I was instantly sent to bed, more in punishment than as a way of speeding my recovery from this gastrointestinal shock.

Tea in the afternoon with Granny was a ceremony—and a delight. Even if only Sis and I were joining Granny, we were served by her two butlers. All was as shining as silver could be polished. Sweets, cakes, cookies, or best of all, cinnamon toast sat on towers of doily-covered trays. Crumpets spilling over with butter were brought in separately and passed around by the butler. It was a feast. I had been taught to sit attentively at tea, quiet unless spoken to, but if Granny didn't have guests for tea we could chatter away as long as we weren't *too* silly.

Only once—and never again!—did Sis and I misbehave with our great-grandmother. It happened during a time when Mummy was visiting; we'd learned the word "belly button" from her as we were taking our baths the night before. Judging by her expression, we understood it wasn't a proper thing to say—indeed, it was pretty naughty. Therefore, we kept repeating it all evening, then falling about with laughter.

The next day we wanted to try it with Granny. As usual, we raced to her room, but then stopped outside her door and, giggling loudly, shouted, "Good morning, belly button!" Then we ran away as fast as we could. Later that morning, we reported our daring to our mother. She'd already gotten wind of it, as it turned out, and was very stern with us. Granny hadn't been amused and, summoning our mother, had chided her on the proper rearing of children. What's more, we learned, our great-grandmother would be in her study before our lunchtime, waiting to see us. Apologies were expected.

Sis and I were gripped with anxiety. But, in the event, it wasn't so bad. Granny smiled while telling us to watch our manners in the future and to remember to show proper respect to our elders. At teatime that day, naturally, we were on our toes, making sure to be extra well mannered—and so was our mother, the inadvertent instigator of the to-do. Granny's approval was equally important to her.

Val Kill, my grandmother's house, was about two miles east of the Big House—and less formal.

Val Kill, where my grandmother's Stone Cottage had been built eight years earlier, offered a much more casual atmosphere than the Big House. Lunch there would be served picnic-style, and we wouldn't have to get dressed for teatime if we stayed on through the afternoon. Our bathing suits would do for sitting around with Grandmère's guests, as they'd be wearing their own. Grandmère served wonderful iced tea with fresh mint (I was limited to two large glasses), as well as cakes and cookies.

It is difficult to separate what I observed as a child from the subsequent legend surrounding the tensions between Eleanor Roosevelt and her mother-in-law, Sara Delano Roosevelt. Over the years, my grandmother's stories, which were repeated by her friends, have become accepted as fact by journalists and biographers. Thus, my Granny has become an icon of the overbearing mother-in-law, a formidable dreadnaught.

Dory Schary, when he wrote the play *Sunrise at Campobello** about my grandparents and their family, cast Granny as the villain. "Every script needs a heavy," said he, after reading his script to those of us my Grandmother had assembled at Val Kill. That characterization, coupled with decades of my grandmother's polite but obviously shaded remarks about her mother-in-law, set in motion her ogress's reputation, a mantle that continues to hang around Sara Delano Roosevelt's shoulders. Moreover, contemporary writers use today's cultural references, imagining that daughter-in-law and mother-in-law let it all hang out as they would in a sitcom.

It wasn't like that. Their style was of two upper-class Victorian women, and neither ever said an improper word about the other. But they could be quite cutting (though rarely in front of the children) without overstepping the "proprieties." For me the uneasiness created in that carefully polite—but poisonous—atmosphere was worse to live with than any direct confrontation or outright rudeness.

The children—my mother and her four brothers, ranging in age from six to sixteen—were a difficult bunch, and my guess is that they provided much grist for the conflict between the two women. Granny made comments about her grandchildren being wild and ill-mannered. Because of her own inhibitions, Grandmère felt herself unable to do anything to effectively rectify the situation. But Granny's observations made her boil. It was during this period that Grandmère wrote to Papa that she had been "horrid to Mama" and that she had apologized. My grandfather received this letter when he was in Florida moseying about on a houseboat. He was not just fishing; he was escaping the chafing dynamic created by his two essential ladies.

At the same time, Granny spoiled my mother and her brothers, particularly Franklin and John when they were teenagers. This probably was aimed at my grandmother, though Grandmère's only protest was to complain loudly to my mother or her friends. When these tensions flared, my grandfather held him-

---

*It opened on Broadway, in January 1958, and ran for 556 performances, winning four Tony Awards, including Best Play, Best Director, and Best Actor. In 1960, the film version was released, with Ralph Bellamy repeating his performance as FDR. My grandmother is reported to have said of it, "A good play, but as much like the Roosevelt family as some people from Mars."

self aloof, doing little other than nodding agreement when his wife complained of Granny's "spoiling the children."

My grandmother was less ambivalent, however, about her mother-in-law's largess when it came to paying the school bills or, for example, providing $1,000 for Jimmy to go to Europe—indeed she acknowledged being grateful for it. My grandparents each had independent incomes and pooled their resources to make ends meet, but it was never enough. While living relatively modestly, they nonetheless continued to live in the style to which their class was accustomed. Granny made this possible by supplementing their income while they were raising their children.

Though she acknowledged Granny's generosity, it was a difficult situation for my grandmother. Perhaps the worst tensions between the two women occurred after FDR came down with polio. After having had her own home for the previous ten years, in Albany and Washington, my grandmother had to live with, or adjacent to, Granny either in New York City or at Hyde Park. It was easier this way, especially financially, for the crippled FDR, but all this support my grandmother found intrusive.

Grandmère's memory of her relationship with her mother-in-law could be selective. One of her favorite stories concerned Granny's role after she and Papa had returned home from their honeymoon in Europe. Sara had rented them a small house on 37th Street between Park and Lexington. "My mother-in-law had completely furnished it," my grandmother would say, with a touch of incredulousness, "down to the last cup and saucer, and she'd hired the servants as well!"

Yet Grandmère's letters to Granny, written while still abroad, are full of thanks to her mother-in-law for having done, or planning to do, exactly what my grandmother found so outrageous. Not knowing of this correspondence at the time of the telling, I laughed with everyone else at Granny's temerity.

Even the National Park Service rangers who guide visitors through the Big House acknowledge the tension between the two women, archly explaining that "Sara" sat at the head of the table with "Franklin" at the other end, and "Eleanor sat anywhere." I see this as feeding the popularized, one-dimensional image of my great-grandmother. It was Granny's house; where else should she sit but at the head of the table? FDR became the man of the house after his father died in 1900. Seating was always arranged for the evening meal, and Granny would surely see that her daughter-in-law was seated befitting her status, probably next to an important guest or family member, such as Granny's brother.

The Park Service guides also draw one's attention to two tall and impressive swivel chairs in front of the fireplace in Springwood's library. They represent the two terms my grandfather served as governor of New York. Papa always sat in one. Grandmère insisted that Granny take the other because, as my grandmother said, she was "always moving about." But I have also heard my grandmother tell the story differently. "Oh, I sat anywhere," she would note with a shrug. In fact, I remember well my mother, my aunts, even my uncles, saying, "Mummy, why don't you sit here?" and my grandmother declining, choosing to perch herself on an arm of the couch instead. Grandmère was complicated! She condemned self-pity, but she also indulged in it.

My grandmother's ordinarily scrupulous politeness and fairness toward people seems to have been set aside whenever Granny was the topic under consideration. She always looked down upon her mother-in-law's "vanities." What she meant by this was Granny's unembarrassed practice of a lifestyle that was completely passé. My grandmother had a keen sense of the reforms needed in our society, and in her view, her mother-in-law was living in the past, in a society where "knowing your place" was the norm, a desirable value.

Granny, though, was not self-indulgent compared to others of her class and position in society. While enjoying the role of the mother of the president of the United States, she made no undue display. She liked being received at Buckingham Palace or at U.S. embassies when she traveled in Europe. And she took the opportunity to have tea with Mussolini, noting that she thought him ill-mannered.

Granny was proud of her son. He had triumphed over adversity to become a world leader. Yet she never displayed—nor approved of—the recognition-craving antics of her grandsons, my uncles, or the outrageous behavior of Hall Roosevelt, FDR's brother-in-law who, according to his daughter Ellie, regularly insisted on a ringside table if in a night club and demanded that his wife

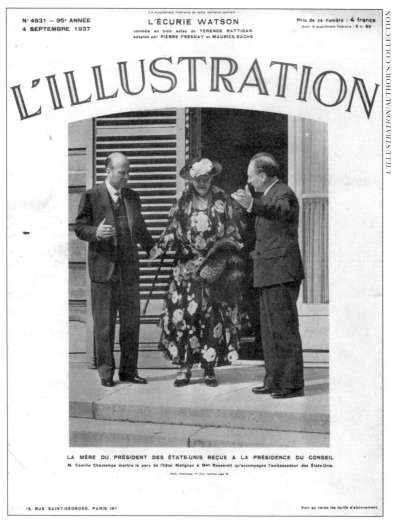

Granny's visit to Paris in September 1937 made the cover of the French news weekly, *L'Illustration*.

play the piano for everyone. My grandmother was willing to tolerate these lapses by her children and her younger brother but never missed an opportunity to point at Granny enjoying the presidential limelight.

The relationship between these two strong-willed women wasn't always strained, however. Granny's letter of April 2, 1926, to FDR, "Dearest Son," gives a different picture. Her second paragraph, mentioning Dad and my mother, "the young lovers," waxes on about life at Hyde Park: "Eleanor has the boys [at Val Kill], but they came over here for some hours today and tomorrow they lunch here. We three [Granny, Dad, and my mother] are invited for supper tomorrow at the cottage and they all lunch here on Sunday. Eleanor is so happy over there that she looks well and plump, don't tell her so, and I hope she will not grow thin."

Without hesitation, Granny invited to her dining table anyone my grandmother or grandfather ever requested be included. She sometimes complained about Grandmère's preference for staying at Val Kill—only because, she said, she disliked losing her company at the Big House. But the fact is that she never approved of Grandmère's friends Marion Dickerman and Nancy Cook, because in her mind it was unseemly for two women to live as a married couple. At the same time, I remember Granny always being polite and friendly to them, and Aunt Marion confirms this in her memoir.

Both women were keen to do their duty toward others, but Granny's noblesse oblige was carried out in her limited world, the estate of which she was mistress and the small circle in which she circulated. Grandmère's turf was America and, eventually, the world. Both women were equally formidable, but one was a crusader, and hence rather righteous, and the other was not, taking her upper-class role for granted.

Neither my grandmother nor my great-grandmother indulged in excessive emotional displays. They both valued self-control. The difference, though, was that Granny spoke quite freely about her likes and dislikes and how she felt about things. Grandmère was more guarded, and her expressions of disapproval were usually couched in thoughtful phrases, or even just a tone of voice, that managed, all the same, to convey her strong sense of right and wrong. From the same cultural background, Sara Delano Roosevelt and Eleanor Roosevelt were both intelligent and imposing. Both were equally focused on the Protestant ethic of duty.

While most historians have tended to see my great-grandmother as the heavy, the Dory Schary stereotype, I am comforted by the knowledge that my uncles shared my view of Granny. Although they certainly never hesitated to

My mother's and my sister's horse, Natoma, hitched up for an afternoon's buggy ride, perhaps over to the Vanderbilt's estate.

offer up amusing stories about the grande dame who was the family matriarch, they nonetheless adored their grandmother. And I knew my mother, when she wasn't trying to please her own mother, revered her, too.

In the Hudson Valley the weather was often humid and gloomy. In fact, the family had built its northern retreat at Campobello Island, a Canadian island at Maine's northeastern tip, for its mosquito-free, healthier summertime climate. By the time Sis and I came to Hyde Park, the riverside marshes along the Hudson had been cut back, much diminishing the chances of contracting malaria. When my grandfather was a little boy, however, families like his left the region for July and August, and he'd begun spending those months on Campobello in 1883 when he was a year old. FDR loved it there—it was a great place for sailing. My sister and I, because we could go riding, preferred to stay at Hyde Park all summer—in spite of the mosquitoes.

At the Big House we didn't bother with lawn furniture; a card table would do. Sarah, Uncle Jimmy's eldest child, Sis, and I gathered around our grandparents—with the dogs, of course.

Life at Hyde Park slowed to a crawl whenever there was a long rainy spell. At least it did for me. I might be left to "read" in the library, to entertain myself. It was a treat, really, since the library was my favorite room, one my grandfather had added to the house when he remodeled it in 1911. Only four years old, I practically disappeared in my chair, enveloped in its deep cushions and high arms. Propped up in my lap was the *London Illustrated News*. I studied pictures of the British royal family, the war in Ethiopia, and the latest model Rolls Royce.

While we were at Hyde Park in the summer, Papa would leave the White House to come north and visit. He'd take the train from Washington, through New York City, up the Hudson River, and when it reached our estate, just before the town of Hyde Park, it pulled off onto a special siding. This privileged access hadn't been laid down with taxpayers' dollars. It had been built by James Roosevelt, FDR's father, to accommodate *his* private car. I was impressed. Your own railroad car! My great-grandfather had been a major stockholder in the Delaware & Hudson Railway, which helps explain such an indulgence.

Sometimes Papa would arrive after my bedtime, but if he'd traveled all night, his train would arrive in the morning, and Sis and I, and any other family, would join Granny and Grandmère meeting him. (Grandmère sometimes walked the near mile down the steep hill to the railroad.) Secret Service cars would also have come down to the siding. Back at the Big House, all the servants were waiting for "Mr. Franklin" in excited anticipation, too.

Boarding the train, we'd run to greet him, always stopping first to say hello to his usual porter, the one assigned to the president's private railroad car. It was a special car provided to him by the Pullman Company, named the *Ferdinand Magellan*. Our grandfather would have a few of his close aides with him such as Missy LeHand, Bill Hassett, a longtime assistant, Grace Tully, another secretary, and maybe one or two others. Turning the big Secret Service cars around on the small dirt track was a challenge, but once that had been accomplished, we were on our way. Breakfast awaited us all in the dining room of the Big House.

At Hyde Park, Papa attempted to do as little work as possible. A special telephone had been installed in his small study, connecting him to the White House switchboard, but only the most urgent calls were put through. Missy, who had her own room in the Big House, might take some dictation, particularly if there was a speech to be drafted, but work was held to a minimum.

What Papa really liked to do for relaxation was work on his stamp collection. He might use Granny's desk in the library, spreading his books around, peering at an unusual stamp with a magnifying glass, totally absorbed—but not so engrossed that I wouldn't be welcomed if I wandered into the library. He'd invite me over and explain what he was doing, showing me a stamp from some exotic place, such as Samoa, and I'd then get a brief geography lesson— until my mother came in and, finding me interrupting him, led me away.

In the evenings, friends might be invited for supper. FDR enjoyed the company of Grandmère's two close friends from Val Kill, Aunt Marion and Aunt Nancy. They were both active in Democratic Party affairs and talked politics knowledgeably, the subject that dominated all conversation in the family. Also asked over might be FDR's Secretary of the Treasury, Henry Morgenthau, and his wife, Elinor, who had an estate south of us, at Fishkill. The Morgenthaus were sufficiently close friends that Sis and I called them aunt and uncle, too. Aunt Elinor, a confidante of my grandmother, was a shrewd observer, and Grandmère often shared insights with her. In Washington, the two of them regularly went horseback riding together.

With Papa around, there was a kind of electricity in the air, his presence changing everything. We had our morning ritual of greetings, stopping to say hello to him first before seeing Granny. We usually found him in bed, wearing one of the same old sweaters, his breakfast tray on his lap, completely engrossed in the newspapers. But without the people crowding around his bed, it wasn't half so much fun as in the White House. Papa might look at papers and even do some dictation, but there was no excited retinue; the president didn't hold court.

Another way Papa relaxed at Hyde Park was to go out motoring. When Papa had been elected president in 1932, Henry Ford had volunteered to adapt a car to his special requirements, a dark-blue four-door convertible.* We jumped at the opportunity to join him! He knew all the little roads that dotted the estate, since his own childhood had been spent exploring them on horseback with his father.

As soon as we climbed into the backseat, off we'd go! A pair of Secret Service cars would immediately fall in behind us. (They had big open touring vehicles like the kind seen in Hollywood gangster films.) One of the two challenges Papa set for himself was to confine his rallies to small estate roads— either our own or those on neighboring lands—avoiding any public route. The second challenge was to shake the detachment of agents at his heels. Taking the first opportunity, he'd be off down some small rutted lane. The game was

---

*It can be seen to this day in the Roosevelt Library's museum.

on! Looking back at the men in the car on our trail, I could see the grins on their faces.

But first we might meander down to see the ice pond where every winter ice was cut, brought up the hill on a horse-drawn wagon to the icehouse to be stored, and then used in the kitchen icebox all summer—right up to the time of my grandfather's death. We traveled along slowly in the forest, our grandfather calling this or that interesting tree to our attention as he drove. I was fascinated as I watched his hands move rapidly up and down the steering shaft to shift gears and apply the brakes as one would a hand brake, as well as steering.

One time, he suddenly spotted a small, really narrow road and veered off, accelerating. Both Secret Service cars gamely swerved as well. As we raced along, my head swiveled back and forth, first to watch where we were headed and then to see how the agents in pursuit were doing. On a particularly sharp turn, my grandfather grinned and whooped, slowing to see how the vehicles behind would make it through the same space we'd just squeezed through. Only one of them managed it; the other was no longer visible. In the meantime, we roared off.

We now whizzed along the edge of the field, ducking into another small road, little more than a pathway. "Look ahead!" my grandfather gleefully alerted Sis and me. Massive trees stood on each side of the narrow trail, forcing him to slow almost to a crawl in order to maneuver the little Ford between them. But we made it, all of us giddy with triumph. Turning around, we could see that the remaining Secret Service car had not. We waved at the agents, and they waved back.

Papa was awfully pleased with himself as we racketed on down the woodland road. His out-driving the Secret Service agents was just the kind of story he loved to regale everyone with over cocktails. Yet, when we emerged back into the open, onto the dirt road leading to one of the tenant farms, there was the second Secret Service car waiting for us, the agents in it beaming. We laughed and shouted. They were, after all, protecting a president and must have drawn a map of all the possible routes so as to secure his safety.

My nursery school in Washington, D.C. Can you imagine sending your child to a school named "The National Research Council for Children"?

CHAPTER 8

T hough it was inevitable at the end of every summer, it was wrenching to leave Hyde Park behind. In 1934, we were returning to Washington and the White House, where my sister would be resuming her classes at the National Cathedral's primary school. As for me, a surprise awaited, my mother said. The determined enthusiasm of her manner made me nervous. Something was up.

Like so many parental decisions couched as "surprises," this one was not about anything on my own personal wish list. What my mother now announced was that I was to go to school, *just as Sis did*. To be like her, following in her wake and doing whatever she did, always brightened me, but I knew that school also meant being with strangers—which is to say, other children. My face must have clouded over with the worry I felt. The more Mummy spoke of "how good it would be for me," the more doubt flooded into me. Nor was I encouraged when I heard the name of my "school": the National Research Council for Children.

The next day, a chauffer drove my mother and me in a White House limousine to a large but modest-looking house with a good-sized yard, where a quite matter-of-fact lady kindly took me by the hand. My mother said good-bye. I sniffled. My new keeper and I walked to the area where the other children were playing. I felt that they were staring at me—as though I were odd—an experience I was to have a dozen times in as many years at subsequent schools. I stared back shyly, aware that, indeed, I was different. In the weeks that followed, I managed to adjust, and I behaved as expected of me and played with everyone. Though I have no memories of what we did there, I have some photographs that show me apparently enjoying myself—as ever, quite willing to pose for the camera—at a school party.

Early on, probably on the first day, I had to go to the toilet. My need of assistance, in learning where to go, at least, must have been obvious, so I was taken upstairs to the bathroom. The teacher who escorted me showed me in and, to my shock, closed the door behind me. I was alone in a bathroom for the first time in my life! Normally, my nurse would undo my pinafore and place me on the pot. After peeing, I would be removed, buttoned up, and my hands washed and hair straightened, made presentable again.

All of a sudden, without any warning, I was on my own in a strange bathroom. But I *did* it. Undoing the buttons was the most difficult, since I'd never buttoned or unbuttoned anything before. God knows what the lady waiting for me outside the bathroom thought, for it must have been an extremely long time before I emerged. Quite triumphant I was. However, all was not completed. She said, "Haven't you forgotten to flush the toilet?" I was stunned. I thought I'd done so well. And flustered: I'd never flushed a toilet before. I wasn't aware of what went on after I'd finished. Beebee took care of all of that.

So, with truth on my side, I responded, "In the White House we never flush the toilet!" Years later I heard my grandmother repeating this story to White House guests.

A few months later, there was another surprise, or at least, that's how it felt to me. A letter from my mother makes it clear that my sister and I had been introduced to John Boettiger at least once before she married him in early 1935. But my first memory of learning about this important new person in my life came from the announcement made to us that he and my mother had been married and were on their "honeymoon." I didn't know what that was, and it wasn't explained. All I knew was that I'd been told that Mummy and my stepfather would return to the White House in a few days. I still do not know where they were married, who was present, or anything about their honeymoon. My half-brother, John, searched for this information when writing his memoir of my stepfather and mother's life together but found nothing.

John Boettiger, I would later learn, was a reporter for the *Chicago Tribune*, first known in his native Chicago for his work as a crime reporter. His only book, *Jake Lingle, or Chicago on the Spot* (1931), is now, I'm told, a sought-after collector's item for aficionados of gangster literature. It was the result of his dogged investigation into the murder of an underworld figure with ties to the *Chicago Tribune*, as well as to the city's violent underworld. With a higher profile as a result, John was assigned to the 1932 presidential race, which is when he met my mother.

Sis and I were mostly kept in the dark. Perhaps from embarrassment, my mother made no effort to explain to me that she was getting married again (nor did she tie it to the six weeks we had spent in Nevada). Even the label "stepfather" had to be defined for me. Once it was, I couldn't help but wonder where that left Dad. He hadn't been mentioned, and the impression I got from my sister was that a replacement was coming in for a father we already had. From my grandmother, I further learned that the return from the honeymoon was going to be a joyful event.

When that day arrived, we waited to be summoned for the reunion. Beebee's extra attention to the way we were dressed only increased the suspense. The moment we were summoned, I followed Sis, racing down to the second floor and then along the long corridor to the East Hall, and finally to the door of my mother's room. Sis, arriving first, had already knocked, and so we were told to enter.

Greetings and hugs! My sister and I spied two stuffed animals propped up on my mother's bed. Sis grabbed the one I had my eye on, a curled-up leopard, leaving me the stiff-haired dog still sitting there. The disappointment on my face was obvious, and my mother told my sister, "You ought to give Buzzie some choice." Sis stood by the bed, looking at me with a resigned expression.

My mother with my new stepfather, John Boettiger, 1936 (fourth and fifth from the right).

My mother said, "Now, which do you choose, Buzzie?" I remember my new stepfather's detached, tolerant amusement at this small scene of sibling conflict. I also remember that I did what was expected of me and picked the dog. I later found someplace to stash it in my room.

What to call John Boettiger? My mother told me that she'd discussed it with my sister and that they thought "Uncle J." would suit. How did I feel about it? I must have looked blank. I hadn't thought of calling him anything. But I nodded, although it had to be explained to me what the "J" stood for. My sister, hearing this, sighed loudly, thinking me awfully dumb.

Shortly afterward, the newlyweds moved to New York City where Uncle J. was beginning a new job. He'd been named executive assistant to Will Hays, president of the Motion Picture Producers and Distributors of America. Known as the Hays Office, it was supposed to monitor films that might violate the nation's accepted morality and also functioned as a public relations operation for the motion picture industry. As my half-brother later described it, "the new job was politically acceptable to the White House, and carried a salary more in keeping with the imminent change in John's social status."

Being poised to become the president's son-in-law had been a problematic position for John Boettiger. He could not continue as a reporter covering the White House, especially for the *Chicago Tribune*, with its well-known anti–New Deal bias. Colonel Robert R. McCormick, the *Tribune's* legendary publisher, was enough of a fan of my stepfather that there'd been rumors he eventually intended to offer Uncle J. the managing editor's job. In the meantime, however, he proposed an executive position in the Chicago offices that might ease the political conflict of being the president's son-in-law while being employed by "the opposition." However, I doubt that my mother and grandmother felt such a move eased the situation enough—Chicago was awfully far away, after all—and so the sinecure at the Hays Office in Manhattan it was to be.

I couldn't imagine a life without the routine provided by the White House. New York City was a place where you changed trains, from Pennsylvania Station to Grand Central, or vice-versa, not somewhere I could ever picture living, except for those occasional nights I was used to spending at the family's house on 65th Street. Sixteen-hundred Pennsylvania Avenue had been my home for three out of my five years; leaving behind the stability it provided was not an idea I could contemplate without feeling fearful. So I was delighted to hear that Sis and I would not, for the time being, move to New York.

───────

Up until the late autumn of 1935, Sis and I were left "on our own" at the White House, while my mother and Uncle J. lived in New York. I settled in at my nursery school, and we spent the summer of '35 at Hyde Park. When we returned to Washington at the end of the summer, however, it felt as though a bomb had fallen on me. When I got to my third-floor bedroom in the White House, Beebee wasn't there. All my mother would tell me was that she'd left.

Her explanation was clear; the bottom line was that I was too old for a nurse. I was a big boy now—five years old—and able to sleep alone in my room.

I felt abandoned and devastated. My reaction to losing Beebee, in fact, seems to have so traumatized me that I've blotted out all memories of this disaster. Looking at pictures of my childhood—there are *a lot* (though I have none of Beebee)—and reading the relevant correspondence has brought back many memories. I've been able to piece together many of the events of childhood and my feelings about them. Still, thinking about Beebee's exit from my life provokes only a vague but deep sense of anger.

Neither my mother nor my sister would ever talk about it with me. When I asked for details, they either didn't remember or referred to her leaving as a perfectly normal part of "growing up," one not requiring comment. All I remember is my mother's defensive tone as she dismissed my inquiries, which made me feel as if I'd done something wrong.

The departure of a beloved nurse, usually to be replaced by a governess, was a rite of passage in families like ours, and it was often handled as insensitively as it had been in my case. In that sense, my mother's behavior was standard operating procedure. But that fact has not diminished one whit my resentment over the loss of the person I loved most.

Very shortly, our new governess, Mademoiselle Deschamps, arrived to take charge of Sis and me. She was given her own room, and I was now to sleep alone. Although she woke me in the morning and helped me dress, I was now expected to wash on my own, comb my hair, and present myself for breakfast. Although each day proceeded in the same efficient manner, life without Beebee was very different in tone and style. The other black servants on the third floor seemed somewhat inhibited by this new keeper, who was not only a proper governess but a foreigner as well.

Our "Mademoiselle" was actually Belgian, not French; she was quiet, soft-spoken, and spoke English with a charming accent. She also seemed quite young. One of her tasks was to converse in French with us at mealtimes, further evidence of the changed order. Our old gang, with whom we had once felt so at home, now kept a polite distance.

In truth, Mademoiselle tried very hard to get to know me. But how could she fill the gap created by Beebee's departure? She, too, may have been lonely, living with children and servants on the third floor. After Sis and I went to bed, what else did she have to do besides read in her own room? Beebee had had a built-in social life with the other residents of the third floor. Yet by the time we left to live in New York City, I'd begun to feel a bond with this new person into whose care I'd been placed.

Mummy's absence over the past year hadn't worried me, nor had it made that much of a difference to our everyday existence. Now she was with Uncle J., and we'd be joining them, and all I knew that fall was that my world, even with Beebee missing, still maintained its accustomed patterns and relationships. My nursery school had by this time become familiar enough, and every day I looked forward to playing there with the other children.

But the moment had to come, and when we finally left the White House just after Thanksgiving Day, 1935, it was a real jolt. My unhappiness at surrendering what I considered my home was intensified by hearing my mother say to one of my uncles that "the White House isn't good for Buzzie." I already knew that my father wasn't good for me, and neither were my uncles. I'd even overheard my mother say that "Hyde Park with Granny isn't good for Buzzie." Was "our gang" at the White House not good for me, either? Apparently not. "They spoil Buzzie" was said of my wonderful allies, clearly within my earshot.

Uncle J. was now being "talked up," and I was told it would be good for me to have a man in my life. In fact, Grandmère highly approved of John Boettiger. The two of them always got on well, and his nickname for his mother-in-law was Lovely Lady. In response to Grandmère's enthusiasm, I simply nodded and smiled. My resistance was automatic, instinctive, and implacable, but with all the propaganda I was being bombarded with, I felt that I had to comply with the wishes of my grandmother, my mother, and my sister. Although I did not take to Uncle J., I tried to respond to him just as my sister did. When she hugged, I hugged; when she kissed, I kissed.

We were to be "the Boettiger family," even if I didn't really know what that actually implied. It was new territory that I didn't wish to contemplate. I had

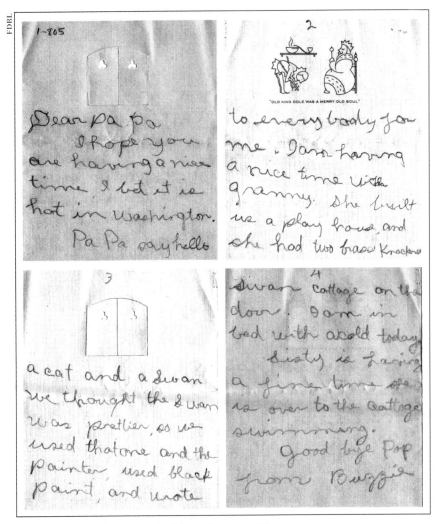

A letter I sent to Papa—not bad for a five-year-old.

little identity other than as one-half of the "Sistie-and-Buzzie" tag-team at the White House. Limited though it may have been, that's who I was. And that identity was one that had been supported by all the people within its corridors.

Thus, despite all the efforts to present our move to New York as "exciting," my good-byes at the White House were tearful. The next thing I knew, I was in a strange place, a Manhattan apartment at 2 West 53rd Street, not the family house on East 65th Street that I knew. The only positive change was that it was the first time I felt I really lived with my mother. Never before had I known her in such close quarters.

My new room was tiny, its window looking out on a ventilation shaft—a typical New York apartment servant's room. Katie, whom Sis and I knew well, was now to be my mother's maid, as well as our cook. The man she lived with, Ivan Holness, was to be our butler and chauffeur. Beebee was still much on my mind, but I dared not mention her. I knew what my mother's reaction would be, and I didn't want to be impolite to Mademoiselle. She, in turn, had been cautioned not to get too close to me and to avoid my becoming too dependent on her. But Mademoiselle was neither cold nor aloof. I think she sensed the depths of my loss.

At my new kindergarten in Manhattan, Miss Smith's, I lost some of my shyness and even sang with the other children. I improved my reading and writing, and adjusted to new activities—naps on pallets after our lunch, playing in the small yard in back. We were a group of children of mostly the same age and roughly the same social background. No fuss was made about my White House past or my grandfather. I got along with the other children quite well, much to my mother's surprise.

Ivan drove us to our respective schools in our new four-door maroon Chrysler, and he picked us up at the end of the day. It was my introduction to congested traffic and crowded city streets. Washington was a little hick town compared with New York. In the mornings, Ivan had to hurry, since he had to return to the apartment to pick up my stepfather and drive him to his office. My mother once teased Uncle J. about being chauffeured to a building only a few blocks away. He was not amused; humor never was one of his strong suits.

Our apartment in New York would today be considered on the grand side. We lived on the top two floors of a late nineteenth-century townhouse belonging to the Rockefeller family. (They owned a whole row of houses there and subsequently contributed this real estate to the Museum of Modern Art.) The ornate five-story building had a tiny self-service elevator, and Sis and I would compete to be the one to press the button up or down.

I also felt it was temporary. My mother, for her part, was oddly apologetic about our new home, speaking of it as cramped. But it had a prestigious address, just off Fifth Avenue, and it was explained to us that Uncle J. would benefit from entertaining here. What it lacked in space, it made up for in cachet.

Although we'd been in New York only a few weeks, we fully expected that we'd return to the White House for Christmas. But my sister and I were stricken with chicken pox, and although we were beyond having fevers by Christmas Day, we still looked awful, in every way unpresentable. So we spent Christmas in the apartment in New York. My mother, I know, felt our deep disappointment and probably shared a bit of it. Christmas stockings were placed in front of the fireplace in my mother and Uncle J.'s bedroom, and she did her best to distract us with something resembling the traditional atmosphere and excitement we were used to.

But it wasn't being at the White House with Papa and Grandmère, with all the people and parties, decorations and gaiety, all the coming and going. We also spent time with Dad that Christmas, although that didn't go well, either. Dad made a real effort, I know, to create a festive Christmas atmosphere for us, but my sister's cranky responses, her plainly wishing to be somewhere else, soured the mood.

The White House seemed very far away.

<hr/>

For the rest of the winter and throughout the spring Sis and I continued at our New York schools, but come the weekends, we were off to Hyde Park. Some weekends we went to visit Dad. What I remember most about our times with him were the Princeton football games, where at halftime a band played and we marched hand in hand with Dad around the playing field.

In June, in Philadelphia, my grandfather received the Democratic nomination for president by acclamation, which was expected but also thrilling. I listened to it on the radio with Katie and Ivan in the kitchen. Sis and I then spent our summer with Granny at Hyde Park. As autumn loomed, I began to face the prospect of first grade at a real school.

It was to the Buckley School, where all my Roosevelt uncles had gone, that I was headed, and I started off there guarded and unsure as ever. Despite making good progress amid the cozy group that comprised Miss Smith's charges, I still felt reluctant to completely relinquish my "specialness." But so many of my classmates came from prominent New York families that my status as "the president's grandson" counted for very little, really. Besides, many of the boys came from staunchly Republican families, with mothers and fathers who hardly celebrated FDR. Being one of the few from a family of Democrats was my only distinction.

Nonetheless, as the weeks passed, I began to gain confidence—and it wasn't based on my White House identity. I liked Buckley and was starting to feel at home there. I now look back on this period and see that it might have been possible, had I remained at Buckley, to put aside much of my dependency upon the cocoon provided by "the goldfish bowl." Those three months in the autumn of 1936 offered me school experiences the likes of which I would never again enjoy.

On November third, Papa defeated his opponent, Kansas governor Alf Landon, in a landslide at the polls. He was not going to leave the White House, I understood, for the next four years. This made me excited and happy, and I began to wonder when I would return to Washington. But there was a cloud looming on my horizon. Mummy and Uncle J. began to speak of "moving to Seattle."

The move was presented to me and Sis as a marvelous opportunity for my stepfather. William Randolph Hearst, the legendary owner of a string of newspapers, including the *Seattle Post-Intelligencer*, had personally wooed my mother and stepfather to come west to run his paper, despite the fact that Uncle J. had little, if any, prior experience in management. My mother was to be named an assistant editor with responsibility for the women's page. The *P.I.* was an ailing paper at the time, having earlier been shut down for three months owing to a Newspaper Guild strike, and it consistently lagged behind the city's leading paper, the *Seattle Times*, in circulation and advertising. Hearst offered his new publisher much more editorial and news autonomy than he usually allowed, exhorting him to make it "the best paper in town."

My mother and Uncle J. set off for the West Coast in mid-December. Katie and Ivan were to follow as soon as a suitable house was found and rented. In the meantime, Sis and I were to stay with Papa and Grandmère while all the necessary arrangements in Washington State were made. To me the whole thing was an incomprehensible maze. We were to move again—and not back to the White House or any of my "homes." I'd never even heard of Seattle! I had no idea how far away it was, but I had some notion of a major displacement when I overheard Granny inquire whether the Indians out there were still dangerous. What's more, I'd have to start another school. I was stricken to my core at the idea of losing the place I'd made for myself at Buckley.

I also intuitively understood that Hyde Park and the White House, and everything pleasant associated with them, would soon be a vast distance away, quite out of reach, and in ways beyond mere geography.

The sole bright spot for me in all this was our return to the White House for Christmas. For the moment I could blot out thoughts of the changes that lay ahead and simply revel in the way everyone there welcomed us. *We'd been missed*. It was lovely to be back in my room—and all the old, familiar, pleasurable routines were quickly resumed. Although I knew I was supposed to be missing my distant mother and Uncle J., I'm quite sure that I gave them little thought as Christmas Day, 1936, approached. It was too exciting, being a six-year-old boy with presents to open, engaged in all the festive hoopla, to worry about obligations or be concerned with how I was *supposed* to feel.

CHAPTER 9

Eleanor Roosevelt greeting Prince Bernard and Princess Juliana at the White House.

Christmas at the White House will always stand out in my memory, not just because of the excitement and the many receptions, but because it broke down my grandmother's normal reserve. The capital boasted a heavy social schedule during the holidays, in which the president and First Lady were expected to play a central role. All the preparations and festive merrymaking were permeated with a feeling of gaiety, and everyone, especially my grandmother, embraced the old-fashioned yuletide spirit.

The city turned into a frenzy of festivities, as every government office threw parties. But invitations to the White House receptions, each for a different sector of the political population, were naturally the most coveted. Presided over by my grandmother, these events required almost military-like preparation and were hosted in the various public rooms of the White House: the Red Room, the Blue Room, and the Green Room, with the East Room reserved for exceptionally large groups.

Waiters worked overlapping shifts. Well-trained military aides helped shepherd the guests, waiting in long reception lines, through the rotunda to be greeted personally by the First Lady. Mrs. Edith Helm, the White House social secretary, who'd gotten her start working under the second Mrs. Woodrow Wilson, and Tommy, Grandmère's secretary, had a game they played while serving coffee and tea to the guests, probably to help relieve the boredom. Courteously fulfilling their duties, they competed to see who could hand out the most cups. Even Sis and I always wanted to know who'd won.

In some cases, children accompanied their parents to these Christmas receptions, and they always received a paper cornet filled with candy—paid for with my grandmother's own funds. My mother once made the mistake of questioning such extravagance, suggesting that spoiling other people's children at Christmastime might be more than was absolutely necessary in the way of hospitality. She received from her mother a measured reply to the effect that it was exactly how she wished to spend her money.

The president was expected to be present at only a few of the events, perhaps to greet all the ambassadors. He'd enter the East Room, swinging himself forward on his braces, his cane supporting him on one side and a military aide on the other, and take his place at the head of the line. Quite soon, though, he'd retire to a chair in one of the reception rooms. If the guests were people with whom he felt comfortable—for example, members of his cabinet or senior White House staff—he would have himself wheeled in, waving his arm, cigarette held high, in greeting (the other arm holding onto the chair for balance). He'd then be steered around among the guests, chatting briefly with everyone.

It was wonderful to see the pleasure that my grandmother took in welcoming the hundreds of invited visitors, wishing them a merry Christmas, presenting a gift to a child. She was in her element, and one could never doubt the fact of her enjoyment. FDR was equally warm and personal, but my grandmother set the tone for Christmas, and everyone responded.

I loved circulating among the crowd—and getting their attention—the coming and going, the state rooms thronged with excited, happy people, all reveling in the spirit of the season. Of course, everyone worried that I might get lost in the crowd, so I was kept under one or another grown-up's watchful eye. I was told to stay away from the candy cornets, which were for the *visiting* children! Occasionally, if there were presents to be presented to children, Sis and I would be recruited to help.

It wasn't until years later that I learned about the unsolicited presents for "Sistie and Buzzie," sent by well-wishers from all around the country, and what a headache they'd been for the White House staff. They arrived by the hundreds, and some, I'm told, were pretty extravagant. Of course my mother and grandmother decreed that so many gifts were "unsuitable" for us—harmful to our developing sense of values—and so we never saw any of those offerings from the citizenry. We were permitted to receive gifts only from family members or from close friends, which included "second grandmothers" like Missy or Tommy. The mountains of presents from unknown admirers were shipped off to children in nearby orphanages and hospitals, though first a record was made of each package, which would later be acknowledged by a note from my grandmother, Mummy, or one of the White House secretaries.

There was, in fact, a "present room" on the third floor, a windowless space with lots of shelves and a big table for wrapping, where my grandmother stowed her cache of gifts for us all. She shopped for Christmas gifts all year long, taking advantage of the brief periods of time between appointments to pop into a store, seeking the perfect present for someone on her long list. I know from shopping with her in later years that her approach to gifts was very focused. Into "the present room" the purchases would go, marked with the proper name.

Not surprisingly, it was pretty exciting news when I got wind of the contents of this special room. The door, of course, was always locked, but one day I noticed it ajar and peeked in. Such a treasure trove! How could I not tell Sis what I'd seen? As usual, it was a big mistake. She squealed on me to our mother, who promptly told Grandmère. I was called on the carpet and told sternly that it was "a violation that wasn't funny!"

Just before Christmas Day, Grandmère went into even higher gear, adding the family Christmas preparations to her already overcrowded schedule. Everyone around pitched in to help. It didn't matter who they were or what they did—White House social secretary, maid, nurse, servant, secretary, or family—all joined my grandmother in the wrapping of presents.

As family members began to arrive in Washington, the arrangements steadily grew more complicated. Finding bedrooms for all my uncles and aunts, the bawling babies, and their nurses meant a good deal of juggling of rooms. Granny and Aunt Betty, widow of my grandfather's older half brother, James Roosevelt Roosevelt,* required special attention.

Aunt Betty, or Elizabeth Riley, as she had been, lived only a quarter of a mile from Granny's Big House in what we called "the Red House." She had met her husband-to-be when he was a widower and First Secretary at the American embassy in London. Prudish New York society held it against her that she had originally been his secretary and that they'd most unconventionally married onboard ship while sailing home to take up residence in America. Reserved at first, Granny warmed to Aunt Betty, finding her good company during the many years both of them were widows.

There was a good chance a dance would be organized for one of my unmarried uncles between Christmas and New Year's. It all seemed a huge effort and exhaustingly frenetic, but my grandmother appeared to relish it. Even a strictly "family" meal might consist of twenty or more adults sitting around the table, because there were always extra people. Our children's table up on the third floor also overflowed with visitors.

---

*The double name was to avoid using "Jr." Everyone in the family called him "Rosy."

Beginning a night or two before Christmas Eve, my grandfather would start to read aloud selections from Dickens's *A Christmas Carol*. It was a performance that all of the family, except our younger generation, had heard countless times before, but that didn't matter; the point was how much pleasure Papa took from it. Holding his audience, he gave it his all, being dramatic in ways that the adults found hilarious and that quite scared us children, especially the arrival of Marley's ghost, dragging his chains.

What I loved about this Christmas ritual was the sense of our family gathered together—a rare occasion when the usual conflicts and tensions were subdued and less competitiveness was on display. After Papa had read one or two chapters, we children would be sent to bed. It was cocktail time for the adults, all except my grandmother. She still had crucial preparations to oversee.

Late on the afternoon of Christmas Eve, the family, plus a few close friends, joined to watch the first lighting of our private Christmas tree, placed in the East Hall as it was about twenty feet tall. This was a moment of high suspense and anticipation mixed with anxiety. Real candles, each about three inches high, had been placed on all the branches. Buckets of water and sand, meanwhile, stood ready in case of a flaming disaster. During the couple of hours leading up to this climactic moment, my grandmother, uncles, and aunts had been decorating the tree with colored balls and tinsel. No friends were allowed to help—only family, only adults—with this tricky exercise.

The candles were the last ornaments to be attached, and they were carefully placed so that they would not cause the tree to catch fire. Papa came in to watch the last half hour, commenting drolly on the decorators' efforts and bestowing his approval on the placement of each colored ball. He could be corny at such times, but, even then, his humor, his delivery, had an unmatched style.

Now it was time for the lighting. Illuminating all the candles on our tall tree took several minutes. Stepladders were brought in to reach the higher branches, and my six-foot-plus uncles took care of the top ones. When the last taper had been lit, a great sigh of relief could be heard, although nervousness still hung in the air as we sang, rather poorly, one or two verses of "Silent Night." Then we grandchildren were told to take a last look before the candles were extinguished. We'd get to see the tree lit one more time, when presents were distributed the next afternoon, Christmas Day. It was a short-lived, if thrilling, phenomenon.

It was, in fact, my grandfather who insisted on real candles being used rather than electric tree lights. At Hyde Park, the family had always adhered to this old-fashioned tradition for the Christmas tree in the library of the Big House. FDR wanted it that way in the White House, as well. I'm told that the government maintenance officials, horrified at the potential fire hazard, simply closed their eyes when told that the president insisted. The sight of the tree with its candles burning is a memory I cherish, and the last time I saw a fir lit with candles was in the library of the Big House on Christmas Day of 1944, three months before my grandfather died.

Later, my grandmother went to the midnight service with a few other family members. Afterward, she stopped in at Tommy's apartment to visit and exchange presents before returning to the White House. (Miss Thompson was separated from her husband, and since she was alone, with no family nearby, Grandmère stepped into the breach.) Well after midnight, she returned to join my mother and aunts as they started filling stockings.

After that, she'd be busy arranging all the Christmas stockings around the bedroom fireplace in Papa's bedroom so that they'd be in place long before Sis and I arrived. In those days, of course, I firmly believed in Santa Claus, even though the logistics of his chimney maneuver did raise some doubts in my literal mind. I was five years old before my sister confronted me with the reality that Santa didn't exist. I told her *I'd* known that for a long time; having an older sister required maintaining such ever-alert defense mechanisms.

For the Christmas of 1936, Grandmère was especially marvelous. With Mademoiselle, we and our cousins dawdled over breakfast, since our appearance at Papa's bedside was set for 8:30 A.M. In Mummy's absence, Grandmère came upstairs to join us at breakfast and then took us in tow to the awaited rendezvous. Our grandfather was propped up in bed wearing one of his old pullovers. We kissed him—his cheeks were scratchy as they always were in the mornings before he shaved—but my eyes couldn't help but be riveted on my bulging stocking, propped up by the fireplace, too heavy to hang from the mantel.

Before I could claim it, though, we had to wait—and wait—for the last of the family members to arrive. They didn't seem to have the same Christmas spirit I had. And when they did finally show up, they seemed more interested in chatting than in appropriating their stockings.

Sis and I sat on Papa's bed, and still we waited impatiently for the last of the grown-ups to pull themselves together and appear. The Roosevelt rule was that no Christmas stockings could be received until everyone was present, a trying experience for the younger family members. While waiting, we would have identified our particular stocking, overstuffed with presents—truly overflowing, as my grandmother always liked to add just one more small item to an already full stocking.

Now, at last, Papa could give the word, and we kids rushed to the fireplace, where we crowded around to claim our stockings. I took mine to a corner of his bed, being careful to avoid his unmoving legs. Tearing off the wrappings, I showed him what I'd got from Santa. They were all small items, mostly useful—socks, mittens, handkerchiefs, a toothbrush—but occasionally there would be three or four of the English-made lead soldiers I was collecting. Santa was well informed. He knew I wanted U.S. marines in full dress uniform, marching with rifles on their shoulders.

I piled my booty in front of me. At the bottom of the stocking were always two special items: a five-dollar bill and an orange. Oranges in those days were an exotic treat, and a fiver was a fortune, which, normally, my mother took to put in my piggy bank "until I found something I really wanted." The adults were slower about emptying their stockings. Still, it was fun to watch them. I'd rush from one to another, eagerly checking what they'd gotten. Without my mother there to save it for me, I put the money in my pocket. The bill never burned a hole as it might have for other kids; I could never think of anything I especially wanted. I kept my $5 for months, changing it from pocket to pocket, like a keepsake or remembrance, until it was lost, perhaps in the laundry.

Then, all dressed up, we'd proceed to church. We'd head off in a long cavalcade of cars. Granny went with Papa and Grandmère, followed by Sis and me and all our uncles, aunts, and close friends. My eldest uncle would take over from Gus to support FDR "walking" on his braces down the aisle of the church. As the church was packed, we squeezed into the front pews.

The rest of Christmas Day remained full of things to do, and some of our amusements were designed to keep us grandchildren well out of the way of the many official duties facing the president and First Lady. But Sis and I were included in the household staff party, where the room was dominated by black faces—men, women, and children all dressed up for the occasion. To my amazement even the little boys were wearing long trousers. It was Grandmère and Papa they were there to see, I'd been told, but the parents made a point of bringing their kids over to meet Sis and me.

In the late afternoon, the adults quickly took their tea, standing up, and then the family and our friends all gathered around the family Christmas tree in the East Hall of the second floor. The wondrous candles were again lit, a hymn was sung, and then the candles were snuffed out. Each person might have a present or two under the tree. These were the "big presents," that is, the ones that didn't fit into a stocking. The only present for me in this category that I remember was an Erector set. It was made up of an array of interesting parts, with which I could build a house or a bridge or nearly any structure. I enjoyed it for years, sometimes just making different abstract shapes, though I didn't bring it out too often since it required sustained attention, something I was already short of.

By the Christmas of 1936, my sister and I were acting as hosts to our young cousins dining with us on the third floor. This responsibility demanded more of my sister, befitting her senior status. Our Christmas supper seemed to me to be exactly like my birthday parties, with little favors at each child's place, crackers to pull that had a "surprise," some trinket, inside. Parents and nurses stood around to see that it all went without tears, or reasonably so.

There was a big cake and lots of ice cream for dessert, but I don't remember the food being otherwise different from our daily fare. After the meal—all the mothers having descended for the cocktail hour—the nurses would try to organize a game, but it would be pretty tame. Anyway, only Sis and I, and perhaps our slightly younger cousins, Sara and Bill, were old enough to join in the simple games. When the older family members trooped up from Papa's study, full of noisy good cheer, to say good night, Christmas Day was over for the children.

I was sad to miss Christmas at the White House. My grandmother's letter tries to cheer me up.

In the choice positions to review the Inaugural parade in January 1937. Sis and I stand on either side of the president, who just happens to be our "Papa" as well. It poured rain.

rom 1793 through 1933, the United States had inaugurated all of its presidents on March 4th. But the Twentieth Amendment to the Constitution, intended to shorten the period of lame-duck leadership, now decreed that incoming presidents take office on the 20th of January. In 1937 FDR was only succeeding himself, and the country was still in the throes of the Depression, but modest celebrations were nonetheless in order, especially given his landslide victory.

Just in front of the White House, right on Pennsylvania Avenue, a replica of President Andrew Jackson's house in Tennessee, the Hermitage, was being built. We were told that our grandfather would watch the inaugural parade from the porch of this structure. Although only a shell, to us it looked like a large dollhouse. Built in less than a week, its construction progress was great fun to watch. Unfortunately, though, it provided little shelter from what would turn out to be a very wet day. (*Time* magazine later would refer to my grandmother's hat as "resembling last year's bathing cap" and described the White House lunch as attended by "500 recently soaked notables.")

The first thing my grandparents had done that morning was go to church at St. John's on Lafayette Square across from the White House. Sis and I went, too. Although we did not attend the swearing-in ceremony on the steps of the Capitol, we did get to be Papa's honor guard as he reviewed the inaugural parade. We stood on either side of him, an undeniably privileged position (which my mother, out in Seattle, heard about from my disgruntled uncles and aunts, who'd all been relegated to seats behind). The official picture of the event—actually a drawing—shows our heads barely visible above the railing of the Hermitage, next to our grandfather.

In a letter Grandmère wrote to my mother in Seattle, describing the day, she told her, "You would have been proud of Buzz taking off his cap whenever Pa did and standing by him all through the parade."

Despite the cold rain, the military showed off. The army, infantry, cavalry—mostly tanks but with enough horses for nostalgia's sake—and the field artillery, mostly horse-drawn caissons but also several of the new motorized units, sloshed by. The tanks and armored cars belched so much smoke that spectators held handkerchiefs to their noses. Overhead, the Army Air Force buzzed past, much more slowly in those days, since they flew noisy prop planes.

When Papa and I spoke during the parade, we had to do so loudly, as my grandfather couldn't bend down to my level without losing his balance. I thought the navy marching men seemed unimpressive and told my grandfather so. He reminded me that sailors didn't have the space to drill on the decks of their ships. The marines following them were much better, but the best were the West Point cadets. Their ranks were splendid, trim straight lines about twenty across. Both Papa and I, inclined to the navy, had to admit that the Annapolis midshipmen fell short of their rivals' standard.

What I enjoyed most were the bands. Papa explained that they were spaced intermittently so that each one's performance would not interfere with the next. Otherwise, the marchers might get confused as to which drumbeat to keep in step with. There were many floats, and Papa explained that some of them were political spoofs.

The other disappointment of the parade, as I saw it, was the silly men—Shriners, I expect—trying to look like clowns, but not succeeding very well. Maybe it was the rain. On the other hand, their band seemed odd as well, seemingly unable to play a straightforward march, always jazzing it up to accompany their antics. Up there on the presidential stand, I frowned in disapproval.

When Papa signaled that he was ready to leave, my grandmother said Sis and I had had enough as well. We followed our grandparents from the podium. My grandfather slowly and laboriously made his way down the ramp, assisted every moment until he could reach his wheelchair. Then, surrounded by people partially screening him from public scrutiny, he was wheeled back into the White House. We followed along with Grandmère until Mademoiselle appeared, ready to take charge.

There was no inaugural ball or ostentatious official party. This was because "tens of millions of citizens" were living under the "pall of family disaster," as my grandfather described in his address that day. But it would not have been my grandparents' style anyway. There had been no inaugural ball in 1933 either. Sheltered as I was, I knew little of the Great Depression's reality for the majority of Americans.

The period right after my grandfather began his second term coincided with Sis's and my preparations for leaving the White House. We were about to embark on what everybody explained to me was a wonderful opportunity—an adventure! Hearing this, I'd just smile vaguely, not wanting to seem out of step with the party line, especially in the afterglow of the inauguration. But my heart wasn't in it. I had my own idea of the "pall of family disaster," one that had little to do with the suffering of my fellow Americans and everything to do with a place called Seattle.

Here I was, a small boy who disliked, even feared, change. I was now being made to leave behind everything I loved—all that underlay not only my emotional security but my special identity. That my mother was waiting for me across the country, a new husband by her side, was hardly something I was approaching with any kind of anticipation. But I didn't dare share these blasphemies with anyone. Basking in my Buzzie-dom, betraying any hint that I liked and depended upon my special circumstance, was out of the question.

To help relieve the tedium of the very long trip that lay ahead of us, my grandmother had the ingenious idea of presenting me with a brand-new Mark Cross attaché case, small enough for me to carry on my own. It was heavy, I remarked as I lifted it for the first time, and I saw her smile. It's filled with presents, she explained, and there was a new one for me to open on each day of the journey. I grinned, tingling with anticipation.

Since we were to be nearly a week en route to Seattle, changing trains several times along the way, it was a tremendously thoughtful gift. A real attaché case, it featured, right below the small gold-embossed Mark Cross emblem, my own initials: C.R.D. The use of my full initials turned out to be a subject of controversy with my sister. "Mummy won't like that," she proclaimed. *What did she expect?* I wondered. Dressed smartly for our departure in my navy-blue double-breasted coat with its gold buttons, and my Buckley School cap on my head, I solemnly hefted my new possession, holding on to Mademoiselle with the other hand.

Before going to the station, we joined Dad for supper at a nearby hotel. It was his idea, and he wanted it to be a special occasion. He had mentioned at an earlier visit in New York his unhappiness at our going so far away, but now he tried to make our last supper as jolly as he could. I, at least, had a good time. He professed himself to be most impressed with my new case, particularly with its CRD initials. Try as I would, I couldn't hold back my sobs when we parted.

Recently, I came across an exchange of letters between my mother and my grandmother that dealt with this good-bye dinner. In her letter, my mother expressed her fear that my father might be capable of . . . anything.

She warns Grandmère that he might "pull something" and adds, "I don't trust him. . . ." Then she goes on: "I think it would be wise to have a Secret Service man accompany the children to Curt's hotel room, stay outside the door, and if they go down to the dining-room for supper, stay near enough so he can see them. While I do not believe that Curt would really try any funny business, I can never be too sure, and would feel much safer if a Secret Service man kept track of them during those two hours."

Could she really have imagined that our father might kidnap us? Try to spirit away two of the best-known children in America? Maybe hold us for ransom? Not even a criminal mastermind would have been able to get away with such a scheme on the paltry income my father was living on. For years, without any Secret Service agents accompanying us, Dad had been having Sis and me for visits. Beebee or Duffie or Katie always accompanied us, just as Mademoiselle was there with us during this pre-departure supper. Evidently, our grandmother empathized with my mother's concerns. She assured her that all the requested precautions would be taken.

Grandmère met us at Union Station after our supper with Dad and settled Mademoiselle, Sis, and me onboard the night train to New York. My great unhappiness over leaving my homes in the east and going west into the unknown wilderness of Seattle made for a large lump in my throat as we said good-bye. Grandmère kept emphasizing how we'd

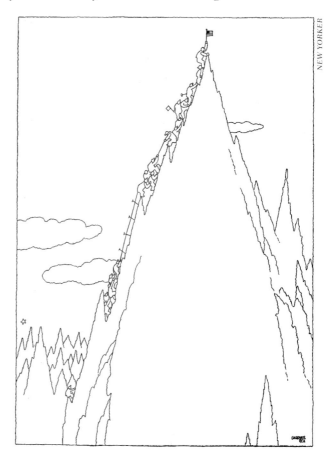

NEW YORKER

"*I name thee Mt. Buzzie Dall!*"

A *New Yorker* cartoon. No comment!

soon be together again with my mother and Uncle J., not understanding that the people now being left behind were those with whom I felt most at home, not the mother and stepfather I was about to be reunited with.

I couldn't speak to my sister about the distress I felt. For her, we were now "the Boettigers," a better version of what we'd been before, avidly supported by my grandmother. And while I didn't dwell on it, I was very aware that my mother, once Mrs. Dall, no longer answered to the same name I did.

The whistle sounded. Waving to Grandmère, we were off. The next morning, in Pennsylvania Station, we changed trains. Seattle lay 2,900 miles to the west. Whatever was happening, I was along for the ride. I did not feel rebellious; that wasn't my style. But my grandmother's plan for distracting me, making each morning of the trip one I might more cheerfully anticipate, was a welcome palliative. Each morning, in our little compartment, I opened one of the gifts in my leather bag—while being steadily carried further into exile.

CHAPTER 11

FDRL

My grandmother's first visit to Seattle—a rare sunny day in spring, 1937.

W hen my mother and John Boettiger first arrived in Seattle in early December of 1936 to begin their new life, finding a suitable house for all of us to live in was their first consideration. Beyond the usual challenges of finding a house that was attractive, spacious enough for everyone, and affordable, they were faced with the very real problem of security. It was never discussed in front of my sister and me, but prominent in their minds was the fact that kidnapping was an ever-present threat.

In fact, a few days after my mother and Uncle J. arrived in Seattle, Charles Mattson, the ten-year-old son of a wealthy Tacoma doctor, was abducted from his family's house by a masked man with a gun. This horrifying event, occurring little more than thirty miles away, was front-page news in the Northwest, and despite the massive publicity and the all-out efforts of law enforcement officials, the boy was never seen again. (To this day, it remains an open case on the FBI books.) The year before, nine-year-old George Weyerhaeuser, of the prominent timber industry family, and also from Tacoma, had been kidnapped while walking home from school in broad daylight. A $200,000 ransom was paid, and the boy was released after being held for a week. The criminals were eventually apprehended, but it, too, was a sensational case that riveted the attention of the region.

My mother had other anxieties beyond our physical safety. Our arrival in the Northwest was news, and the ensuing publicity surely confirmed that William Randolph Hearst had been savvy in his hiring of my mother and stepfather.* This brought to the fore my mother's perennial worry that people might seek their acquaintance because of her close connection to the president. Ever since we had moved into the White House, my mother was preoccupied with "being used." She was channeling Grandmère's adamant view that no family member should ever be a conduit to the president or in any way let themselves be open to "improper influence," even the least whiff of it.

And now, three thousand miles away, Mummy was on her own, weighing the motives of a myriad of new acquaintances. How could one know what lay behind the hand held out in friendship? Normally, an introduction on behalf of a friend was just simple kindness. But if your father was President of the United States, it was a different matter. Her dilemma was real. Her experience was that even proven friends were not above asking for a favor.

On the real estate front, there were still other considerations. We needed a house in a "good" neighborhood, but we did not want to appear snooty. We

---

*My uncle Elliott had already been on the Hearst payroll, becoming manager of the Hearst radio chain in 1933. After World War II he became "aviation editor" for the Hearst papers.

weren't snobs, though we were old money (and aware of our class background). Yet these distinctions could be hard for real estate agents to grasp as they struggled to show my mother "appropriate" houses. Uncle J. had no objection to being near the local country club, but my mother put her foot down, unwilling to be seen as joining the "country club set."

This real estate exercise would be reenacted every year for the next three. Moreover, a major plank in the party line was that Sis and I were not to be snobbish like the children of the country club set allegedly were. But where was our place? It was left to me to sort that one out.

In the end, when Sis and I finally arrived in Seattle, we liked our new house. It was in Lawtonwood, a woodsy suburb, where the city took on a more countrified air. Mademoiselle's and our bedrooms were upstairs, with Katie and Ivan in connecting servants' quarters over the garage. Sis had a large double bedroom with its own bath. Mademoiselle had a room across the hall with her own bath. I had a small bedroom with a large dormer and shared Katie and Ivan's bathroom. Although the heavy-hanging tree branches outside my window made the room dark, it had a cozy feeling that suited me.

Without a pause, on literally the day following our moving in, we were slated to enter our new school, Magnolia. Since it was February, there was no way we'd be able to simply take our place in the crowd, sliding in inconspicuously. On top of that, it was a public school—a change for both of us and a distinction Sis seemed to grasp better than I did. I'd always thought schools were schools, but I quickly saw that the kids at Magnolia looked very different from my Buckley School crowd.

Mummy made it clear that my new school was going to be "good" for me. I would come into contact with "less-privileged children" and in the process I would become more "regular," she intoned. I had heard this before and it always aroused my suspicions. When Mummy referred to Buckley when explaining the dangers of exclusiveness, I looked down at my shoes.

What sealed the deal for my mother was how much Grandmère liked the plan. Later I learned that none of my uncles had ever been to a public school, but as an abstract notion, it was highly pleasing to her that I'd be seeing

America from another perspective. She herself liked to have as much exposure to *real* people as she could manage. Both my mother and my grandmother felt that it was desirable for children to see past the narrow snobberies of traditional upper-class behavior.

———

On that first morning at Magnolia, my mother took Sis and me to the principal's office. I couldn't hold back the tears, and the stoic demeanor I was trying to maintain crumbled. But Mummy quickly left. She had to get to her office, she said, reminding me that big boys don't cry. A lady then took Sis in hand, while the principal led me to my classroom. Every head turned around as we entered, and the teacher beamed a greeting. I was introduced as "Buzzie, President Roosevelt's grandson, who has been living at the White House in Washington." The forty-odd other children stared in disbelief.

Embarrassment is not adequate to describe my profound sense of wishing I was elsewhere, anywhere else. Shortly afterward a loud bell rang. I sat there, but everyone else got up quickly and ran out. The teacher said it was time to join the other children outside since it was now "recess." It wasn't a word I knew. But, getting the idea, I stumbled into the hallway where several children—some older and not in my first grade class—demanded to know whether what the teacher had said about me was true.

I wasn't prepared for such an inquisition. I nodded, smiled, and tried to be polite. But the other pupils' questions left me feeling like someone from a circus sideshow. The loud bell went off again. Recess was over, and everyone rushed back to their classrooms. I followed—forgetting for an instant where I'd been sitting but then, finally, locating my desk again—and then waited for the next thing to happen.

Breaking for lunch, and the mad free-for-all that ensued, was equally daunting. Nothing in my experience had prepared me for it. My mother had been told to give us money to buy lunch tickets so we could line up in the cafeteria with everyone else, but the lunch money came with no instructions.

I watched the others ahead of me, first grabbing a fork, knife, and spoon and then holding up their trays to be served from behind the counter. When I said "thank you," the serving lady smirked and nudged her colleague.

Once we'd claimed our food and paid, we rushed to the long tables, found space to sit, and ate from our trays. It was a far cry from the Buckley School back in New York, where we ate quietly under the supervision of teachers. At Magnolia, it would be a while before I was pushing and shoving with the rest.

Finally, the shocks of the first day ended, and I went out to find Sis and the Secret Service man already waiting for me in the car. What a day. I had never before in my life felt so exposed and vulnerable. I found my fellow students' questions intrusive and exasperating. I didn't know how to reply, and I instinctively knew that what I offered in floundering explanation was as incomprehensible to them as their questions were to me.

As the days passed, I was asked regularly about "life in the White House." The teachers seemed equally interested. In the corridors of Magnolia how could I explain about life in a unique atmosphere that, I knew, was utterly foreign to them? I tried, but I'm sure it ended up sounding boastful.

After only a single day in our new home, my mother sat down and wrote to Grandmère about how Sis and I were faring: "She [Mademoiselle] has him more under her thumb than I like, and I am hoping that school and rubbing shoulders with many different types of boys will help him acquire more independence and confidence. Sis will have a so much easier time in life than Buzz. She takes everything in her stride and has such an open, happy nature. Buzz hides so many of his feelings, partly because Sis overshadows him and partly because his emotions lie very deep and it is hard for him to know exactly how he feels about things that are happening to him."

This letter is typical of the correspondence between my mother and grandmother; the two women were always writing for each other, saying what they thought would elicit approval from the other. My mother was right about the way I submerged my emotions. But any insights she seemed to have into my sister and me were simply made up for Grandmère's consumption. Far from lending me independence and confidence, Magnolia had exactly the opposite effect on me. My sister struggled as well. Mummy simply did not grasp the disabling effect upon us of this radical change in our life.

I'd like to think my mother and grandmother were a bit less like the blind leading the blind, but that is not the case. For them to clearly see what was happening to me as I floundered in the world outside of the White House would have meant examining their own relationship to power and privilege, something they viscerally blocked.

⧉

The three newly recruited Secret Service men assigned to our family in Seattle—one for each eight-hour shift—were primarily stationed as guards for Sis and me. Mr. Carmody, whom we soon took to calling "Mody," was our day-time Secret Service man, and Hazen (I never did learn what his first name was) took over from him at 4:00 P.M. Bunker, a man we rarely saw, watched over us from midnight to 8:00 A.M. Not trained for the job the way the very professional and circumspect White House Secret Service men had been, Mody and Hazen turned out to be as starstruck with us as the kids at school.

Each morning, Mody drove Sis and me to school. At recess periods and during the lunch hour, he stationed himself in the schoolyard. "Buzzie has his own G-man," the kids would say. When anyone asked, I replied casually that I'd *always* had someone protecting me. That only made matters worse.

Mody would patiently field questions from the kids who crowded around him. Yes, he did carry a gun, he admitted, and after much persuasion, he pointed to the bulge under his jacket. In time, he became more expansive, and stories poured out of him, various adventures he'd had over the years. He'd worked in a sheriff's office, he said, sometimes as a prison guard.

I found some of his tales a little far-fetched, but what did I know? I liked having Mody around. I was able, simply, to join his audience and laugh appreciatively at his stories, just like everyone else.

Once I was invited to a birthday party by one of my classmates at Magnolia. My mother was hesitant, wanting to know something about the family of the boy, but she finally approved. For the occasion I was dressed in my proper clothes, my good short trousers and blazer with my shirt collar folded neatly over my jacket. Knee socks, polished shoes, and my blue overcoat and cap completed the outfit. It was exactly what I'd worn for my grandfather's inauguration in Washington a few months earlier.

Hazen drove me to the birthday boy's home that afternoon. Upon entering the house, I said my howdoyoudo to the boy's parents and then stood at the edge of the noisy bunch of kids. No one else was dressed as formally as I was, nowhere near it. Other parents stood about, assisting with the party. Several turned immediately to me, engaging me with questions they'd heard and read about "Buzzie." I was happy to oblige—anything to avoid showing my awkwardness with the other children. It was soon discovered that my keeper was outside. All the kids ran out to see a real "G-man." I was left with the adults, fielding more questions—and feeling more at ease.

The arrival of the birthday cake arrayed with candles shifted everyone's focus, both children and adults, and shortly thereafter I made my excuses and left. It was such a relief to get into the car with Hazen. He asked if I had had a good time. I looked at him, puzzled. I didn't know how to respond. Not only did I find the phrase "a good time" odd when applied to me, but the question of how I felt about something was also unfamiliar. I replied that I didn't know, and that was the truth. Hazen looked confused! He must have thought me a strange kid.

In Seattle, in my new house and my new school in this new place, I had entered into a landscape that was almost, if not quite, the real world. Sis and I arrived home from school each day just after three o'clock. We'd been introduced to Don and Jack Clark, children of our immediate neighbors, a year or two older than we were. After some initial timidity, we hit it off remarkably well. I'd never played cowboys and Indians or cops and robbers, though I had heard of these games. The problem was that Sis and I hadn't been allowed to listen to the radio—except to Papa's "fireside chats"—nor had we gone to any movies.

But we quickly caught on. I was introduced to cap pistols—and caps with real gunpowder. Whether as a G-man or a bad guy, it was BANG! Gotcha! And then running like hell to hide behind the next tree. For me it was a totally new—and thrilling—experience.

My mother, hard at work at the newspaper with Uncle J., assumed that either Mademoiselle or one of the Secret Service men was watching over us. But neither did, having the good sense to simply let us play. So there we were, with no supervision, no nannies curbing the running and shrieking. Freedom! I'd had outings with my school classmates in New York's Central Park, but nothing like this. I waited for that familiar brake to be applied to my enthusiasm, the stale old "Buzzie's getting overexcited," but it didn't come. Gross hilarity, vulgarity, to which I took quite naturally, was now something I could gleefully indulge in.

The Clark boys were utterly amazed to learn that I'd never seen a comic book, so they lent me some old dog-eared issues of Flash Gordon and Tarzan. As soon as I made the mistake of showing off these treasures to my mother, though, she ordered them returned immediately. She wouldn't even touch them, disturbed that they were grimy from being handled by all the other kids.

I am not sure how long the great fun I'd been allowed went on after this, but probably no more than a few weeks. Soon Mummy decided to speak to Mrs. Clark. Her boys were a little old for me, she explained, adding that I was very impressionable. To me, she said that Don and Jack were "too rough"—I might get hurt. But I suspect the real reason she brought my fun to a halt was that they were too different from the children at Buckley's or Miss Smith's, which, decoded, meant "not like us." It was one thing to theorize about changing the tone of my social life, to explain "that school and rubbing shoulders with many different types of boys" would be good for me, and another thing altogether to actually countenance it.

Finally, having discussed my budding hooliganism with Uncle J., my mother told Mademoiselle that I was no longer to play with the neighborhood kids. Mody was further instructed to see that Sis and I bought no more caps. (They were technically illegal, but Mody knew where to obtain them.) So, into a drawer went my cap pistol. Mademoiselle was asked to get me started on "something of my own, something useful" that would occupy my after-school hours. My mother suggested putting in more time on my French, something constructive.

Alone, with playmates banished and so much time on my hands, I began to do something that would have long-lasting consequences. I slipped into a dream world, a landscape composed of the turf I'd left behind—Hyde Park, the White House, and all the people in those places who accepted me.

All of us gathered in our living room at Lawtonwood—where I was told by my mother, "You *are* home!"

CHAPTER 12

Instead of roughhousing with other children, a totally new experience for me, I now got into the habit of spending long hours with my toy ships and soldiers. I was able to keep myself happily occupied this way for vast stretches of time, arranging and rearranging them. Using my imagination, I restaged scenes I remembered from my days in the White House, lining up my marines and organizing my armada as Papa had told me they should be.

After a few months in Seattle, I asked plaintively, "When are we going home?" I don't, in fact, recall whether I addressed the question to my sister, to Mademoiselle, or to Mummy. It didn't matter, since my mother heard it, and the response she fired off was instantaneous and angry: "YOU *ARE* HOME!" I never brought up the subject again.

As the school year progressed, I gradually became less of an oddity. I remained shy, but I did get to know the other children's names and hung around the edges of their groups. Handball, the most popular activity, was more than I could handle. I was afraid of getting hurt.

One day, following the other boys' lead, I came sliding down the banister of the school building's stairway, and a teacher saw me. "Buzzie!" she said loudly. "What would your grandfather say?" I'd never been scolded publicly like that before, and I took her reprimand to heart. I stammered an apology as the kids standing around all laughed.

In the classroom, citing the assumed disapproval of one of my grandparents became the standard way to reprimand me for one small failing or another—for example, not paying attention or forgetting to blot my copy paper. (We used metal quill-pens, dipping them carefully into a small pot of ink.) The possibility that I might be sensitive to such remarks apparently never occurred to my teachers.

Advanced by half a grade after two months I was still bored, and I began daydreaming in class. I was petrified that I would answer incorrectly when it came my turn to respond to a question. For someone as sensitive to criticism as I was, any rebuke was awful. Yet even with my increasing anxiety about being caught out, I found it difficult to concentrate on what was in front of me. Slowly I was becoming wrapped up in my dream world, pushing reality aside. Even as I retreated into my fantasies, I knew that this behavior would bring disapproval. Fear of exposure was constantly with me.

Reports sent home noted my inability to pay close attention, but I still got fairly good marks. That was all that mattered. Mummy and Uncle J. simply assumed I must be making new friends. I kept quiet.

<hr>

We'd been in Seattle only a few months when both Grandmère and Granny proposed visits. However, they didn't want to come at the same time, which made obvious good sense. Granny came first, and having her with us was a real tonic for me. Just being near her I could practically smell Hyde Park and taste something of my life "back east," as my mother referred to it.

Entertaining Granny was a problem since my mother had a difficult time deciding who'd make a "good fit" socially with her class-conscious octogenarian grandmother. It was easy to sense my mother and Uncle J.'s relief when her visit finally drew to an end. But I was sad to see her go.

During her stay, I managed to overhear some grown-up conversations. In one of them, my great-grandmother expressed once again the deep-seated reservations she had regarding this "unsettled country," to which Mummy and Uncle J. had brought Sis and me. To a woman born before the Civil War, it was still the Wild West. What's more, when she was told we were attending public school, she reacted with shocked disbelief, undoubtedly blaming our grandmother's "new" ideas. It had been explained to her that attending a public school was indeed "good for Buzzy, bringing him more into the real world."

In those days one could freely roam about airports, meeting relatives right at the plane door. Sis, me, and my mother and stepfather, greeting Grandmère.

Most important to me, in the end, however, was Granny's firm expectation that Sis and I would eventually be sent "back east" for schooling. In fact, the only direct comment I can remember Granny making about our Seattle life related to Magnolia School. *And* it was said in front of me, which was highly irregular. In just a few months, she noted, I had picked up an undesirable accent and now was using words and phrases "not at all in good taste"—undoubtedly language I'd learned at school. She wanted to know what Mademoiselle was doing about it—which, I feel sure, was a polite way of asking what my mother was doing about it.

In her opinion, this would not have happened at "a proper school." Are there none available? she asked. Mummy's answer was that putting us in public school saved money; besides, public education was very good in Seattle—everyone said so. (Six years later, too late for me, my mother had changed her opinion.)

On Granny's return home, she must have tackled the subject straightaway with the other person just as concerned about our welfare, since my grandmother, visiting us soon thereafter, offered to subsidize private school tuition for us. My mother told her—repeating to me what she'd said—that I was doing "just fine."

My mother had been writing to Grandmère about Sis's and my progress at school, pointing out that we'd each jumped half a class. In one letter to her mother, she wrote:

"Sis is tickled to death with everything out here. Buz is having greater difficulty adjusting himself. I am sorry to say that he does not like his school, though I honestly think that as time goes on he will get more accustomed to the large classes, the new children and teachers. He needs a little more of the roughneck in his system. . . ." That was, I suppose, one way of explaining—avoiding understanding—my general malaise.

Time continued to hang heavily on my hands after school. Sis had schoolwork, but I still had none. So I escaped to my dream world, a diversion that proved as reliable as television or video games for today's child. On one occasion, I decided to use the playroom to set up my navy ships and marine platoons, spending several days arranging an elaborate display that spread over most of the available space. I intended to show off what I'd done to Mummy, Uncle J., and the rest of the household.

I'd never attempted anything on so magnificent a scale before. I found blocks of wood, cardboard boxes, and enough toy cars to make a motorcade. The scenario that I'd written in my mind involved FDR visiting a U.S. naval base, like the one at Bremerton, just across Puget Sound. Papa was in the lead vehicle. The Secret Service followed with one car on the right edging parallel to the president's car and another positioned on the left rear, just as I knew it should be from riding in that very motorcade many times. Sadly, I didn't possess any toy motorcycles for the usual outriders.

Finally, by Sunday, I was ready to unveil the spectacle I'd created and excited to explain everything. I gathered my audience—Mummy, Sis, Uncle J., and Mademoiselle. I pointed out the buildings and docks surrounded by boxes representing hills, and in the harbor naval ships would be firing their twenty-one-gun salute. Of course, I explained, the band was playing "Hail to the Chief." It was just as I remembered, and I assumed my audience, too, remembered it all happening.

Condescendingly, Uncle J. remarked, "And I'll bet you're riding with Papa in the first car." His meaning didn't escape me. My sister smirked. I was frozen, completely exposed. I don't remember bursting into tears or anything else that would have helped release my feelings. I was too stunned.

My mother said something to try to ease the situation. Shamed, I made my way quickly to my room. Mademoiselle picked up my ships and soldiers for me. If the episode made more than a passing impression upon my mother, it isn't indicated in her letter to Grandmère that describes that Sunday. "It has rained all day so we played ping-pong, dart throwing, coits and 'parade' with Buz's soldiers, in the playroom. John wrote two editorials and I did our accounts. . . ."

From then on, I found a spot to seclude myself when bringing out these soldiers and ships, and I put them away before anyone else could witness the private world with which I continued, secretly, to be engaged. I don't remember ever using that playroom again.

⸙

What was left of the school year dragged on. Finally, summer vacation arrived. After a stay in Wisconsin with my father, another two wonderful weeks at Plum Lake, we were ready to travel on to Hyde Park and the Big House, where Granny awaited our arrival. The relief I felt at this homecoming invaded my every pore.

There I was, back in my old bed in the nursery, with Duffie nearby, installed in one of the two rooms for the children's nurses on the stairwell landing. Lying there, just as always, there were the night noises of the train alongside the Hudson River, its coal-fired engines chugging slowly up the grade on its way to Albany. The late-evening thunderstorms were just as fierce as ever.

The best part of coming home was simply its deep and intense familiarity, the rooms in the Big House, their furniture and the smell of polish, the tall trees in the spacious grounds outside, the gardens, and, of course, the people.

There was also for me the enormous security of being with Granny, sensing her aura even when I wasn't with her. It was her place, the Big House and the surrounding estate. I identified with it and with her. Formidable though she might be, I knew I had her unreserved love. Where she was, I felt I belonged.

The big library room at Hyde Park, where I felt completely at home.

CHAPTER 13

A lovely picture of Granny (on the left) with Papa, my mother, and us kids (1933).

I had always been a picky eater, yet I liked mealtimes with Granny. She enjoyed her food and had high expectations of her English cook, Mary, who still used the wood range in the kitchen, insisting it was better than any of the new gas or electric stoves. Vegetables at Hyde Park weren't boiled until tasteless; meat had the proper pink tinge. We ate slowly and, emulating Granny, appreciatively. She would always note with pride that everything served came from our family farm, and in this way, she was both of her time and way ahead of it.

When we returned to Hyde Park that summer after our move to Seattle, it was soon clear that my deteriorating manners needed correction. I was taught how to serve myself from a platter held by the butler and to always say thank you, how to use my knife and fork with the proper style, when to use the butter knife—and when not to!—how to drink from my water and milk glasses, and above all, the importance of not spilling anything.

When lunching with Granny, it was essential that Duffie make us "presentable." If Granny had a guest, we usually did not eat with her, except if the guest was a family member. Lunch at the big table was properly served by both butlers, who would first serve Granny, the guest, then Sis and me. We commenced with a soup served from a tureen and ladled into a soup bowl. The large spoon on the right side of my bowl that sat waiting to be used was quite heavy. In my small hand it required close attention if I wasn't to spill. Then came a meat course. I was expected to cut my own meat and do it smartly. Sometimes, as in the European style, the vegetables were served as a separate course. If there was fresh corn on the cob, I could eat it with my fingers! Not too much butter on it, please, and don't gobble. Then came salad. Before dessert, the butler set down in front of us a finger bowl with a dessert plate underneath. I learned to dip just so much of my fingers into the bowl—not to "take a bath"—before carefully picking up the finger bowl, with its doily underneath, and moving it up and to the left, just above my bread plate. It seemed to me quite unnecessary, but it was a formality I associated with being an adult, so I didn't mind. For dessert Granny liked the sweet and heavy variety, but quite often we had ice cream, made that morning in our kitchen. I was then ready for my nap. Granny would nod meaningfully to us, and we would dutifully ask, "May I be excused, please?" Her response was, "You may get down." For me these rituals were fun.

Granny's instructions or admonitions never seemed burdensome. Even when she corrected my pronunciation or pointedly frowned when I used a questionable expression learned from my Magnolia classmates, I was not put off—the reason being that I was where I wanted to be, with someone I felt I belonged with. Granny's love was unreserved, and her caring for me was straightforward.

Whenever Sis and I sat with Granny, she chatted easily with us. During lunch she'd discuss with us the guests she might be having that evening or for tea, what she'd done that morning, what tenants or neighbors she'd visited—perhaps an ill person she's called upon. In her company, items from the morning newspaper might also figure. My sister and I were expected to listen carefully, even ask a question.

Occasionally, Granny's sister, Aunt Kassie—Katherine Delano Robbins—who lived in Tuxedo, an exclusive community, gated, close to New York City, would visit during our summer stay. (Granny had ten siblings, although not all of them lived into adulthood.) If Sis and I were included at lunch with her, we were to put on our best clothes. From our mother, we knew two things about Aunt Kassie. First, she was something of a dreadnought, and second, she was an arch-conservative whose opinions drew the disapproval of our grandmother.

Upon entering the library, we'd dutifully peck a kiss on Aunt Kassie's cheek and then seat ourselves close by in two straight chairs. When the moment came, we'd follow the two grandes dames into the dining room where the best china and silver had been laid. Sis and I mostly listened, with the conversation usually featuring gossip about Delano family members, which meant little to us. We'd nod politely at what seemed like the proper moments; otherwise we'd keep silent except to say "thank you" or "no thank you" when being served.

One of the most memorable visitors to the Big House was Dora Delano Forbes, known as Aunt Doe, another of Granny's sisters, who for many years had lived in grand style (more than she could sensibly afford, Papa liked to note) in Paris. Compared to Granny and Aunt Kassie, who were both ample sized, Aunt Doe was a petite woman. She and Granny always spoke French together, and it was in this language that she addressed Sis and me whenever we joined them. My sister managed to hold her own, but I came up short, not having made much progress with Mademoiselle.

Still, I was happy to sit with my cambric tea and watch such an exotic creature as this. Through her eighties Aunt Doe crossed the Atlantic regularly on an ocean liner to visit the Delano clan. She smiled far less than Granny, but she had a very expressive face that would change subtly with pleasure or amusement. Around her neck she wore a black velvet choker with a modest diamond clasp, the sparkle of which always caught my eye. I remember her as always dressed in black. Although she'd been an expatriate—very Francophile—for many years, Aunt Doe was proud of being a Delano and of the family's long heritage of building and sailing ships.* My grandfather later gave me a book about Massachusetts's seafaring history, written by Samuel Eliot Morrison, and his inscription to me on the flyleaf points to Aunt Doe's initials just above his own signature.

⌘

Life changed substantially each summer at the Big House after Granny departed for her annual month at Campobello. For one thing, the butler returned to England for his holiday and so did the cook. Jennings, Granny's maid, usually accompanied her to Campo, but if she couldn't, Granny "made do" with a local staff recruited by the resident housekeeper there, Mrs. Lilian Calder.

With no Granny at the center of it all, the Big House seemed empty. Our ordered life, however, stayed the same. After breakfast we would go riding, a routine for my sister and me as much as visiting Granny or having tea. Every summer the army grooms brought our horses from the White House stables to Hyde Park. To us it seemed quite normal to learn to ride horseback under the supervision of the U.S. cavalry, but it was quite a perk. My grandmother, who rode her horse, Dot, every day, noted in a letter to my mother: "Buzz considers Dot his horse!" The paths, usually on our neighbor's property, were endless. Sis rode better than I did; she, like Mummy, wanted to be a good rider. I fell off more than once from not paying attention. I was distracted by the hayfields and trees, especially apple trees. I could pick apples right from the saddle.

While Granny was away, Sis and I took our afternoon tea on the back screened porch with the servants. It was quite a different scene. Duffie told sto-

---

*Aunt Doe's husband, William Howell Forbes, had risen to become a partner of her father, Warren Delano, in Russell & Company, once the largest American trading house in China.

After falling out with "Aunts" Marion and Nancy, my grandmother built her own house at Val Kill.

ries and we sang simple songs like "Mama's little baby loves shortnin', shortnin', Mama's little baby loves shortnin' bread" . . . or "Comin' through the Rye." Duffie led, while Sis and I and the white servants joined in shyly. It was a delight.

When our great-grandmother departed, our grandmother, to the extent that she was available, kept an eye on Sis and me. When she was at Val Kill we'd go over at least once a day. After our morning ride, we often joined Grandmère for lunch. I loved the casual atmosphere there; there might be hamburgers or hot dogs grilled on the barbeque—which resembled a big fireplace set on the lawn—and guests joined in with the preparations and serving. My grandmother didn't know the first thing about cooking, but she was quite willing to flip over a burger if someone told her when to do it, though it would invariably be well-done if she did.

Grandmère for many years had enjoyed Val Kill with her dear friends Nancy Cook and Marion Dickerman. The three of them had been ardent political activists together, as well as business partners, in the 1920s and early

'30s, sharing quarters—the Stone Cottage, built for them by my grandfather—there on the property. Whenever she had a free day or two, my grandmother would escape to Val Kill, considering it her home away from Granny and the Big House. She spent several weeks there during the summer, but always moved back to the Big House when my grandfather was visiting.

The cottage industry they'd idealistically begun in 1925—originally known as the Val-Kill Furniture Shop, and later Val-Kill Industries—at first offered only reproduction early American furniture, including an occasional Dutch colonial piece. Later they added pewter, weaving, and other crafts, all as a way to help local farmers supplement their incomes in the off-season. But this enterprise, never well managed, was already faltering before the Great Depression dealt it a final blow.

After Grandmère became First Lady and her life changed so greatly, new people—friends like Lorena Hickok—entered the picture and became part of her inner circle. Disapproving, and undoubtedly jealous, Marion and Nancy weren't as welcoming as they might have been to Hick and the other newcomers. It probably didn't help that Nancy had not been invited to Washington with a post in the national Democratic Party organization. What had once been a jolly, harmonious atmosphere at Val Kill was no longer.

I also speculate that Grandmère may have finally realized that she was a fifth wheel in the company of her two friends, though she would certainly never mention it. That Nancy and Marion were a couple was obvious to everyone and regularly spoken of (though behind the hand). I suspect that my grandmother put it out of her mind, choosing to ignore, not think about, the remarks about Nancy and Marion uttered within her earshot, and Granny would have done the same.

Grandmère regarded and cherished Val Kill as her own special getaway—and so, after the rift with Nancy and Marion, she decided to build a house of her own, constructing it out of two of the now idle Val-Kill factory buildings. (As Val Kill is now a National Historic Site, this is what visitors see today.)

By 1937, when Sis and I returned to Hyde Park from Seattle, the chill between our grandmother and Nancy and Marion was obvious, even to us children. In fact, our mother had actually given us warning that things had changed at Val Kill. Even though we could see plainly that Grandmère now had a house of her own, we knew that we were still to call her ex-chums Aunt Marion and Aunt Nancy, and they continued to be invited to the Big House for a meal whenever Papa came home from Washington to visit.

When we arrived, Grandmère's house at Val Kill had only recently been finished. She felt, she said, "for the first time in my life" that she really had a home of her own. The pine paneling throughout had a pleasant rustic feel, and the rooms were decorated just as my grandmother always styled her homes, in a simple, homey good taste, with book-

My grandmother loved her house at Val Kill and enjoyed showing famous visitors around.

cases and pictures—mostly of family and friends—covering the walls.

An unpretentious staircase led to the second floor, where the narrow hallway led to Grandmère's modestly sized bedroom with its big screened-in sleeping porch. Lacking any grandeur, the house had a character that embodied my grandmother, as a person and as a hostess. While the house carried echoes of her Victorian childhood, Val Kill also expressed my grandmother's rebellion against what she considered the dated atmosphere of Springwood and the embedded class distinctions so naturally expressed by her mother-in-law. Though there was still a lot of family silver in the dining room, Val Kill's atmosphere was never formal. Even when Grandmère served tea with all the trimmings, the effect was casual, the ritual never imposing.

Enjoying the company of others, she filled the house most weekends with visiting friends and relatives—there were numerous guestrooms in the

Nancy Cook: "Eleanor, please, nobody cooks, not even on a barbeque, with their purse hanging from their arm!"

rambling structure. She was never alone, even on weekdays. Of course, with her demanding schedule, my grandmother was rarely at Val Kill for more than a few days at a time. The exception was summertime. Then she'd come more frequently and stay longer.

The screened porch off my grandmother's bedroom was where she slept during the warm and humid summer nights. She had the largest daybed I've ever seen. It had been made to order at the Val Kill factory for my 6-foot 5-inch uncle, John Roosevelt, her youngest son. But since he had never used it, she took it back and put it on the sleeping porch. I loved lying on it for afternoon naps, occupying less than half its length. I have the daybed today, and I still take naps on it.

That year, as a summer project, each of us in my class at Magnolia had been asked to write a history of the Dewey family in our own words. Not connected to the famous admiral of Manila Bay fame—or to the creator of the library decimal system—the local Deweys were known only to regional historians and the public school system of Seattle. In class, we'd reviewed at length their progress in covered wagons across the Great Plains and over the Rocky Mountains, at which point, unlike most pioneers, they'd turned north to Oregon and Washington, rather than south to California. In scenes straight out of a Hollywood western, the doughty Deweys were attacked by Indians, forced to circle their wagons and fight off the marauders, finally arriving at a place that seemed right for settling and making a farm. There they prospered, the city of Seattle being the result, built upon Protestant virtue and hard work.

I believed it all then, and I still admire their journey. What could be more uplifting—or provide me with a better behavioral model? Although it was an ideal quite beyond my reach—I was a bit challenged in the rough-and-ready department—their true grit nonetheless offered a goal to strive for—and fodder for my dream world. But rather than daydream, I had to write my own version of this saga and illustrate it. There was to be a prize for the best report in the class.

So every afternoon that summer at Val Kill, after my nap, and before I was allowed to go swimming, I sat in a rather odd chair, Val Kill–made, next to the huge daybed in my grandmother's sleeping porch. It was a writing chair with an egg-shaped arm extending up and out on the right side, with enough room on it to place a notebook or pad of paper, or to set your book for reading. (Left-handers were out of luck.) My grandmother, despite the strained relations between them, had asked Nancy Cook to review my work each afternoon. Aunt Nancy took her assignment seriously, pronouncing me too inclined to daydream and dawdle, but, with much encouragement, I completed it by summer's end.

Summers always seem to stretch out endlessly at the beginning, and this one was no different. When I arrived at Hyde Park, the fact that, eventually, I'd have to leave again was not on my mind. I was too happy to be there. But the time slipped by, and soon Grandmère was reminding Sis and me that we'd soon be leaving for Seattle to start school again. We'd wait for Granny to come back from Campobello—she insisted upon seeing us before we headed west—but then it was the train to New York, where Mademoiselle would meet us for the long trip back across the country.

I felt like a balloon with its air released, utterly deflated. Duffie tried to comfort me, reminding me that I'd soon be seeing my mother and Uncle J. But I felt more at home in the Big House, with Granny, and at Val Kill, with Grand-mère and Tommy. Leaving their company was what occupied my mind.

After buying their tickets to view the Big House, today's visitors will pass by the Rose Garden and then, to their right, behold Springwood. Not looking to the left, they will miss the long, tree-lined entrance drive, which the family always used—most poignantly for me, for my departures.

Today, visitors to the Timberline Lodge in Oregon will find this picture, only I am cut out of it so that children can stick their head through the hole to have their picture taken with FDR.

S is and I were seasoned train travelers, but as we crossed the wide open spaces on our way back to Seattle, the days hung heavily. Finally we reached the Rocky Mountains, and an open car was attached for passengers willing to risk being rained on. Since it was still summer, Mademoiselle relented. The open car, where the three of us squeezed into one seat, reminded me of the open trolley cars in big cities. There were no seat belts, and often, as the train took a long curve, the car leaned over, and we had to hold on to keep from falling out of our seats. It provided extraordinary views of the deep ravines below, even if it wasn't very safe by today's standards. The scenery was spectacular, and the train, going very slowly, turned in a mesmerizing snake-like fashion, so that we could see the engine up front at the same time that we could see the last coach.

Back in Seattle, my mother sprang a very unwelcome surprise: it was now Mademoiselle who was going to be leaving us. I'd grown very fond of my Belgian governess, and the time we spent together had offered the only companionship I remember having during that period. Before we left Hyde Park, Mummy had written to my grandmother: "It is so hard to make a decision about Mlle. The children are terribly fond of her, and having her has been a help to me while the work was so heavy. But she is not good for Buzz, is a big expense, & has not taught the children how to speak French. My plan is to tell her I do not need her any more when the children are settled into their school lives again—probably about the 20th of Sept."

Sis and I were both devastated by this news. In fact, the correspondence indicates that my sister continued to be so upset after Mademoiselle's departure that our mother led Sis to believe in the subterfuge that her governess would be returning. Nothing could cheer me up—until we learned later that autumn that Papa was headed in our direction. He was to tour the Northwest, where he would inspect large Public Works Administration (PWA) projects such as Oregon's newly opened Bonneville Dam on the Columbia River. And most importantly, from my perspective, he would visit us.

⟶⟨⟩⟵

I was beside myself with anticipation at the prospect of seeing Papa and being part of his entourage again. The plan was for Sis and me to go with my mother and Uncle J. to join the presidential train in Oregon and travel with him for several days. Once we'd boarded, our first stop would be the new lodge on Mt. Hood, Timberline Lodge, a PWA project, which he'd be dedicating. (I didn't know it at the time, but construction of the lodge hadn't yet been completed at the time of our arrival, and officials had scurried to make it presentable for the occasion.)

For reasons that are still unclear to me, I found myself seated next to my grandfather at the gala luncheon. Such a thing had never happened before in all my years of living in the White House. The only sensible explanation is that the photographers on hand wanted pictures, as they always did, and my grandfather liked to include family, particularly us kids, whenever he could.

So there I was, proudly at Papa's side, with an array of knives and forks before me and Granny's distant voice in my ear. I was quite conscious of the flashbulbs popping. The first course was a whole tomato, cold and tough, filled with something I didn't recognize. I watched my grandfather deftly extract the slippery stuff from his tomato and get all of it to his mouth, not once missing a beat in the story he was telling. My own portion kept sliding off my fork. Out of the corner of my eye, I glimpsed the reporters and their cameras. I was mortified. Still, I had no choice but to continue gamely. Suddenly Papa's fork swooped over to my plate, lifted out a large forkful of whatever it was, and set it beside my tomato. All of this he did effortlessly while carrying on with another story.

I was familiar with our train, the *Magellan*, having occasionally traveled on it from Washington to Hyde Park before moving to Seattle. It wasn't as sumptuous as other legendary private cars, such as those belonging to famed bon vivant Lucius Beebe, but it was still pretty wonderful. Because space was limited at the dining table, Sis and I ate our supper earlier than the grown-ups, and after we were finished, we'd briefly join everyone else at the back of the carriage for cocktail hour in an open lounge area. The air there was filled with smoke, and everyone was talking at once, with lots of laughter.

Papa—who always smelled of tobacco, since he was a habitual smoker—sat in his chair, his trademark cigarette holder in hand, the center of attention. Our arrival stopped the conversation. I said my good nights and kissed even people I didn't recognize. Sleep came quickly in the top berth of the tiny compartment we shared, as the train rumbled along.

Far too soon, it was time to return home to Seattle. Papa stopped off to see where we lived, but it was only a quick look, as he had to be on his way, continuing his tour. We accompanied him in the back of his car. Unknown to Sis and me, Papa had asked to be driven past our school. Magnolia's principal had lined up all the kids outside to watch President Roosevelt drive by. I didn't mind being seen by my peers in my grandfather's company, though I tried to hide my excitement. My sister, modest as ever, hid on the floor of the limousine as the cavalcade swept slowly past our classmates.

With the conclusion of this distracting interlude, I became a schoolboy again. When my grandfather departed, so too went the comforting sense of being enveloped in his powerful and protective aura. In class, my teacher reminded the other students why I'd been absent for nearly a week. So that everyone could see, she held up a large news photo of Sis and me in the open car with Papa on his way to board the *Magellan*. Any pride I may have felt evaporated, leaving me embarrassed and tongue-tied. She then suggested that I tell everybody all about my trip with the president of the United States. Did I admire my grandfather, she asked?

I found I couldn't say anything except to mumble that I'd had a good time—and, yes, I admired my grandfather. When asked if I wanted to be like my grandfather, however, I said I didn't know. With my nearly inaudible answers, the grilling finally stopped. The teacher and my fellow second-graders probably thought me awfully dull, as I seemed not to understand the questions asked of me.

As the school term dragged on, I sank deeper into my dream world, maintaining something of an acceptable facade at school and at home, but in truth, increasingly immersed in another sphere. My grades at school declined, and teachers told me I wasn't paying enough attention. At home my preoccupation with my other world went unnoticed, or at least, nothing was ever said to me. With Mademoiselle's departure, Sis and I now ate alone.

We did join Mummy and Uncle J. for cocktail hour when they came home. It was like a sacred ritual. Mummy and Popsie began by raising their martini glasses to each other and mouthing silently (but visibly) "I love you." Sis and I would turn away and look at each other with resigned expressions of disgust. We were very prim. I think we also sensed this exercise surely excluded us. Still, we wouldn't have been left out for anything. After a short time I was sent to bed, my mother and stepfather coming up to kiss me goodnight.

Then, just before Christmas, came news that cheered me up. Grandmère had changed all her usual holiday plans and would be flying to Seattle to be with us. This was a surprise! We knew it wasn't a simple matter for her to get away for the holidays; she had a bumper crop of parties to preside over, and Christmas was one of her favorite times at the White House. The Christmas of 1937 was the first time I would not be spending my winter holiday in the East, and I felt much better about it knowing that my grandmother was coming to be with us.

Much later I would learn that Grandmère's real reason for coming to Seattle was that my mother had not been feeling well. (It was a serious issue, and my mother later had a hysterectomy.) My grandmother had decided her only daughter needed her assistance to put on the right sort of Christmas for her family.

Since Mummy had been ordered to rest—literally to stay off her feet—her normal anxiety about whom she and Uncle J. should invite to meet her famous mother was not an issue. And, as it turned out, it was the only visit of my grandmother that I remember as being relatively easy on our household. It was short and strictly a family affair. For two days, we ate together with my parents, and because it was the school holidays, I could stay up later than usual. My grandmother's presence made a real difference.

Grandmère brought a surfeit of presents with her. In fact, her own suitcase was much smaller than the great bag of gifts she carried. In my stocking on Christmas morning, I found special presents from Papa: new ships to expand my private navy. That afternoon we did invite some of the neighbors,

Christmas with Grandmère and some neighborhood kids at our house in Lawtonwood, 1937. A jolly time.

including their children, to meet our visitor. Grandmère had presents—or else my mother, cleverly, made sure some were at hand—for all the kids who came over.

The biggest surprise on Christmas Day was a very special telephone call. Papa had arranged with the telephone company to hook up all the family members—all my uncles and aunts and Granny—on the same circuit at the same time (taking into account the three-hour time difference from coast to coast). This was quite a technical feat in those days. Sis and I were each allowed to say "Merry Christmas" to Papa and to hear him offer a similar greeting to each of us. This brief exchange provoked lots of excitement and was repeated with little variation—most of the phone call involved each family member asking "Who's that?" My grandfather must have been exhausted afterward, although Grandmère reported later how pleased he'd been by the success of his idea.

The next afternoon, my grandmother returned to Washington, and we resumed our lives without her. We had a few more days' vacation, but I dreaded going back to school. I knew I'd be asked by my teacher to offer yet another report on my family and what it was like spending Christmas with Mrs. Roosevelt. It didn't matter that "Mrs. Roosevelt" was my grandmother, since her public persona always trumped the private one.

While Grandmère had been with us over Christmas, Sis and I had listened to Mummy and Uncle J. give her glowing reports of how well both of us were doing in school, repeating what she'd written to her earlier: "There will be 35 to 40 children in Sis' and Buz' classes, but I have watched them at work and the children seem to learn a great deal, to be very much interested, and the discipline is excellent." Sis and I were too well mannered to contradict anything my mother said and only nodded as she prettied up our experiences at school for our grandmother. (My sister entered a private school the following year.) Yet, reading their correspondence sixty years later, I was pained to see how our mother rationalized fitting Sis and me into the "adventure" the Boettigers were having in Seattle, running the *Post-Intelligencer* and being a force for "liberalism" in the Northwest. We were perforce supporting players.

In the New Year, I continued to underperform at school, but other than the warning that I must improve my performance in spelling—on the occasion of my report card arriving at home—no pressure was put on me to take stock, concentrate, pay attention. At home, meanwhile, I played by myself. Occasionally, my mother would make a plan for a neighbor's son, a boy about my age, to join me after school. But neither he nor I enjoyed it. For my part, I found it a strain to "entertain" him, something I felt I was expected to do.

Probably these arranged visits seemed strange to him, too, since I acted more like a courteous, nervous host than a playmate.

With one difficult year in Seattle just about behind me, I couldn't have been more shocked when mother and Uncle J. suddenly informed Sis and me that we were moving out of our house in Lawtonwood and to a neighborhood closer to their jobs, nearer the center of the city, which would cut their driving time in half. So we began packing.

A few of the kids gathered around the Secret Service's car on Galler Street, the closest I ever came to being part of a neighborhood gang.

Our one-year lease in Lawtonwood was extended just long enough to get us through the Easter vacation. The rent, my mother explained, had been raised simply because she was a Roosevelt—or so she believed. But it was a fact that living on Capitol Hill would cut in half her and Uncle J.'s driving time to their office. For me it meant leaving Magnolia for another school.

After Easter we moved to our new house on Galler Street in one of Seattle's older residential areas. Houses on our new street were substantial, and their lawns well kept with up-market cars in the garages. Most enjoyed a good view from the steep hill. Immediately surrounding us were smaller houses. Children from both areas mixed at Stevens, the public elementary school, although some of the kids from the big houses went to private schools, as Sis now did.

For the first week or so, Mody drove me in the Secret Service car the short distance to Stevens School. But then, as a mark of my being a third grader and more grown up, Mummy decided to allow me to walk the three blocks to school on my own. This was exciting, and I felt very proud. It was, in fact, the first experience I had had of being out "in public" on my own. The two blocks to my destination required navigating two intersections, neither of which had traffic lights. My instructions were to look twice in one direction and twice in the other, and then, if there were no cars coming, I was to quickly walk across.

My new freedom felt wonderful! Venturing out on my own the first morning, I skipped down the street, looked at other homes, cars in the street, the occasional person on his way to work. It seemed to me that things appeared quite different when you were on your own. I was very careful at the intersection, waiting and waiting for the moment I could safely proceed. When I got to the second block, where the school playground began, I made sure to straighten up and march properly, half expecting that every teacher in school would be watching me.

Soon I grew more confident and began, cockily, to calculate whether a car approaching one of my crossing places was far enough away to allow me to dash across. However, this didn't go on for long before my mother confronted me. She firmly scolded me for taking foolish chances—not following the rules she'd laid down. Why did I think I could get away with this, she wanted to know. I was confounded: *how did she know?* I couldn't figure out the mystery of her omniscience.

My sister clued me in. Mody had been slowly following me, with Sis in the car, on the way to her new school. Sure enough, looking over my shoulder the next day, I spotted my tail. The game was over. I waited until they caught up with me, held up my thumb, and climbed in. Later, I told Mummy I would just ride with them and be dropped off. I'd been had.

Life at my new school was very much like that at Magnolia, with large classes and work that was not challenging. I was able to get average grades with little effort. Lost, as ever, in my dream world, I simply seemed "doze-y" to the teacher, who conscientiously reported my inattention to my mother. In one area, however, I was a star. Back in those days, children were graded on "deportment," and here I was at the head of the class. My unfailing politeness astonished my teachers. I got along well enough with my classmates, but I remained shy and distant, never joining in the handball or tag they played together. I was even hesitant about playing musical chairs! Although I desperately wanted to belong, I nonetheless kept on doing my best to block this from happening. My specialness was more important; I clung to it.

This choice—not exactly a conscious one—led me to an isolation I couldn't break through. My identity as "Buzzie" provided security, but there was a price to pay for this protection, a high one.

One day, Hazen picked me up from school and overheard some kids talking about a pick-up baseball game on the playground later on that day. It was to be right after supper, when there'd still be plenty of light. Sensing that it would do me good to join the other kids, Hazen asked Mummy if he could take me, saying that he knew I'd never seen a baseball game before. My mother gave her permission, and I was full of anticipation as we headed back to Stevens.

The game was already in progress when we got there, so we joined the sidelines, where the other parents and kids were sitting. I found what I was seeing confusing, and Hazen's explanations only made things more bewildering. When there was a break, he asked if I couldn't have a chance at bat. I tried to get out of it, but it was too late.

Stepping up to the plate, I was petrified. Bat in hand, I was told how to stand—and to swing when the ball was thrown by the pitcher. Ready? The ball sailed toward me. I swung. My God, I hit it! I just stood there. "Run! Run!" everyone screamed. But where? One of the boys caught my confusion and gestured wildly at first base. I ran, but by the time I reached it I'd been thrown out. It didn't matter to me: I was on top of the moon. I'd hit the ball. What my teammates thought, I can just imagine. By the time we got home, it was dark. Thrilled and very pleased with myself, I announced—repeatedly—that I'd hit the ball! I went into the kitchen to tell Katie and Ivan of my triumph.

First thing the next morning, I asked when I could go again to watch baseball. My mother looked doubtful, pointing out how long past my bedtime we'd returned. I had been too worked up to fall asleep, she noted. Perhaps, she proposed, I could go with Uncle J. one Saturday to see a Seattle Rainiers game at the new Sick's Stadium. (The Seattle franchise was part of the Pacific Coast League and played such teams as the Oakland Oaks, the Portland Beavers, the Sacramento Solons, and the San Francisco Seals. Back then there was no major league baseball west of the Mississippi.) This promised outing didn't happen right away, but when we did finally go, I enjoyed the excitement, and so did Sis. Our discovery there of Cracker Jacks, heretofore unknown to us, made it even better.

Sis at this stage was starting to have friends whom my mother, after vetting the parents, would allow her to visit. But such social protocol wasn't observed by boys of my age. My new milieu was the impromptu world of the street. Where we lived now was a genuine neighborhood. On Galler Street alone there were children of all ages. In the long evenings they played in the street, the occasional car passing by slowly. I hung around the edges. Gradually, I joined in their hide-and-seek games, which offered wonderful adventure. We would hide in the alley until an opportunity came to run to home base without being tagged out. As the light waned, our fun would increase in the hazy twilight. Poor Hazen, however, couldn't always discern my whereabouts. It was a problem that soon gave my mother an excuse to shut down this fun, too. The Galler Street gang was a "little too rough for me," Mummy explained, and the Secret Service didn't want me out after dark.

With my street games curtailed, I focused on the approaching summer vacation. For me, the sense of urgency was barely containable. Before me lay Hyde Park, the Big House, and Val Kill. We were also to meet Dad and go once more with him to Plum Lake on our way east.

After moving to Seattle, the subject of our father came up only when there'd be some communication from him, usually relating to arrangements for a visit. His desire to continue to exercise his visiting rights with his children was considered tiresome by my mother and sister, an undesirable interruption. Mummy remained skeptical of my father's intentions. She wrote to Grandmère in July 1938: "His sentiments for the children [have] grown by leaps and bounds since his separation from them [since our move to Seattle], and now assume terrific proportions in his mind." Uncle J.'s pointed silence on the topic of Dad signaled to me that he shared my mother's attitude. I can't blame him for that, but, for me, it inhibited any parental role.

One evening, as my sister and I ate supper together, with my mother hovering nearby, Sis announced that henceforth we would—or, at least, *she* would—cease referring to our father as "Dad." From now on she intended to call him "Mr. D." Didn't I agree? I wish I'd had the guts to say no, but I didn't. After an initial hesitation, which provoked strong looks from my sister, I nodded. What to say? I was a wimp. The move to Seattle had isolated me from the few people—such as Granny and Papa—who held sympathetic attitudes toward Dad.

Soon, Sis abandoned the idea of Mr. D. for the even more depersonalizing "The Man from New York." I thought she was teasing, but she took my amused smile for acceptance, and that was that. Whether my mother had anything to do with this, I don't know. In later years, my mother swore that it was Sis who'd been the one to invent this final effacement of his identity.

I don't remember what I called Dad; naming him had become such a potential trap. Part of the problem was practical. Visits with Dad had been frequent enough to maintain our relationship with him when we lived in New York City and then in Washington. But now that we were three thousand miles away in Seattle, I saw my father once a year. I lost contact.

In retrospect, I can see that my mother, and also my grandmother, simply assumed that I would welcome a stepfather into my life, shifting my loyalty from Dad to Uncle J. Of course, it suited them to imagine this. Neither woman allowed for the possibility of my continuing to identify with my father. After all, I was named "Curtis." So, with John Boettiger as the male head of our household and my mother and sister revolving around him, it was easier for me just to go along. While never embracing this new father figure, I don't recall feeling resentful, or even expressing any reservation, toward my stepfather. To do so would immediately have incurred reaction from all of the women in my life. Besides, as my mother had noted, I kept it all inside.

As summer drew near, Mummy announced that she'd planned a surprise for me. Before Sis and I were to leave for Plum Lake and then east to Hyde Park, I would spend two weeks at a place called Camp Discovery. Two weeks, to me, had the sound of an eternity. It would be my first time on my own in a strange place without someone—like my governess or my father—closely attending. The camp was located on Puget Sound, about two hours away, and my mother was to drive me there.

As we left Seattle and the surrounding towns, we entered the forests of tall cedars and firs that crowd right to the edge of the sound. It must have been a beautiful drive, but my mother seemed anxious. Her jaw was set, and we didn't speak. Although she may well have had other things on her mind, I interpreted this as some kind of disapproval of me. My mother had repeated several times her mantra that this experience would be "good for me." But I couldn't understand why it would be better than all of the neighborhood play and games I'd been steered away from.

After getting lost, we found the dirt road that led to Camp Discovery's secluded site. We arrived at a big building made of rough-hewn logs and were met by a young woman counselor, who showed us to my cabin. After my mother left, I began to cry. I couldn't help myself. But it was too late; she was gone. The counselor, though only a teenager herself, quickly saw that I didn't know what to do with my clothes, that I didn't know what to wear, what shoes to put on. In fact, this new boy didn't know anything, really. Being sympathetic, she helped me unpack. Once my other bunkmates came in, she sent me off with them for afternoon milk and cookies.

Discovery's small rustic cabins, each housing four boys, were scattered around a large field that extended down to a rocky beach. Everyone ate together in a big dining hall enclosed by screens to keep out the enormous flies and mosquitoes. At the end of each meal, the campers scraped their plates into a large trash bin. This was yet another activity new to me. I always finished everything—I knew not to put too much syrup on my pancakes—so this ritual never had been necessary. But, still, I wanted to belong, so I joined the queue.

I learned three useful things at Camp Discovery. One was how to tie my shoes. (My ignorance of this amazed my fellows.) Second, I learned how to put on my pullover while holding on to my sleeves so they didn't end up above my elbows. And the third was how to pick up the dry part of a road apple—left by the animals who grazed on our center field the other ten months of the year—and throw the turd at the older boys who were housed in the cabins on the other side of the field. That was great fun, limited only to a few minutes, just before lights out. Not much older than some of their charges, the staff joined us in our dirty game. I don't remember washing before going to bed in my cot. Whatever my mother might have thought of this sport, I slept well.

After I had settled in at camp, Mummy and Uncle J. came to Parents' Day. I had lots to demonstrate, just like the other campers who wanted to show off for their mothers and fathers. But it wasn't hard to see that Mummy and Uncle J. were different. Cordial to everyone, but distant, they were aware of "who they were," and thus stood a bit apart. It wasn't that they were putting on an act, exactly. They were simply more at ease once they'd been recognized as the Boettigers, the president's daughter and son-in-law. Indeed, after that, everyone, including me, seemed more comfortable.

Back in Seattle, I was in for a shock. Returning to our house, I found that my teddy bear had disappeared, gone from its place on my pillow. When I tearfully asked where it was, my mother replied that I was too old for it now and that she'd disposed of it. I had held this teddy bear closely night after night. He was like a thousand other teddy bears, but this one was my closest companion. I confided in him. In time, I got over his sudden disappearance, as was expected, but it was a loss I still resent.

Camp *had* been good for me, but, like a homing bird, I couldn't wait to depart for Hyde Park. Katie would accompany us on the trip to Chicago, where she'd hand us over to Duffie. Duffie would travel with us to Wisconsin to be with Dad at Plum Lake and then would stay with us at Hyde Park for the rest of the summer. With her easy manner and sense of fun, having her minding Sis and me was always enjoyable.

Once at Hyde Park, we followed our usual routine, which I loved. That summer I learned to swim. Grandmère recruited her friend, Earl Miller, who had helped her get over her fear of water, to teach me how to swim in the pool at Val Kill. While he was instructing me, Earl remarked to my grandmother, "Buzzie seems afraid of everything."

Swimming was something I'd watched my grandmother do with her trademark self-imposed discipline. Usually in the late afternoon she would walk from her house to the pool at the Stone Cottage, a bathrobe worn over her swimming suit. Her daily swim was a routine, for "exercise," she said. Standing on the side of the pool, pumping her legs, she got off the edge with a low dive. Actually, it was more like a belly flop, which brought schoolboy derision from any of my uncles standing by. She took two turns each length, one breast stroke and the other side stroke. (The breast stroke, the back stroke, and the side stroke were considered, I was informed, most appropriate for ladies.) After this, Grandmère got out and lay down by the side of the pool to sun herself for a few minutes. Then she went back to work.

⤬

What stands out most in my mind about that particular summer, when I was eight, was not the time I spent at the Hyde Park estate but rather the times I left it. Two trips took me past its borders, the first one all the way to Boston, where my youngest uncle, John Roosevelt, was married to Ann Clark at Nahant, on the North Shore. I rode to Boston with my great-grandmother in her old limousine. Her chauffeur, Mr. De Pew, sat at the wheel, and her maid, Jennings, sat up front beside him. The age of both Granny's limousine and her driver was regarded by the family with some resigned trepidation. Her firm stance was "Both Mr. De Pew and my car will last me out."

It is still a long journey to make by car today, but in 1938 it took *all* day. Very few towns on the two-lane route were bypassed, which meant we frequently slowed down to twenty miles an hour when entering a village. I didn't mind; I was entranced by everything I saw out the window. Also, Mary, our cook, had prepared a sumptuous picnic basket. After lunch by the side of the road, I curled up for a nap, lying on Granny's lovely car rug on the floor of the backseat. With the jump seats up, there was more than enough room for me.

For the wedding ceremony, I had been designated the role of ring bearer, and I was thrilled—and nervous. It pains me even now to confess that I flubbed it: the ring somehow slithered off the satin cushion I was proudly holding in front of me and fell to the floor. The good news is that this catastrophe happened in the rehearsal. Nonetheless, at my mother's insistence, I was quickly replaced—by Uncle Jimmy, the groom's brother and best man.

Papa arrived the morning of the wedding, with my mother, on the presidential yacht, the USS *Potomac*, anchoring off the coast along with the navy destroyer that escorted it. Indeed, it was a very public wedding. As Blanche Cook recorded in her biography of my grandmother,* the headline in the *New York Times* blared "Thousands Cheer at Nahant Church." It was, as Cook described, "an extraordinary testimony to a popular president. A crowd of thirty thousand lined the streets to cheer FDR's party from Salem's dock all along the ten mile route to the reception at the Nahant Tennis Club." I was in my element. But I wonder how the Clark family felt about all the "Hurrahs," all of which had nothing to do with their daughter.

⁓

The second memorable outing of the summer came when my grandmother decided to take me and Sis to the little Hudson River village Tivoli, New York. This was where, in 1892, as a little girl, she had gone to live with her grandmother, Mary Livingston Ludlow Hall, after her mother, Anna Hall Roosevelt, died of diphtheria. Eleanor's father, Elliott Roosevelt, brother of Theodore Roosevelt, was out of the picture. He'd been banished to Virginia, where he was battling his own demons of drink and depression. Anna, separated from

---

*Blanche Wiesen Cook, *Eleanor Roosevelt, Volume 2, The Defining Years, 1933–1938* (New York: Viking, 1999).

Elliott Roosevelt with his adored and adoring daughter, Eleanor, along with her younger brothers Elliott and Hall. It was not a happy family.

him, had requested in her will that her children be cared for by her mother. Elliott died two years later, leaving my grandmother an orphan.

The Halls, Grandmère's mother's family, were in the habit of splitting their time between their Manhattan townhouse just off Fifth Avenue on West 37th Street and Oak Terrace, their country place in Tivoli. Eleanor's grandfather, Valentine Hall Jr., had been dead a dozen years. He'd been a puritanically religious man; while he was alive, a clergyman had lived with the Halls to conduct morning and evening prayers. Valentine (known as "Vallie") and Edward, his only two sons, had become unruly, mostly owing to alcohol, after their father's death. Their mother was little able to control them, and for the young Eleanor, along with her brother Hall, deposited into the family as they were, their much older uncles presented an ongoing problem.

I could sense my grandmother's anticipation as we drove north, parallel to the Hudson River. It is less than twenty miles between Hyde Park and Tivoli, but it felt like we'd made a longer expedition. Writing from a perspective of seventy years later, I realize that this was how it felt at the time because what we were *really* traveling with her was psychic distance. Journeying into her childhood, as she was doing, made Grandmère unusually expansive.

Along the way, her steady stream of stories of her time with the Hall family kept us enthralled. She had been eight when taken into her grandmother's household, the same age I was, listening to her. She fondly recalled a tennis lesson with her two uncles (both were champion players), explaining how she didn't play well—always feeling awkward—but enjoyed their attention. And she noted the pleasure of stealing off to hide in a shaded nook behind a tree where she could read uninterruptedly.

Grandmère also told us that she felt sorry for her grandmother, who had been completely unprepared for assuming the parental responsibilities when her husband had died. Grandmother Hall didn't know how to write a check; she had never known where the money came from when her husband gave it to her. Grandfather Hall was "really very thoughtless," Grandmère noted.

As we drove through the gates of Oak Terrace, I immediately noticed how unkempt the grounds were, so unlike the Big House or Val Kill, neither of which could have been described as "manicured." A long, rutted driveway brought us to the large, three-storied house with its handsome mansard roof. Paint peeling and shutters askew, the house was quite as neglected as the grounds. There is no one here to take care, noted Grandmère rather wistfully. Her grandmother had long since died, and the children didn't bother themselves with the place. Money was a chronic problem.

Key in hand, she preceded us into the house—I guess to make sure Uncle Vallie wasn't lurking. He was supposed to be away, possibly at yet another sanatorium, drying out, but you never could tell. Inside, it was spooky. There were white dust sheets over the furniture, and the place had a deserted feel. "Haunted," my sister whispered to me. Our grandmother gave us a tour that covered most of the rooms, but soon enough she suggested that we go outside to sit on the lawn to share the lunch we'd brought with us. We were only too happy to comply.

The stories Grandmère told about her childhood in the Hall household made a great impression on me. Though her own memoirs tread lightly on this era—emphasizing her affection for the widowed grandmother who offered her love, however straitened—and though her biographers have found episodes of pleasure and lightness there—campfires and games and twilight picnics—that isn't what my grandmother conveyed to us.

Though she was fond of her own grandmother, her feelings were mixed. My grandmother enjoyed the attentions of her aunts—three were alive when my grandmother arrived to live at Tivoli: Elizabeth, or "Tissie," as she was known; Edith, or "Pussie"; and Maude.* She spoke happily of occasions when one of them, usually Edith or Maude, would invite her young niece to join her and her current beau on a picnic. But their rapport was limited. Several years older and more frivolous than she—her aunts were much engaged with the fast set in New York City—they had little else with which to occupy themselves except each new infatuation. It was not a very nurturing environment for a shy and awkward girl, one who took religious dictums seriously.

Even at my young age, I could sense that in the midst of her many relatives—her grandmother and young uncles and aunts—my grandmother had been alone. Indeed my grandmother would go on to write plainly of her loneliness during this period of nearly eight years. She had been looked after dutifully but always at a remove.

More than anything else, what Grandmère emphasized to us was the sober atmosphere. At Tivoli, Grandmère explained, life had been highly disciplined, a trait she had "found useful in my own life." She spoke of being made to walk while pressing a cane against the small of her spine, forcing her to remain erect as if she were carrying a book on her head. Realizing how permissive she had been with her own children, Grandmother Hall emphasized order, insisting that only the Bible or a prayer book could be read on a Sunday. There were no cards or any playing of games. As Grandmère put it, "It was the Lord's day, but we were bored stiff, in spite of going twice to church on Sundays." She was always given "outdated clothes" and hence was "terribly embar-

---

*I came to know Aunt Maude quite well in the 1950s. By then an old lady, she was charming, a real flirt, always dressed for dinner wrapped from head to toe in colorful chiffons.

Grandmère visiting her old home at Tivoli. The picture says it all.

rassed" when in company. The whole thing had the air of a Victorian melodrama, with my grandmother as the orphan heroine. I'm sure it's not exactly what she intended, but it's how it came out.

At the same time Grandmère's disapproval of her aunts and uncles was obvious. In her view, her aunts were "unfortunately" feckless and unable to keep their emotions in check. As for her uncles, when sober they could be brotherly, but Vallie's and Eddie's lapses were frequent, and my grandmother dreaded the times "when they were out of control."

Sis and I got the point. It was at this moment that I began to have a clear notion of what Grandmère referred to as "the slippery slope," that archetypal downward slide that begins slowly, starts picking up speed along the way, and inexorably morphs into seriously bad behavior. Her Uncle Vallie's unfortunate habits—above all, his drinking—had made Grandmère actually fear him. She had to double-lock her bedroom door at night, she told us. Here was an example of someone who'd plummeted straight to the bottom of the pit.

Her uncles' lack of self-control had indisputably darkened her girlhood. Although Grandmère saw drunkenness as a transgression, it was the expression of weakness and loss of control that bothered her the most. Along this line, her giddy aunts came in for some stern tones of censure.

The single greatest lesson I took away—though I was not conscious of it at the time—was about the way strict morality can engender its opposite. Grandfather Hall, believing in self-denial, above all, had devised a repressive regimen for his wife and children. His lessons, however, did not take, and once they slipped his yoke, his children seemed to go to the opposite extreme of self-indulgent excess. Listening to Grandmère's stories made me anxious.

The matter of self-control was to wear many faces in my life—most literally, the ones of my grandmother, my mother, and my sister, all of whom far surpassed me when it came to such self-governance. I did not have the self-discipline to curtail my dream world enough to achieve anything like work or accomplish a specific task. In my fantasy world, I was my own master and could do just as I wished. Satisfaction came easily. In the real world, I was either wildly overexcited or paralyzed by fear. Any disapproval from my grandmother, mother, or sister scuttled my ambition. Spontaneity was lost to me. I didn't know what I might achieve or of what I was capable. But since none of these flaws in the real world afflicted me when I escaped from it into the cosmos of my personal fantasy, its strength continued to grow.

Even now, I imagine the firm, loving hand that might have guided me into feeling the satisfaction of doing something well in the real world. At age eight, with some caring support and personal attention, I might have broken the grip my dream world had on me. However, my mother—and nearly everyone else in my life—was too involved in the demands and excitement of proximity to the presidency to offer such guidance. She was otherwise occupied—just as I was.

CHAPTER 16

With Shirley Temple—having never been to a movie we couldn't guess what a movie star would look like!

PHOTOGRAPH BY CLIFFORD M. SMITH/RICHARD R. CAIN COLLECTION

Before our summer was completed, Mummy and Grandmère's hypocritical attitude toward the media—avoiding the press whenever possible, but then arranging for Sis and Buzz to be photographed—was again tested. A studio-managed visit by Shirley Temple was proposed by someone at MGM. Although my sister and I hadn't yet been allowed to see any movies, we knew all about this Hollywood celebrity who was just a year older than I. Though we'd had more than our fair share of publicity, Shirley was in a different league.

My grandmother was reserved when the matter was broached. The studio executives carefully pitched the get-together, explaining that it was Shirley who wanted to meet *us*. That made my grandmother smile, I know, but she acquiesced. She stipulated that there be no photographers or reporters present—just Shirley and her mother, and Sis and me.

My sister and I were the official hosts, with Grandmère watching over us. We were just as nervous as Shirley was; none of us knew what to expect of the other. Saying hello shyly, we suggested going swimming before lunch. Immediately, Mrs. Temple was worried about her daughter's "perm" and the preservation of her ringlets. But Shirley insisted on joining us in the pool, promising to keep her head out of the water. So off we went for a limited splash. After that, we played hide-and-seek. Shirley's mother stayed out of the way while we ran around.

A shout from Grandmère summoned us to the barbeque she'd ordered prepared—the usual hot dogs,* hamburgers, and potato salad, accompanied by iced tea. "Not too much dear," warned Shirley's mother, explaining that Shirley put on weight easily and so had always to watch her diet, with the studio demanding she stay slim. Despite her mother's concern, Shirley helped herself to both hot dog and hamburger, as well as a generous portion of potato salad.

Shirley made polite conversation with our grandmother during lunch and, in fact, was more socially graceful than her mother. Sis and I were impressed. But when the chocolate cake arrived, she naturally acted her age and begged to be allowed a slice. With a little encouragement from Grandmère, she had two, her mother looking on horrified. Then, with lunch over, Shirley wanted to take snapshots of me, Sis, and Grandmère. I was awed, having believed only adults ever had cameras. Very professionally, America's sweetheart lined us up, just as the press photographers did. Then it was her mother's turn to snap Shirley with Sis and me.

For souvenirs, our guest had brought us badges inscribed with Shirley Temple Police, made for her by the Los Angeles Police Department. I don't

---

*My grandmother, who preferred entertaining picnic-style, famously served hot dogs not just to Shirley Temple but also, the following summer, to George VI, the visiting king of England, and, much later, to Nikita Khrushchev.

remember what we gave her, but I know we exchanged autographs. I had to be helped with the spelling of my name. Was it Buzzie or Buzzy? (In fact, no one spelled my name consistently; my mother and grandmother used both versions, sometimes "Buz," in their correspondence.) We were relieved when it was all over, though it had gone better than we'd expected, due to Shirley's precocious sophistication. Inevitably, pictures were published, and as usual, Sis and I didn't see them.

<hr />

Back in school in Seattle, nothing much was being demanded of me—certainly nothing that stretched my intellect. To my classmates, I was more a curiosity than a classmate. In Washington and New York, where I'd attended private schools, the other children were, more or less, like me. I don't think I would have been allowed at the Buckley School to daydream and coast as I did in Seattle, where I was always "Buzzie," the president's grandson.

As the autumn school term was getting under way, I learned to my surprise and delight that we'd soon have Granny with us again. Our great-grandmother wanted to see our new house on Galler Street and, I suspect, knew my mother was a few months pregnant, something I wouldn't learn until a couple of months before my half brother was born. Granny arrived in Seattle accompanied by her maid, Jennings.

While staying with us, Granny had a serious talk with my mother. She expressed her growing concern about the undesirable habits she felt Sis and I were acquiring. She then listed those we should acquire, such as church attendance, which she considered to be part of our education. She had observed that ours was less than regular. In fact, we had stopped going to Sunday school after just a couple of visits. (At Hyde Park, Granny always took us to church, unless she was away, in which case, we went with Grandmère.) Mummy, hearing her grandmother's predictable criticisms, merely kept to her party line, which was that I was doing well at my school, it was good for me, and I liked my life in Seattle. Granny was cool to her remark that "the children didn't like Sunday school."

There were other behavioral issues that Granny took exception to while she was staying with us. Once she caught Sis and me listening to *The Green Hornet* on the radio. (Listening to "the trash" on the radio was held to be distinctly inferior to reading a good book.) To Sis's and my delight, Granny decided to be a good sport about it—at least it had Rimsky-Korsakov's "Flight of the Bumblebee" as its theme song—and listened with Sis and me to the adventures of crime-fighting newspaper publisher Britt Reid, whose secret identity was known only to his valet, Kato.

In other ways, I made an almost unbelievably good impression on Granny. She wrote to Papa during this visit: "Dear Son, . . . Sisty had a headache & a tiny bit of fever last evening & Buzzy sat by her & was so solicitous & troubled. . . . Buzzy is so sweet and sensible that he frightens me. . . . He made griddle cakes for me and sent them up on my tray . . . "

In the weeks leading up to Granny's appearance, the usual slyly negative comments about her can be found in the correspondence between Mummy and Grandmère that crossed the country. My grandmother wrote teasingly to her daughter, "I hope you come through alive!" And a week later, in another letter, she wrote: "I hope Granny is feeling well and that she can refrain for the week she is there from trying to plan your lives! She seems to be aging fast but she still takes so much interest in all of us that she would be glad to direct all our actions even in the future."

For the most part their letters were playful, but a few days into the visit, my mother sent back this report from the front: ". . . her . . . grievances began cropping up one by one: Pa's house on the top of the hill, the cottage, your friends . . . , your apartment, her uselessness, and so on! I did manage to keep her fairly well in line in front of the children, though not always." All of these issues were long-simmering old chestnuts. Granny's "uselessness" was more in her mind than it was in actual fact, for this eighty-four-year-old matriarch still was actively in control of her domain. Granny *was* opinionated and openly expressed herself, but one could see her frankness as refreshing. Most people did. I certainly preferred it to the veiled remarks and innuendos of the other women in my life.

⁂

That Granny was visiting us because my mother was going to have a baby was something I did not understand at the time, though Sis definitely did. But I would soon have to adjust to a new order. Just before my ninth birthday, my mother gave birth to my brother. I'd had difficulty engaging in the general excitement prior to the event, but when Grandmère arrived on the scene just before my mother was due, bringing an enthusiastic Tommy with her, even I fell in with the contagious sense of happy anticipation. My sister hoped to share with the baby her birthday, the 25th of March (it was Uncle J.'s, as well), but John Roosevelt Boettiger arrived five days later, on the 30th.

My mother's return home from the hospital was celebrated with champagne. Uncle J.'s pride in his new parenthood made him expansive, and for the first time, I really warmed to him. The large guest room across the hall from Mummy and Uncle J.'s bedroom was made into a nursery for Johnny and his nurse. It was there that I was allowed to come and look at him and, finally, when he was a few

With Johnny just a few weeks old, I still thought my kid brother was a cute addition to the household.

weeks old, to hold him. He was awfully cute and had a charming little smile—but I couldn't understand how he could be gurgling one moment and screaming the next. The startling inconsistencies of infant behavior kept me off balance. I was bemused and, at the same time, enchanted with my half-sibling.

That summer we were to move yet again. Leaving the house on Capitol Hill for Seward Park, a neighborhood right on Lake Washington, meant that I was to be enrolled at another new school, my third in three and a half years in Seattle. One day, as we were preparing for the move, my family was gathered in the living room for what I could see was an important discussion.

Without preliminaries, my mother began. Sistie thought, she told me, that it would simplify life, make us more of a family now that Johnny had arrived, if we all used the Boettiger name. Sis was embarrassed by the kids at school constantly asking, "Why is your name Dall and your parents' Boettiger?" Before I could say anything—perhaps a troubled look had crossed my face—my mother quickly assured me, "You don't have to make a decision this minute, of course. Why don't you think about it?"

I understood the problem my sister was talking about. In those days, divorce was a serious scandal, particularly in the provincial atmosphere of a Seattle public school. Children of divorced parents couldn't help but feel the personal stigma. Among my classmates in public school, I knew of none whose parents were divorced. Undoubtedly there must have been some, but children kept silent for fear of exposure to the taunting remarks of the other kids.

I always used the name Dall on my schoolwork and of course responded to that name. If pressed, I would say that my mother and father had been divorced. Sometimes I acknowledged that John Boettiger was my stepfather, but my experience had been that this designation only led to more questions. If I could, I simply avoided saying anything.

The arrival of Johnny provided my mother with the opportunity to present the Boettiger family as a single face to the world. I can now see why she would want that, but at the time, I felt uncomfortable with becoming Buzzie Boettiger or Curtis Boettiger. I can't place all the blame for relegating my father to the sidelines on my mother and sister, though. In the end, I went along with using my stepfather's name, and I continued using that name until I was eighteen years old, about a year after my mother's second divorce. It was then that my grandmother suggested that I use my middle name—Roosevelt—as my last name, dropping both Dall and Boettiger.

The issue would always be a complicated one for me. While living in the White House and at Hyde Park, I had no doubt about what family I belonged to. It was the Roosevelt family. Moving to Seattle and using the Boettiger name muddied it.

Indeed, my formative years, until the age of seven, had been spent almost entirely among my Roosevelt relatives at Hyde Park, in the house in New York City, and at the White House. In Seattle, whether I was called Dall or Boettiger, my "family" had remained the same. It was who I felt I was.

Still, I was confronted with other members of my family, who could be quite proprietary about the Roosevelt name. Years later, when I had returned to New York to live, I was making martinis in Tommy's kitchen for my two uncles, Franklin and John, along with a couple of other guests. Thinking I couldn't hear, one of the guests asked, "Who is Curtis Roosevelt?" Franklin replied, "Oh, he's not a real Roosevelt!" He and John laughed loudly. My uncle explained his remark by adding, "He's Anna's son."

The fact that I was always known as Buzz or Buzzie added another layer to this complex sense of identity. I'd be asked where the nickname came from, and the accepted answer was that it had been my sister's nickname for me, her baby brother. I was a teenager before I recognized that neither my mother nor my grandmother ever wanted to call me by my father's name. The name Curtis or Curt would be a perpetual reminder of something distasteful, which made it all the more startling, some years later, when my grandfather inscribed a book with "To my grandson Curtis Roosevelt Dall." I had nearly forgotten.

Little Johnny stealing the show. Christmas, The White House, 1939.

CHAPTER 17

Nearly nine months after Johnny's birth in 1939, three of my mother's siblings, children in tow, along with four "Boettigers," assembled at the White House to celebrate Christmas. With that crowd, my grandmother was hard-pressed to allot the limited number of guest rooms, especially the choice ones. When we arrived, I was stunned. We had been given the coveted quarters on the second floor of the White House in the East Hall. (I had fully expected to be bunking with some other grandchild on the third floor.) Sis even had the privilege of staying in the room our mother had occupied when we first lived in the White House, the one that only six months earlier had accommodated the wife of King George VI, Queen Elizabeth. Grandmère's motive for this largess was, she said, "to keep the Boettiger family together." It was hard not to feel spoiled by everything, down to the knife and napkin on a plate holding a pear or an apple, placed neatly by my bedside table every evening.

My uncles and their wives were not best pleased. Though my uncles affected their usual casual air, any practiced observer of Roosevelt family dynamics would have noted their jealousy, and disdain, of my mother *and* their new brother-in-law. Correspondence shows two of my uncles being sharply critical of their sister's choice of a second husband before they married, and they hadn't warmed to John Boettiger. The world in which they dwelt was a far cry from Uncle J.'s Chicago boyhood, one in which he'd dropped out of high school and joined the navy during the First World War. Moreover, they did not like the special relationship he enjoyed with their mother.

My younger uncles had also resented my father—an "older man" in his early thirties when he married my mother—because he treated them as unruly teenagers, which indeed they were when Dad was around from 1926 to 1932. Now, although they were still younger than John Boettiger by about fifteen years, the newcomer tried to treat them as pals. But it didn't work.

I was disappointed to learn Uncle Jimmy wouldn't be at the White House that Christmas. He had a wonderfully engaging manner, with a sophisticated way of gently mocking almost everything. That was the way I wanted to be when I grew up. And his wife, my godmother, Aunt Betsey—one of the famously glamorous Cushing sisters*—was mesmerizing. I was stricken when I overheard, later, that they looked bound for divorce court. My grandfather, I gathered, was going to be equally sad to lose Aunt Betsey's charming company. I remembered their exchanges—asides and giggles, mostly shared just between the two of them. *That* was really being an adult, I intuited. I longed to be included.

Because Sis was then twelve years old—going on thirteen—she announced to me, with a superior air, that this Christmas, she'd be eating dinner with the adults. However, much to her displeasure, I, too, wound up being included at the grown-up's table. Our mother explained to my sister that it would be impractical to do otherwise. Besides, I was deemed "old for my age" and never had any trouble fitting in with adults.

---

*Each of the three beautiful debutante daughters of Boston neurosurgeon Harvey Cushing—Barbara ("Babe"), Betsey, and Minnie—married well, and more than once. Aunt Betsey divorced Uncle Jimmy in 1940; two years later, she wed the much richer John Hay Whitney. *The Sisters: The Lives and Times of the Fabulous Cushing Sisters*, by David Grafton (New York: Villard, 1992), tells their story.

Knowing I was having my picture taken, I decided to appear absorbed listening to my grandfather address Congress. Granny's brother, Frederic Delano (behind me), seems not to have found it so interesting. Left to right: Diana Hopkins, Sis, me, Uncle Fred, Grandmère, and Granny.

When eating in the private family dining room—a smaller but still sizeable room adjoining the State Dining Room—we were never less than a dozen sitting down, and at holidays we filled the large oval table to its maximum of two dozen. The conversation buzzed. Especially at dinner, jokes, laughter, stories, and good cheer generally abounded, with the usual family competitiveness being set aside—most of the time. During these meals I was alert and paid close attention; thus began my real education.

In 1939 it seemed important to me that everyone on the White House scene should recognize the difference between who I was now and the little Buzzie, age three, who'd come to live in the White House six years earlier. The servants instinctively understood and started calling me Master Curtis. (My mother was always "MissAnna"—all one word.) I was delighted with this new recognition, but once my sister got wind of it, she told our mother, who scotched it immediately. "He is already likely to think too highly of himself,"

Mummy advised Duffie. Then she explained that I didn't wish to be called Curtis, anyway. Disappointed as I was, I kept quiet, lest I risk tarnishing the luster of "the Boettiger family."

One lovely aspect of being at the White House that Christmas was the presence of Granny. Seeing her always made me happy. Aunt Betty, the widow of my grandfather's half brother, "Rosy" Roosevelt, accompanied Granny.

My father was in the picture that Christmas, as well. A visit to him was scheduled while we were on the East Coast, though my mother spoke only of "getting it over with" and my sister grudgingly asked, "Do we have to?" In the end, the visit was planned to be brief, so that we'd miss little of the White House family festivities. We would join him in New York for a couple of days, spending most of the time at his mother's house in New Jersey.

Mary Bean Dall was my other grandmother, whom we did not know well, as we saw her so infrequently. We called her DeeDee. She was a traditional-seeming, gray-haired woman with a sweet, tired face. She lived in a comfortable white clapboard farmhouse with a big barn behind it. My impression was always that Dad was very tied to her. He'd speak of her with a feeling that bordered on reverence; to him, she seemed to represent everything he valued in life.

My father had gathered together at DeeDee's home other members of his family. Everyone sat down together for a big feast. Afterward, we sang Christmas carols, with Dad sitting at the piano. The two presents he gave me that year were both rather extraordinary, and they were not gifts I might have received from anyone else. The first was a hunting knife from Abercrombie and Fitch, six inches long with a bone handle. Its leather case was monogrammed CRD. It was beautiful, and I treasured it. It said to me that I had come of age.

Dad also gave me, to my great surprise, a .22 caliber (short) rifle. Only about three feet long, its bullets were tiny, around half an inch. He told me I was old enough to begin to learn how to handle a gun, and he would teach me. At first I was scared of it. My mother and sister were neurotic about the noise guns made, and I'd internalized their aversion. But Dad introduced me to target practice, patiently explaining how to sight and then slowly squeeze the trigger. His enthusiasm was infectious, his pride in me obvious, and so I gave it my all. Afterward, we cleaned the gun, and he showed me several times how to dismantle and reassemble it. He also instructed me at length on how to carry the rifle safely. He was serious about the proper handling of guns, and I listened carefully. It was a rite of passage, a part of my father's world.

Dad's wonderful Christmas present to me when I was nine years old—this was the only time I ever fired the rifle.

On the train back to Washington, Sis informed me that Mummy wouldn't let me keep the rifle. She was right. My mother wrote a stiff note to our father telling him that I was too young to have a gun and that she would keep it for me, safely out of reach. Back in Seattle, in fact, I was occasionally allowed to take it out and dismantle it, clean it, and reassemble it, pull back the bolt, ram it home, cock it, aim it, pull the trigger, and enjoy the click—all of which I did alone. The beautiful knife I was permitted to keep in my bureau drawer, though wearing and using it was frowned on.

Back in Washington, the Christmas season was in high gear. It was during this holiday that I fully grasped what "first cousins" were: family members of the same status as Sis and me, though mostly much younger. I wasn't sure what I thought of this category. We'd been for so long, it seemed, the only grandchildren, certainly the only ones in the White House. Now it was my uncles' turn to proliferate; among them, they'd eventually wind up with sixteen wives and nineteen children.*

---

*Jimmy went on to have four wives and six children; Elliott, five wives and four children; Franklin Jr., five wives and five children; John, two wives and four children. Jimmy and Elliott adopted other children.

I remember Sara and Kate, Uncle Jimmy and Aunt Betsey's two children, and closer to my age, arriving at the White House for a brief day's visit. Sis and I were in awe of their very proper clothes—*obviously expensive* my mother noted—and their formidable governess.

After dinner on Christmas Day we all adjourned to the East Room to sit in front of the tree. There all the grandchildren present (Sara and Kate had left) joined together for a family picture. My baby brother, nine months old and restless, wriggled on my mother's lap, so she set him on the floor. He crawled out in front of everybody, eliciting much amused comment, and producing great pride in my mother and Popsie (as we now called my stepfather). The aunts who were still dutifully holding onto their own infants were not as amused. Johnny had stolen the show.

We had a very special treat that New Year's Eve. A screen and projector—having to change every reel—were set up in the long hall of the second floor so that we could watch *Gone with the Wind*, which had had its premiere in Atlanta on December 15th. I wasn't allowed to stay up for it, though Sis was. She made sure to lord it over me the next morning, telling me all about Clark Gable and Vivien Leigh—whom I'd never heard of.

That year, leaving the White House for the first leg of yet another long journey home by train, we all felt an extra dimension of sadness. Grandmère and my mother both had made it plain to Sis and me that there would be no White House Christmas a year hence. Not for us, anyway. Papa would have served his two terms, the traditional limit, and a new president would have been elected.

While I grasped this, I couldn't help but be depressed. I was leaving the place that had been my "home" since I was three years old, and it was hard to conceive of other people living in the White House.

In a letter to my grandmother, upon our return to Seattle, my mother wrote: "Buz has finally recovered from his sadness at leaving the W.H." She described the attention I'd received from Papa's naval aide when I'd visited Annapolis and how "puffed up" I was about it. She continued:

He . . . said it was terrible to think he might never have another chance to stay in the W.H. It was all a very normal reaction, and . . . [he] falls for pomp and glory! Sis had a somewhat similar reaction tonight when she opened the evening paper and saw a picture of you and all the movie and radio stars grouped together at the W.H. Her remarks had to do with what she was missing by not being at the W.H.! Of course, with Sis, all is outspoken and quickly over, and with Buz it is more difficult because he keeps it all within him and broods. Anyway, I think that for the moment we're over the worst with Buzz.

My grandmother always said—though I don't fully believe it—that she would be happy to be quit of the White House and being First Lady, and my mother, as expected, emulated that attitude. Yet it's difficult to imagine that Mummy and Uncle J. were not acutely aware of how life would change for them in Seattle—no more Secret Service chauffeurs, for one thing. More important, would W. R. Hearst renew their contracts with the newspaper? Doubtful.

I wondered to myself, what would my grandfather do after he left the White House? Would he go to some other job? It was clear to me how gripped my family was, how immensely we would be affected, by the end of FDR's two terms as president.

"Mrs. Roosevelt saved the situation to an unusual degree—and that is not mere empty praise. . . ." My grandmother addressing the delegates at the 1940 Democratic convention. Sen. Albin Barkley is behind her.

CHAPTER 18

Several months earlier, on September 1, 1939, Hitler's invasion of Poland had marked the beginning of World War II in Europe. By 1940, it increasingly appeared likely that France would have to surrender, and my mother and Popsie talked of little else. Sis and I, joining them during the cocktail hour as usual, followed the dark clouds of war. For a twelve-year-old and a nine-year-old we were quite well informed. For several years I had pored over the newspapers and magazines that were regularly brought into the house—publications like *Life, Time, Look, Liberty, Newsweek,* the *Saturday Evening Post,* and *Collier's.* I surprised our adult company with my knowledge.

There was a personal family angle to the tragedy unfolding as the German army rapidly advanced on Paris. Aunt Doe, Granny's sister who so fascinated me at Hyde Park, still lived in Paris and refused to leave. At ninety-three, she was increasingly frail, and Papa was gravely concerned for her welfare. The State Department had even expressed its concern about the possibility that once the German army occupied Paris—which was fully expected—the Nazis might take this aged aunt of the president into custody on some pretext, in order to use her as a pawn.

The American ambassador in Paris had been instructed to persuade her to leave immediately on one of the boats leaving for the States. But thus far, his entreaties had been unsuccessful. FDR's pleading with her as a loving nephew had not swayed her either. Granny had invited her to stay at Hyde Park, but Aunt Doe wouldn't budge. In the end, she barely escaped Hitler's invading army. As Papa related to us, she was lucky to find space on the proverbial "last boat." Upon returning to America at last, Aunt Doe took up residence at her and Granny's family home, Algonac, just south of Hyde Park on the Hudson River. She died there soon thereafter.

All through the spring of 1940 my mother, stepfather, grandmother— *everybody*, really—were on tenterhooks as to what Papa intended to do after his second term ended. For Mummy and Popsie, the fallout from FDR's leaving the White House would be immediate. Their status, their public identity, in Seattle and the greater Northwest region, would be radically altered. And their jobs? My stepfather may have been an accomplished newspaperman before becoming the president's son-in-law, but it was his identity as my mother's husband that now colored his résumé.

A third term had never been considered in the 164-year history of the United States, and public sentiment was passionately divided on the issue. At the time, I couldn't imagine that my grandmother wasn't aware of Papa's plans, but all the available evidence I've seen indicates that she, too, was unsure of her husband's intentions.

Mid-July signaled the start of the Democratic convention in Chicago. Yet, even as it began, everyone was kept in the dark. Papa's senior aides were urging him to communicate his wishes in order to avoid a bruising floor fight among the rival candidates who were tossing their hats into the ring for the nomination. Keeping the greater good of the party in mind, seasoned advisers reminded the president that the convention needed to go smoothly. Everyone was edgy.

But in response to such counsel my grandfather would only nod, smile, and proceed to tell an irrelevant story. As the days went on, he didn't relent.

He offered no hint of his plans to those closest to him. He simply sat back, remaining in Washington as the convention opened, giving every appearance of allowing events to take their course. This stance angered many of his supporters, who felt stranded, waiting for him to say yes. In the meantime, they were unable to throw their support to another candidate. Eventually, even my grandmother expressed her frustration with her husband's silence.

Looking back, it seems to me that my grandfather, even though he may have wanted a third term, probably did not know whether it was feasible. Always the astute politician, he recognized that the convention must freely choose him with an overwhelming mandate. It had to be clear to the American people that his party wasn't allowing itself to be manipulated by a popular sitting president and that it was the will of the people that his name be put forward in this time of crises—with Hitler gaining momentum in Europe and the Japanese continuing to stir up the waters in the Pacific. To break the taboo of a third term FDR would have to be nominated by extraordinary acclamation due to extraordinary circumstances.

Finally, with the Democrats assembled in Chicago increasingly mired in frustration, my grandfather let it be known that he would accept the nomination—but only if nominated by acclamation. Immediately, he was nominated to run for an unprecedented third term.

But the delay and the frustration it had fostered among the delegates had a backlash. There was a revolt against FDR's candidate for the vice presidency, Henry Wallace, the Secretary of Agriculture. Wallace was not popular with Democratic Party regulars, nor was he well known to the average convention delegate. Moreover, he was thought to be a "leftie."

The story of my grandfather's 1940 running mate is a fascinating one, but not part of my tale, except to say that my grandfather was adamant that he wasn't interested in any sort of compromise. He wanted Wallace, my grandmother told me years later, and no other, because he thought Wallace was someone he could groom as a successor. Competing names, all duly put forward with their supporters cheering wildly, would not do for FDR.

His stubbornness about Wallace caused an even greater resentment to take hold on the convention floor and in its backrooms. My family and I closely followed this drama from the other side of the country. We all felt my grandfather was asking too much, that he'd gone too far in his refusal to compromise.

Into this divisive mess, Papa now sent Grandmère by plane to Chicago to speak to the delegates. Ostensibly, her appearance before the convention had nothing to do with her husband's choice of a running mate, and it was certainly the first time that the wife of a president had ever addressed such an assembly. Of course everybody knew what she was *really* talking about.

Despite the fact that she never mentioned the name Henry Wallace or even the vice presidency, my grandmother's informal address on July 18, 1940, the final day of the convention, did the trick. Simple words were what she offered, and they were all the more stirring for that:

> We cannot tell from day to day what may come. This is no ordinary time. No time for weighing anything except what we can do best for the country as a whole, and that responsibility rests on each and every one of us as individuals.
>
> No man who is a candidate or who is President can carry this situation alone. This is only carried by a united people who love their country and who will live for it to the fullest of their ability, with the highest ideals, with a determination that their party shall be absolutely devoted to the good of the nation as a whole and to doing what this country can to bring the world to a safer and happier condition.

What my grandmother was asking was, to put it archly, purely a matter of common sense. Still, behind her polite yet persuasive tone was a shaft of steel that crept down the backs of most delegates. Because she was standing up for what was clearly right for the country, the delegates took her message to heart. They now fell into line, although grudgingly, and nominated Henry Wallace. To me it seemed that Grandmère had saved FDR's bacon.

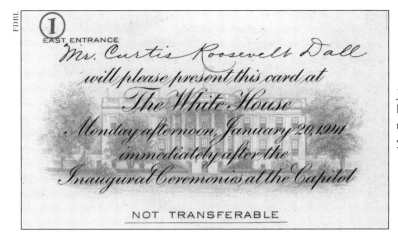

EAST ENTRANCE

Mr. Curtis Roosevelt Dall

will please present this card at

The White House

Monday afternoon, January 20, 1941

immediately after the

Inaugural Ceremonies at the Capitol

NOT TRANSFERABLE

Just a formal invitation, but it confirmed for me that I too had another four years in the White House.

My grandmother didn't stay to see the delegates agree to FDR's choice of running mate, nor did she ever recognize her own accomplishment to the degree that history now does. In a *McCall's* magazine article fourteen years later, she recalled that she went to the speaker's stand quite unprepared: ". . . cold all over . . . I stood there, feeling completely alone . . . I have no recollection now of what I said, but it must have been very simple and to the point, because it held the audience."

Actually, she had handwritten notes outlining the basics of what she intended to say at the convention. In the years to come, Grandmère was emphatic that Papa had given her absolutely no instructions or guidance. He had been advised to ask her to speak and had heeded the counsel. According to my grandmother, all he said was "I am perfectly willing you should go." Nothing more.

Though I do not think anyone in my family, even my politically savvy mother, grasped the full extent of the miraculous rescue that my grandmother had brought about, we were overwhelmed by the moment. Listening to the prolonged applause and hurrahs for Grandmère on our radio, I welled up with tears. Later I felt the same pride for my grandfather when he accepted his party's nomination for president, speaking to the convention over the radio from the White House. Even now, I can summon that deeply felt thrill.

Mummy wrote to Grandmère after her speech: "a *wonderful* job . . . your sincerity and high minded purposefulness rang so true in every word you said." More notably, the seasoned political observer Eddie Roddan wrote to my step-father: "Mrs. Roosevelt saved the situation to an unusual degree—and that is not mere empty praise. The story of what she accomplished at Chicago, aside from her speech, will have to be told to you and Anna at a later date."

What I was left with after these momentous events was a new impression of my grandmother, beyond the idea of her as a committed humanitarian and a remarkable doer of good deeds. Suddenly I saw her as a political figure in her own right. She had influence, a lot of it.

"The Boettigers" at their new home in Seward Park on Lake Washington. With a tennis court and a 26-foot motorboat Sis and I concluded: "We must be rich!"

Following the intense excitement of Papa's nomination, my mother arranged for Sis and me to spend three of the summer's remaining weeks with our Secret Service man, Tom Carmody, at the farm of his brother-in-law. I think Mummy wanted us out from underfoot for a while and saw this as a cheaper alternative to camp.

So Mody and his wife drove us to our destination, a wheat farm in eastern Oregon. From Seattle, it was twelve full hours of riding in a hot car. Along the way, I indulged in bottle after bottle of Coke, along with numerous candy bars—all forbidden fruit. My mother was getting farther away by the mile, and my sister, who ordinarily kept a sharp eye on my behavior, made the decision to join in my sugar orgy.

The land was flat around the farm, with either corn or wheat fields for miles in all directions, and the climate there was hot and dry. A big rambling farmhouse accommodated us all. I had my own small room with a painted iron bed. The names of our hosts, Mrs. Carmody's brother and sister-in-law, long ago escaped me, but I will never forget the attention I received. I knew how to invite it, and here, much to my delight, I was special again. In fact, I managed to stay in bed the first day or two with a mild fever. I was happy with this situation, since my medication consisted mainly of ice cream and ginger ale, plus lots of sleep—not to mention an abundance of loving, tender care.

The third day there, I got up and joined the crowded family dining table. At home, it was only on Sundays that we might have pancakes, syrup, and bacon for breakfast, as a special treat. Incredibly, such delicious bounty was a daily event at the farm. At lunch, there was always corn on the cob and plenty of sandwiches, since the farmhands were also fed at midday. Later, it was meat, potatoes, and gravy for supper. I ate as ravenously as if I'd been out in the fields on the big mower or looking after the animals, which puzzled Sis. Ordinarily, I resisted eating, seeing it as yet another chore.

No doubt I did work up a natural appetite, since I was encouraged to try my hand at splitting wood for kindling and carrying heavy buckets of water. My sister, fancying herself *in loco parentis*, was horrified at my encounters with the ax, but, mostly, I just tagged along after the other kids, who had regular chores assigned to them. The fun I was having was far better than any camp that I'd been sent to!

I even played a game of "I'll show you if you'll show me" with other kids in the hayloft of one of the large barns. My mother, for once, didn't go into crisis mode or engage in any hand-wringing when she got wind of it. To Grand-mère she wrote merely, "As the children in the ranch family are all older, Sis and Buzz came home having learned considerably more about the 'facts of life'—some desirable and some not—but all to the good I think in the long run." (My mother may have had information to which I was never privy, but I don't remember Sis participating in our games in the barn.) When we had to leave the Carmodys' farm, I cried.

∞∞∞

Later that same summer, practically on schedule, we moved again. This time it was to a large place right on Lake Washington, in the Seward Park neighborhood. The Spanish-style house was perched on a steep slope that led down to the lake. Halfway down the two hundred feet to the water's edge was a tennis court. Impressive, I thought, having your own tennis court, and I guessed Popsie and my mother must have got a raise when signing a new contract with Mr. Hearst and the *Post-Intelligencer*. But, in fact, our lease on the house once again was for only one year (as was their contract with the newspaper).

Below the tennis court was a garden in which we raised vegetables. My mother reported to my grandmother: "Did I tell you Sis and Buzz have their own vegetable gardens? What with their gardens and ours we are eating only our own vegetables these days." In fact, what vegetables we harvested were largely owing to the efforts of our Secret Service man, Hazen, who came on duty at 4:00 P.M. and enjoyed gardening.

I had little interest in weeding and mulching and plucking off pests, or anything that required steady commitment. All of this interfered with the time I craved for retreating to my dream world. But I did pick up a shovel and spend hours, most of a day, excavating a large hole in the ground. Occasionally, I would lie down in the dankness of my hole. Or I sat in it, peering out over the edge. Came the rain—which was nearly every other day in Seattle— my hideaway would become mucky with mud at the bottom. When I showed off my creation, everyone said it looked like a grave. What else? It was the right shape. I could offer no alternative reason for creating such an unusual retreat except that I liked hideouts. When we next changed houses, in the summer of 1941, my mother ordered my hole filled in. She worried that the owners of the property would think we'd been engaged in some sort of sinister concealment.

Our house at Seward Park sloped steeply down to the edge of Lake Washington, which was a big lake with lots of frontage. All around it were boathouses and docks. At times, the lake was lovely and tranquil, but often the high whine of motorboats dominated, particularly on weekends when neighbors were out trying to master the new sport of waterskiing. While I could sit for hours idly watching the boats zipping across the water, I preferred it when there was nothing out there but the ducks and maybe a lone fisherman in his skiff.

Because of my mother's uptightness when it came to anything she deemed financial extravagance, I was stunned to hear Popsie announce one day that we were acquiring a Chris Craft cabin cruiser. It was small, he was quick to say, only twenty-six feet in length, but it did have a head, a tiny galley, and bunks for two. The name he'd selected for this most unexpected possession was the *Newshawk*, which, he explained, was a word for a dogged reporter.

Popsie had been hankering for a boat like this for some time. But the actual cost of purchasing it was only the beginning, Mummy reminded him. Next thing you knew, we'd need a boathouse and an electric lift to hoist the boat out of the water. Popsie nodded, irritation crossing his face, but he was determined not to let her dampen his satisfaction.

Sis and I, meanwhile, were impressed with our new status symbol. Over supper, she and I discussed this extraordinary development. It wasn't a yacht, we agreed, but, still, a cabin cruiser of our own was pretty impressive. We finally concluded that we must be rich! Mummy, coming to the same conclusion about how this new acquisition might appear, wrote to Grandmère to justify the seeming frivolousness of such an expenditure at a time when war was raging in Europe.

Despite my mother's anxiety over most everything involved in life on the water, I liked being on the boat. Sharing this experience marked the beginning of some feeling on my part of belonging to the Boettiger family. This included our little stepbrother, of course, but since Johnny was barely a toddler, he was hardly seaworthy. It would be some time before he was included in our outings on the new boat.

Once again, I didn't have an easy time making friends with any of the kids in our new neighborhood. The Seward Park houses seemed isolated, and there was no natural meeting place such as I had on Galler Street. I stayed close to home and played alone. Though my large sandbox and my dress-up uniforms had somehow failed to make the journey to our new house—Popsie had made fun of my Royal Canadian Mounted Police outfit—I was content with my soldiers and ships.

The first day of school brought a watershed moment: at last I was dressed in long trousers. My mother had bought a dark blue pair of corduroys for me, which I'd be allowed to wear when classes began. If I'd been at the Buckley School, all the children would have worn short pants or knickers with longs socks until age ten or twelve. But in Seattle, I had stood out like the proverbial sore thumb in my short trousers. I was very proud of my new stature.

Having worn short trousers all my life, at age ten I finally graduated to long ones. Now I looked like the other boys.

Sis's private school was considered too far away, so the two of us were back to attending the same school that autumn. Registering at John Muir School was the first public expression of our adoption of the Boettiger name. Mummy wrote to Grandmère:

This morning I took Sis and Buzz to their new school. They insisted on registering under the name of Boettiger, saying they were always called "the Boettiger children" and didn't want to be called something different from "Pops"! Don't mention this to anyone, because, while I have explained to the kids that they cannot legally use the name Boettiger, there is always the chance that some busy body might want to relay some garbled story to Curt and persuade him to raise a rumpus. The school people didn't even raise an eyebrow over the children's request. In fact they seemed to take the whole matter perfectly naturally.

Sis and I considered this a non-event, just as the teacher registering us did, but for my mother it made a good story for Grandmère. I had already decided what name I would now use on my school papers: CR Boettiger.

The first day at John Muir followed the pattern I'd become familiar with from my previous two Seattle public schools. Disbelieving stares, isolation, exaggerated attention from the teachers, and the same questions from everybody marked my arrival. After a couple of weeks, it settled down to a tolerable level.

Most of the time I dealt with the strain by retreating to my current fantasies—fed by whatever events happened to be in the war news or maybe some adventure story I was reading. All of it was grist for the mill that occupied my mind whenever I could escape from the world in which I moved about.

Eventually, I acquired a couple of chums, Al and Gorden, and we palled around together until our homeroom teacher seemed to think the worst of these friendships and separated us. Still, she couldn't keep us apart at lunchtime. Mody, who stayed all day parked in the street outside the school, trying to be unobtrusive (and sleeping, mostly), was the culprit who introduced us to the local candy store. Since by now I had some cash in my pocket, for my lunch at school, small purchases were possible if I budgeted carefully.

After school I hung around a bit with Al, who lived nearby, until my sister was ready and we'd drive home. Occasionally, I was allowed to go to Al's home, and there I fell in love with his younger sister, Lois, who became my dream girl—someone to show off to, but only in my imaginary life. She, of course, knew nothing about it.

Only two things really occupied me in the real world. One was a bicycle, which I soon mastered sufficiently to ride in a three-block radius—a distance established by Mummy for "security reasons." Before long, though, this limited circuit proved uninteresting, and so I wasn't disappointed when the Secret Service, for fear of kidnapping, suggested I stop riding altogether. The other was a BB gun that I had begged and begged to order from the Sears Roebuck catalogue. Gaining Popsie's support, I was, against Mummy's better judgment, given the go-ahead to send for it. It was the least powerful gun on offer.

It was at the Seward Park house that I first read an entire book on my own, a story of marauding Vikings on the British coastline. Such an accomplishment may not sound unusual for a nine-year-old, but it was the first time that I remember finishing a book by myself. Sis, during this period, was madly into the Nancy Drew novels that were being passed around by her classmates. I'd started one myself, but my mother objected, explaining it was a book for girls; as a substitute, she gave me one of Albert Payson Terhune's novels about dogs. Apparently, I wept so much over the collie's numerous traumas that the book disappeared, with the less disturbing Viking one replacing it.

My late start in reading for pleasure was not due to any shortage of books. My grandmother had for several years subscribed to the Junior Library Guild for us. Every month my sister and I each received a new book designed for our respective age levels. I never read any of mine. It probably didn't help that Mummy thought we *should* read them, as Grandmère had sent them to us. My mother always seemed to be carrying around some hefty volume on a serious subject, quite likely a book that Grandmère had mentioned as being "important."

On some Saturday mornings, when my mother and Popsie went downtown to the newspaper office "to catch up on the mail," I would accompany them. I was permitted to cross the street to Frederick & Nelson, a local department store with a large book section. I may not yet have read more than a couple of books cover to cover, but I soon became well versed in the current titles and their dust-jacket blurbs. The clerks got used to seeing me absorbedly browsing, and Mummy considered it a safe place for me to occupy myself for an hour or so. In fact, she introduced me to the staff there, making sure everyone in the book section knew "who I was."

One day I surprised the salespeople in the book department by declaring that I wanted to buy a birthday present for my mother. They looked more than ready to assist me, but I assured them I needed no help, as I knew quite well where the books on serious subjects were. I agonized for over an hour about which choice would elicit the most appreciative reaction when I presented it. Finally I settled on the memoirs of a diplomat who'd recently been our ambassador to Moscow. Not only was the subject worthwhile, I felt, but the book was just the right weight and size. In every way, it was impressive.

I was proud of my selection and already could imagine the thrilled look on my mother's face when she received it. When the moment came and we gathered for her birthday party, I eagerly presented my gift to her, insisting that she open it right away. As she took the wrapping off, the expression on her face seemed puzzled, even faintly dismayed. But, recovering enough to thank me for it, dutifully, she noted that it was undoubtedly something she *should* read.

I later overheard her say to Popsie, "What am I ever going to do with that?" To which he replied, "Oh, you can find someone to give it to." "No, I can't!" my mother corrected him exasperatedly. "Buzzie will expect to see it in the house!"

Indeed, I kept an eye on it over the next several years. Although *Mission to Moscow*, by Joseph E. Davies, my grandfather's second envoy to the Soviet Union, looked like it might have been picked up now and then—possibly for dusting—its virgin status was attested to by the fact that its binding had not been cracked.

CHAPTER 20

Sis and I relaxing at our fourth house in Seattle,
a beautiful place on Mercer Island.

S is and I weren't surprised, but we were wary when we learned that
we were about to have yet another change of residence. Not that
I'd made any friends at the Seward Park house, but I would have
preferred sameness and security. Mummy and Popsie were unusually enthusiastic. That's because this was to be our last move,
they assured us.

After three one-year rentals, usually extended to a year and a
half, we were finally buying our own house in Seattle. The main
reason for this decision was that my mother and stepfather's contracts with the *Post-Intelligencer* had just been renewed, on advan-
tageous terms for both of them. So it was with great excitement

that we set off one Sunday morning to visit our new house, which was located on Mercer Island, in the middle of Lake Washington.

Back then the island was sparsely populated, and its face was covered with a forest of evergreens. To get there we drove over the extraordinary, recently built Floating Bridge, which connected the island to the city of Seattle. To me, the very idea of living on an island was a kind of enchanted one, though the big four-lane highway running across the island seemed out of place in such a rustic setting.

Just before reaching the small bridge leading to the mainland on the far side of the island, we drove over a bridge to a slip road on the opposite side of the big highway, and then headed down a dirt track. This was "our property," noted my mother. Just like the small back roads at Hyde Park, the track wound its way for a quarter mile through woods. We waited anxiously for our first glimpse. Suddenly, the barn, which doubled as a garage, appeared and then the house spread out before us, with Lake Washington beyond. Sis and I looked at each other in amazement and stammered words to that effect—much to my mother and Popsie's pleasure.

The place seemed huge and was, in fact, two houses joined together. Because it was still occupied by the current renters, we couldn't go inside, and so we settled for walking down to the shore. A flagpole stood at the water's edge. A dock extended into the lake, and there was more lakefront than we'd had at Seward Park. Popsie showed us where he planned to have the boathouse built for the *Newshawk*. Both Sis and I were rendered speechless by what we'd seen, and on the drive home we completely forgot to bicker.

Meanwhile, the school year dragged on, and in spite of my pleading—possibly I had been *too* enthusiastic about how much I'd enjoyed it—Sis and I would not be returning to the comfortable and welcoming wheat farm in eastern Oregon. At eleven, I needed a more disciplined boys' camp, or so my mother felt, with Popsie backing her up. It would help me become a "more regular" boy, he said. So off I went to the Henderson camp down at the bottom of Puget Sound, with Sis going to a nearby girls' camp.

I liked my camp. There wasn't too much regimentation, and I enjoyed the activities—riding, playing games, and swimming, even if the slimy rocks were less than inviting. My mother seemed pleased at "how good" camp had been for me and so wrote Grandmère.

Popsie wasn't quite as enthused. In a letter sent to William O. Douglas (just appointed to the Supreme Court), he wrote: "Dear Bill . . . have learned of your plan to send your youngster to a camp in our state. . . . Frankly, Anna and I do not feel that our son had quite the degree of 'red blooded' treatment at the Henderson camp. I think you understand what I mean. It is rather on the order of a Y.M.C.A. operation."

My stepfather had usually been silent when my mother presented things that were going to be "good for me." But I sensed his feeling that I wasn't at all the normal boy he felt I should be. We were not companionable and did nothing together as a father and son might. So running across this letter of his doesn't surprise me. No, I wasn't "regular"—and never would be.

There is another dimension. Like many men of his time, John Boettiger had a disparaging attitude toward anything effete, disapproving, for instance, of male ballet dancers or men participating in the arts at all. How the YMCA fit in, I don't know, but he seems to have deemed my camp not robust enough. As I could see later, his manliness was an assumed air, a shell masking fears of his own.

Before leaving Seward Park, I allowed myself the luxury of a parting shot. Our diet at home was composed of the same underseasoned, overcooked, tasteless dishes. It might have been wholesome from a nutritionist's point of view—two vegetables, a starch, some protein, like stew meat, was considered a "balanced diet" for us—but the real problem for Sis and me was that it was half again too much all the time, with food brimming over our plates.

Of all the meals we suffered through regularly, the worst was the greasy liver, which looked and, I imagined, tasted like shoe leather. Sometimes, I'd succeed in smuggling some of the overcooked meat from my plate to one of our two Irish setters, Jack and Jill, who regarded it with more enthusiasm than I did. But such behavior would usually be spotted and reported to Mummy.

One day, carefully choosing my moment, instead of slipping it to the dogs, I had the idea to stick one of my two pieces of liver under a corner of the dining room rug. Sis saw this and seemed awed at such daring on my part. Naturally, seeing her admiration greatly inflated my self-esteem. In a burst of kindly solidarity, she refrained from telling on me, and then I forgot all about it.

Soon after we moved into our new house on Mercer Island I learned that there had been a problem with our old one: something was rotten in Seward Park. The dining room had begun to smell right after Sis and I had left for our respective camps—and no amount of searching revealed the source of the stench. To my mother's horror, it kept getting worse. However, since the important task at hand was organizing the packing, she had had to let it go for the moment.

Then, on the day the moving team came, the blue dining room rug, my mother's favorite, finally was rolled up. Lo and behold, on the corner of the rug there was a quite unrecognizable moldy blob that was clearly causing the problem. After it was examined, the conclusion was that perhaps a wayward piece of meat had integrated itself into the carpet. No one could think of a way to extract it without ruining the carpet, and so the offending square was cut out. My mother was furious at the desecration of one of the more cherished (and valuable) items brought west from Manhattan.

Once we were settled around the dining table in our Mercer Island house, I could see that the annoying incident had become a comic story and that my mother was enjoying telling it. Feeling guilty and scared, I kept quiet, sure that I was going to be exposed by Sis as the culprit. As it turned out, though, the dining room in our new house was slightly smaller, which meant the entire rug had to be trimmed to fit. What a stroke of luck! Better still, my sister only flashed a smirk in my direction—a triumph for me, even though my mother knew perfectly well who the culprit was.

Our new house rambled from one side of our property to the other. Every day we raised and lowered the flag in front of the house, which I thoroughly enjoyed, as I loved rituals. We had the rowboat in which I ventured warily out into Lake Washington. And here, Sis and I, for the first time in our lives, were assigned chores. Though we still had a housekeeper, Mrs. Williams, times had changed, and my sister and I were now deemed old enough "to pull our weight in the household." The house was a big expense, my mother explained, and slacking off would not be tolerated. My assignment was to sweep the porches—there were five of them—plus the big, brick-floored patio, whose cracks stubbornly held the ubiquitous pine needles.

I resented, resisted, and regularly "forgot" these duties. It sounds minor, and typical, for a spoiled kid my age—especially a boy—but, still, I see it as more than that. My response was similar when it came to almost any task presented to me. My failure to follow through extended to a wide range of activities, from schoolwork and appointments to even the most ordinary things of life, such as remembering birthdays or writing thank you notes. It was not willful disobedience; I simply wanted to escape to my dream world. There all "shoulds" fell away, all commands were suspended. It was a life-support system. And I resented anything that interfered.

Life on rural Mercer Island was even more isolated for me than Seward Park had been. My sister and I had received special permission to continue at our old public schools on the mainland, and so we had a tedious commute of over an hour each way. I was glad to avoid changing schools again, but if it had been difficult to get boys from John Muir Elementary School to visit in Seward Park, it was practically impossible on Mercer Island, picturesque though it was. My mother made a few efforts to arrange playdates for me—Al visited once—but she would become bogged down in the elaborate arrangements and soon she gave up. With her job working at the paper, she really didn't have the time.

The Secret Service agents assigned to us still doubled as chauffeurs. But there were limits to what we could ask of them on the taxpayers' dollar. So visits to friends were infrequent, and I didn't press for them. Without thinking about it, my preference was to be alone.

⚬⚬⚬

I had been back at school only a few days when we received startling news. On September 7, 1941, two weeks before her eighty-seventh birthday and without warning, Granny had died. The next day my mother casually announced this to Sis and me at the breakfast table before she and Popsie went on to talk of the day's work ahead of them.

But it was all over the newspapers. The kids at school bombarded me with questions. "Is she a relative of yours?" they asked. I even had to explain what a "great-grandmother" was to some classmates. The whole thing was surreal. It was impossible to convey how close I had felt to her, how much Sara Delano Roosevelt had meant to me.

Although the time when Granny had felt like a surrogate mother to me now seemed quite distant, I felt a keen sense of loss. Still, I didn't mention my sorrow to anyone. My demeanor was surely influenced by the fact that unrestrained emotion was *not* what my mother and sister were displaying. They were deferential but aloof. I didn't want to be odd man out, so I kept the way I felt muted—veiled even from myself.

In a letter, Grandmère described to my mother how she had felt at the funeral: "I kept being appalled because I couldn't feel any real grief or sense of loss & that seemed terrible after 36 years of fairly close association." She also described Papa's demeanor at Granny's funeral: "Father has begun to forget all that was ever disagreeable in his relationship to Granny but he was not emotional & neither was anyone except Aunt Kassie." The truth was that my grandfather had been deeply affected by his mother's death. Not revealing hurt or grief in public was simply his style.

Mummy answered:

My own feelings about Granny are so mixed. Some of my childhood memories of her are grand; others funny, and still others horrible—such as my adolescent qualms and general irresolution when she would bring constant pressure on me to do something about a family situation she didn't happen to approve of! And yet, Granny was definitely a strong influence on my younger years—undoubtedly making my final development slower, but perhaps more thorough! By that I mean her uncompromising consistency succeeded in the end in making me more rebellious and independent than I might have been otherwise!

Phew! This hedging style—on the one hand this, on the other hand that. Mummy and Grandmère's real feelings about Granny—both positive and negative—were, I suspect, just as buried as mine. My mother, at heart, had good memories of Granny, whereas my grandmother, I know, had made her mother-in-law an object of hostility.

For me, Granny had been a place as well as a person. My feelings about her, my memories, encompassed both. When she died, my sense of being anchored at Hyde Park did too. Granny and the Big House at Hyde Park had felt more than anything else like home to me, even more than the White House.

When Grandmère came to visit us the following year, a very unsettling subject was raised. It seemed that the Big House might be turned over to the U.S. Department of the Interior as a National Historic Site and opened to the public. A final decision would be delayed until the end of the war, as my uncles, to a man, had howled in protest at the suggestion. My mother was more realistic.

However, to Papa's simple question to my mother and her brothers, "Can you afford to keep up this big place?" there came no reply. Uncle Elliott made the suggestion that all five children share Springwood, each having two months' use of the estate, something like today's time-sharing arrangements. The rest of the time it would be open to the public. However, everyone instinctively knew such an arrangement was unworkable.

I listened to the practical arguments put forth by my grandmother, who favored the family divesting itself of the Big House and the adjacent few acres. She ticked off her points with sentences that began, "Pa feels . . . "

Even then I sensed that public access would inevitably deprive us of real privacy once Papa retired and the Secret Service protection was withdrawn. People would just come in. Already the building of the FDR Library building, which the National Archives was erecting to house all of my grandfather's papers and collections, had made it different from the beloved refuge I knew so well.

I couldn't envisage what would happen when the U.S. Park Service guides took over and visitors paid their fee to walk through the rooms that for me had been the landmarks of my identity. Nor could I imagine the number of visitors—thousands each day in summertime—so many that they have had to be limited in order to protect the house. Over the years I have adjusted, but I have made a point of keeping my memories intact, of preserving my vision of "home."

For me, Granny's death left the Big House feeling empty.

AP IMAGES

My favorite battleship, the *Arizona*, toppling into Pearl Harbor.

I n the same way that the abrupt horror of September 11, 2001, changed the world, the 7th of December and the two words "Pearl Harbor" seared their way into the consciousness of every American alive at the time. I was close to twelve years old, but I had been mesmerized by the war news since 1939. I heard about it every evening at home, and I knew my grandfather felt we would eventually be involved in the war.

As the Nazis' successive conquests of their European neighbors led to the British-French declaration of war against Germany, the drama escalated daily, ending at Dunkirk, with France defeated and the rise of their Vichy regime under Pétain and Laval. What schoolboy did not thrill to the Battle of Britain, the daring of the Spitfire pilots, and the perils bravely faced by the crews aboard the North Atlantic convoys?

As I followed the brutalization of Europe by the Third Reich, I also kept abreast of the Japanese aggression continuing in China, indeed their threat to the whole Pacific area. My sister and I got much of our information from our mother and stepfather's cocktail hour after work—sitting there sipping their martinis.

All through 1941 tensions between Japan and the United States had increased dramatically, and my mother and stepfather's speculation was fed by tidbits from Papa and Grandmère. Any news on this front carried a special relevance for those of us living on the Pacific coast. In late November and early December of 1941, after my grandmother told us that the discussions with Secretary of State Cordell Hull might ease the situation, my family tracked the Japanese peace mission's activity in Washington.

How wrong we were—as were most Americans. FDR was aware of the real possibility of war with Japan. Not only did he speak about it within the family, but he talked about it in his press conferences. But our fellow countrymen were not moved. They didn't want to consider it any more than they wanted to consider a war with Nazi Germany. When Pearl Harbor exploded, nearly everyone, from bureaucrats in the State Department to the man in the street, was rudely awakened.*

On the Sunday afternoon of December 7, 1941, we had gone walking with a friend of my mother and Popsie, a Seattle lawyer who two years earlier had been appointed Assistant Attorney General in the Justice Department. It was just an ordinary day until we arrived back at the house.

It was then that, turning on the radio, we heard the first Pearl Harbor bulletins. All of us were dumbstruck. No longer could we feel that we were in-

---

*Even an eleventh-hour Japanese peace mission, led by special envoy Saburo Kurusu, had been kept in the dark.

vulnerable to an attack from a nation thousands of miles across the Pacific. Though I knew all about aircraft carriers, the idea of their cruising thousands of miles undetected to attack our fleet seemed somehow absurd.

Sis and I listened to the adults talk, but at that moment they had only their bafflement and conjecture to share. Even when our guest telephoned his Washington office, we could glean no further information. "Well, we're in it now!" was the adults' rather wan conclusion.

The bombing of Pearl Harbor had lasted only ninety minutes, but for our country, World War II had begun. Before, the Pacific Ocean had seemed too vast, and Hawaii well out of range for bomb-bearing Japanese planes. I would later learn that both our army and navy chiefs thought it impossible. Now all illusions of security shattered instantly. To me, it felt personal; my favorite battleship, the *Arizona,* whose photograph hung on my bedroom wall, had been sunk.

That evening my mother was able to speak with my grandmother, who gave her some idea of the extensive losses the U.S. fleet had suffered. Extremely worried about us, Grandmère felt it imperative that we be evacuated to the East Coast, since the West Coast was now, in her words, "completely vulnerable" to invasion by the Japanese. My grandmother was not being melodramatic. In those early days after Pearl Harbor, an attack along the Pacific coast, while not acknowledged by the government, was widely believed to be a real possibility. Grandmère knew the facts directly from Papa, who had received the army's confidential assessment of our vulnerability.

After all, she told my mother, the consequences of a Japanese invasion had to be considered. What if the president's daughter should be captured, along with her children? My mother immediately dismissed this, protesting that her duty was to remain with her husband and that Johnny was too little to be without his mother. As for Sis and me, she'd have to discuss it with us. We were now old enough to have some voice in assessing the situation, she said.

The next morning, across the front page of the "sunrise edition" of the *Post-Intelligencer*, the headline shrieked "WAR EXTRA! WAR EXTRA! JAPAN WARS ON U.S.," while the lead story informed readers, "Roosevelt to Give

Personal Message in Congress Today." (A small Christmas ad below the news stories—"Fifteen shopping days left!"—was a weird reminder of the normality now left behind.)

In a controlled but impassioned bylined piece on the second page, the newspaper's publisher, John Boettiger, weighed in. "War has been brought to America despite our most determined efforts to keep the peace," Popsie declared. "From here on there can be but one purpose of all true Americans, and that is to defeat the war-mad dictators of Asia and Europe."

Later that day, my grandfather went to Congress, asking the Senate for a formal declaration of war against both Japan and Germany. Thirty-three minutes after he spoke, they obliged. I can still summon the somber but fierce determination in his voice that Monday. His speech was broadcast at 9:30 A.M. Pacific time and was carried by five local radio stations. Listening to him on that occasion was unforgettable. Sis, Mummy, Popsie, and I, joined by some friends, stared at the radio with utter concentration, as if we could actually see him speaking.

After declaring that December 7 was a "date that would live in infamy," he went on to tell his rapt listeners:

As Commander-in-Chief of the Army and Navy I have directed that all measures be taken for our defense, that always will our whole nation remember the character of the onslaught against us. No matter how long it may take us to overcome this premeditated invasion, the American people, in their righteous might, will win through to absolute victory. I believe that I interpret the will of the Congress and of the people when I assert that we will not only defend ourselves to the uttermost but will make it very certain that this form of treachery shall never again endanger us. Hostilities exist. There is no blinking at the fact that our people, our territory, and our interests are in grave danger. With confidence in our armed forces, with the unbounding determination of our people, we will gain the inevitable triumph. So help us God.

His last two sentences carried an unforgettable emphasis.

So much had changed, was changing, would change. Closest to home for us was the threat of kidnapping. It had always been a danger not only because we were grandchildren of the president but also because we lived in privilege. But now there was an added, even more pressing, dimension to that threat. The sizeable Japanese population in communities in all the major cities along the West Coast, including Seattle, was immediately identified as potentially harmful—a "fifth column" it was labeled.

My sister and I were not consulted until our mother had talked once again to Grandmère. During this next go-around, Mummy tried to gauge her father's opinion. According to my grandmother, Papa felt that my mother was probably right to stay with Popsie and Johnny but that Sis and I were very welcome to join our grandparents at the White House. This would be not unlike the evacuation of children from the cities of Britain to countryside refuges, which was familiar to all of us.

Grandmère added that in any event, our Secret Service detail (up to this point Mody, Hazen, and Bunker) would be doubled, with two men now on duty at all times. How one more of these very nice, laid-back fellows on each shift would protect us more fully if ravening Japanese soldiers did land, I can't guess.

Faced with the suggestion that we leave Mercer Island for the safety of the East Coast, Sis and I both reacted with instinctive indignation. I was momentarily tempted by the idea of living in the White House again, but, as it did for so many Americans, the war aroused in me a tremendous sense of purpose and swellings of patriotism. I regarded such decamping as running away in the face of the enemy and sensed that the proper stand was to remain with my family.

Every evening, Mummy and Popsie brought Sis and me up to date on the war news. Most of it was most discouraging, a state of affairs that would last many months. There were the Philippines and Corregidor, Hong Kong and Singapore—all defeats. The Japanese army marched on, seemingly invulnerable.

In the weeks following Pearl Harbor, Sis and I witnessed increasing hostility among our classmates toward Japanese Americans, the nearest "enemy" to hand. When the internment of the Japanese populace on the West Coast was announced, the dinner table opinions of Mummy and Popsie and their circle favored the decision. The policy was even framed as being in the interest of our Japanese neighbors—unpleasant, to be sure, but undertaken to protect them. The distinction between "enemy aliens" and American citizens was ignored.

As feelings against the Japanese community ran high, the potential for violence directed at them was increasing daily. The man in the street professed uncertainty about how to tell the difference between "a Jap and a Chinaman." Perhaps the latter might wear large buttons proclaiming "I am Chinese," it was suggested. Community leaders asked for calm and tolerance—and then the detention camps became law, with my grandfather signing Executive Order 9066.

Many kids in school sneered that it was "about time they were taken away." Probably they had heard their parents repeating the widely circulating rumors of Japanese spies among us. There were even rumors that the local Japanese knew about the December 7th attack before it happened. Of course, there was no evidence of any such thing, but many people wanted to believe it just the same.

From the beginning, my grandmother expressed reservations about what was happening. Less than a week after the attack on Pearl Harbor, she flew to the Northwest and posed for a picture in nearby Tacoma with a delegation of young Japanese Americans, thanking them for their support as "loyal Americans." She then visited us and shared her fears. While she understood the expediency behind the action, she also saw clearly that removing all Japanese Americans from the Pacific coast area meant violating the basic rights of U.S. citizens. Sadly, she recognized—and unhappily accepted—that it would forever remain "a real black eye" for America.

But even discussing the human rights issue at length with Papa had not brought to light a practical alternative, she told us. He had noted the immediate hostility Americans felt for all Japanese and said that the American military commanders, especially, were reiterating their worries about a fifth column on our Pacific coast. I remember that as the war went on, my grandmother never stopped being troubled by this decision, which detained or relocated more than 100,000 people.

⸺∞⸺

Our Christmas in 1941 was a somber affair, with fewer presents, a minimum of frivolity, and no "round robin" telephone call on Christmas Day with Papa. There was, though, a surprise in a registered envelope mailed from the White House. "I wish you could have seen & heard Sis [and] Buzz," my mother wrote to Grandmère, "when they saw the amount of the bonds Pa sent all the grand-children! Their eyes practically popped out while they felt the $1000 figure with their fingers & asked me over and over again: 'Is this really mine?'!" It was quite a sum; at the time, I had a savings account with fourteen dollars in it.

As we began a new year, the crucial role of the "home front" was daily hammered into us through newspapers and magazines. Those sterling citizens who pitched in that extra something for the war effort were forever being spotlighted. In the Boettiger household, too, we did our part and worked with some semblance of energy and dedication on the victory garden we'd planted at our new house. An unused chicken coop was cleaned out, hens and chicks purchased, and before long, we had our own eggs. (One of the Secret Service men reminded my mother we would also need a rooster.) Since rationing soon made them a sought-after item, we shared our eggs with our neighbors. My sister and I were assigned to care for the hens, a daily responsibility.

I'd been given a four-month-old black Labrador puppy, which I named Ensign, and he was now an important part of my life. After much pleading, Mummy acceded to his being allowed to sleep on my bed with me, and it was wonderful. Soon this creature was my closest intimate. However, because Ensign was growing rapidly, like all puppies, he needed meat, not just dried food, my mother said.

Since we were on meat rations, Mummy cleverly asked our Secret Service men whether horse meat could be purchased outside the rationing system. Told there were already horsemeat markets springing up, she sent me out with Hazen to buy a two-week supply. Our cook, Mrs. Williams, divided it into portions, freezing what wouldn't be used immediately. She then taught me how to make a simple stew, picking out vegetables and potatoes that were past their prime to add to the meat. I enjoyed this first experience of cooking and did it every third day, storing the leftovers in the icebox.

JULIANNA ROOSEVELT

A boy and his dog.

After feeding Ensign, I would leave the rest cooling on the back of the stove, just as the cook had told me to do. Then the inevitable happened. One evening, when it was her night out, Mrs. Williams had posted instructions for my mother about what to heat up for her and Popsie's supper. Finding my hearty concoction cooling on the stove, Mummy assumed it was their main course, heated it, and served it.

Both of them found it tasty. And all would have gone well if Mrs. Williams hadn't returned later to discover the meal she'd prepared for them still in the icebox and asked them why. Sis and I doubled over with laughter when we heard, but my mother was not amused, nor was my stepfather. I received a stern lecture—about what I'm not sure. The next weekend I learned from the children of family friends that they'd heard the story from their parents, along with the wry admission that my dish had been enjoyed.

Sis and I continued our long school commute, and since wartime gas rationing meant even the Secret Service car was limited to the new forty miles-per-hour limit, we now traveled very slowly. This gave Sis and me plenty of time to quarrel over nearly everything, and as always, I ended up the loser. Then without telling me, she volunteered to help register motorists for gas rationing three afternoons a week after school. Suddenly, she acquired new status.

My mother fretted over Sis's new job, writing to Grandmère: ". . . I tried to impress her [Sis] with the necessity for realizing that while she could get away with being careless at times in school, she could not do this at work, as her carelessness might be harmful to someone else. I wish I had some way of checking up and finding out what kind of job she is doing! School work is still most *un*serious!"

The days Sis worked at her new job, I hung around school, waiting for her to be done so that we could make the long trip home together with Mody or Hazen. Now that I was older, I was occasionally allowed to board the public bus that ran close by school and go into downtown Seattle—all by myself!—instead of just hanging around. On those days, I would usually browse in the classical music section of a record shop that we'd discovered before going to my mother's office. An interest in classical music, which was not Mummy and Popsie's thing,* was the first bridge between me and my sister.

Rather than distracting me, the war, and all the fighting I heard about, provided fresh fodder for my fantasies. Hollywood had been churning out war movies at a furious rate, enabling me to populate my escape universe with such heroes as the studios dreamed up for me: Brian Donlevy and Robert Preston in *Wake Island*; Preston and Edmond O'Brien in *Parachute Battalion*; Errol Flynn in *Dive Bomber*; Flynn and Ronald Reagan in *Desperate Journey*; and John Payne in *To the Shores of Tripoli*,** among many others. I also devoured books about the exploits of real-life heroes. Captain Walter Bayler's heart-stopping *Last Man Off Wake Island* was a particular favorite, and I read it over and over, weaving it into the stories I rolled out in my fantasies.

---

*Several years earlier, to introduce us to "the better things of life," my mother and stepfather had brought home a record of Jeanette MacDonald and Nelson Eddy singing "I'll Be Loving You Always!" Sis and I both groaned and were dismissed from the room.

**After Pearl Harbor, the ending of this film was reshot. The hero reenlists and heads off to war, with his father reminding him to "Get a Jap for me."

Sis, Ensign, and I with Papa in 1942 at our Mercer Island house.

CHAPTER 22

L ate that summer of 1942, just before I was scheduled to start attending yet another new school, Sis and I learned that our grandfather was making an unexpected visit. We hadn't seen him in more than a year, not since early 1941. Now he was a wartime president, Commander in Chief of our armed forces. His journey was confidential—no press coverage allowed—and we were in on the secret.

Sis and I were thrilled. Such anticipation! It was hard to think of anything else. Along with Mummy and Popsie, we would join the presidential train the evening before FDR was scheduled to review the troops training at Fort Lewis (which was named after Meriwether Lewis, companion to Clark on their famed expedition). We'd then travel with my grandfather to Tacoma, where he planned to visit the Bremerton Navy Yard. Crossing Puget Sound by ferry to Seattle, we'd stop at the Boeing aircraft plant, before returning, with the entire motor cavalcade, back home to Mercer Island.

When we arrived at the *Magellan*, it felt like old times. We were shown our sleeping quarters on the train and deposited our suitcases there. As usual, the cocktail hour was going strong in the lounge at the rear of the car when we arrived. There were lots of voluble people making rapid conversation, accompanied by laughter—and smoke. As we joined the crowd, the air was so thick that I remember my mother waving her hand in front of her face in mock asphyxiation. But everyone just laughed and took another puff. My mother quickly accepted a proffered cigarette, as did Popsie.

I had been allowed—after much pleading—to bring Ensign along on the trip, so the two of us were greeted with exceptional interest as we crowded in, following Sis. I found space on the floor—difficult with so many feet in a packed space—and inevitably came the question, "What's your dog's name?"

When I answered "Ensign," most of my questioners looked puzzled. Papa overheard, and with just the right air of seriousness, answered for me, explaining about navy rank and how an ensign corresponded to an army second lieutenant. We, of course, were navy men. I was relieved, and very pleased as I had my eye on Annapolis.

Because there were so many people at the dining table, our mother announced that Sis and I would have to eat early. When we complained, Papa heard about it and proposed—authoritatively—that he was sure space could be made for two extra places. We were grateful, knowing that dinner with the adults would be full of conversation, just as it had been in the White House, except that now it was the war that dominated the table talk. I sat and listened, fascinated as people reviewed Pearl Harbor and the hard time the British were having with Rommel in Africa. There was no mention, of course, of the impending North African invasion involving U.S. troops. My mother told me later that it was top secret.

The next morning I gathered my clothes and went down the corridor to dress in the men's room in order to allow my sister some privacy. Then I took Ensign out for a quick turn. We had already arrived in Tacoma and were sitting in the train station, but all of us in the presidential car had breakfast—which included steaming Cream of Wheat with honey on the side, lots of toast, and bacon—before disembarking to find our places in the motorcade.

For the State of Washington's motorcycle troopers, escorting the president on his route was a rare occasion to show off. They were the outriders, and they indulged in a good deal of macho revving of their engines and jockeying for position. I noticed tolerant smiles on the faces of some of the seasoned presidential Secret Service detail, who obviously felt themselves beyond such provincial antics.

Our mother told my sister and me to stand and wait until our places were designated. The top brass from Fort Lewis, generals all, were to ride with Papa in the backseat of his big open Packard. To my great pleasure, I was to be squeezed into the front seat of that car, between the driver and the chief of the Secret Service detail, Mike Reilly.

Mike and the driver, Monty Snyder, also an old hand I knew, would be the ones to assist Papa as needed. Sis went with my mother and stepfather into the limousine behind the two Secret Service cars. Mike explained to me that he was sorry but that my mother would have to take Ensign.

It was a short drive to the base. Though we were greeted with the usual honor guard presenting arms and the band playing "Hail to the Chief," Papa declined to formally review the assembled troops at Fort Lewis. One can only imagine what a disappointment this must have been to sergeants and officers who'd spent hours trying to get their new and fumbling recruits—a mixture of enlisted men and draftees—to handle their rifles smartly. Instead, Papa drove slowly through the ranks, insisting that the speed be reduced to a crawl so that he could look at the faces of these men who were in the midst of basic training.

He didn't wave or respond in any "political" way as we passed. This was wartime, and he was all business. Addressing the assembled troops, he confined his remarks to extending a brief thanks for serving their country. He acknowledged the personal sacrifice many of the soldiers had made, particularly those who had left behind their families, and wished them the best of luck. Now I know that my grandfather was already aware that within a couple of months, these men might well be on their way to take part in the North African invasion, the first big American engagement in combat on the western front.

Although it wasn't on the official schedule prepared by the commanding general, FDR told his hosts he wanted to see the trainees' barracks and mess hall. After this, time was short, and he had to forego the official reception, which had been prepared by the commanding general's wife. I imagine this provoked further disappointment, this time at a more rarefied level. We did stop briefly in front of the general's house, and my grandfather chatted with those assembled outside, engaging everyone with his usual charm. My mother pointed out to me that by arranging things this way, Papa didn't have to get out of the car and thus didn't have to put on his braces.

After the military brass vacated the back of the lead car, my mother and Popsie came to sit with him. Mummy said it was now Sis's turn to be there. My unhappiness at having to forfeit my privileged position must have been evident. The Secret Service men now generously offered me a place with them, undoubtedly bending regulations.

Being with the Secret Service men in their big open car, the one that stayed close behind him, was an exceptional treat, almost as exciting as riding with FDR himself. The agents made a great fuss over me. I was aware of my mother's wry and knowing smile, but it didn't spoil my pleasure. We roared off, sirens going, the motorcycle police waving off the cars of startled citizens, just the kind of excitement I gloried in. I had to keep a hand on Ensign, who wasn't as thrilled with all the hoopla.

The protection of the president in those days—in spite of the assassination attempt against FDR in 1932, when he was traveling in an open car—would be considered minimal, even casual, today. The Secret Service planned the president's routes, sending ahead half a dozen advance men, but it was nothing like the second-by-second breakdown of events that now precedes any appearance by a president. I know my grandfather always said that if someone were really determined to assassinate him, no amount of protection could prevent it.

At the big navy base in Bremerton, I found myself feeling a little cheated. This was because we weren't there to look at ships; most of the vessels anchored there had been damaged in combat and were being repaired. Instead, Sis and I took Ensign for a long walk while my mother and Papa visited the big military hospital. There, in his wheelchair, Papa was pushed slowly around the wards. Even without his braces, his crippled legs were manifestly obvious to the wounded officers and men. Many had been injured at Pearl Harbor, but some had participated in recent sea battles in the Pacific against the Japanese navy. My grandfather made the rounds, taking his time and talking with the men he saw, asking about their combat experience. Mummy, the only person accompanying Papa, told us that the visit was draining and inspiring at the same time. She had frequently found herself near tears, watching the men as they responded to her father.

As we headed for the ferry to take us to Seattle, we drove past some warships, damaged and in dry dock, and I enjoyed getting glimpses of them, but we were running late. A quick pass was made through the downtown streets. As no news stories had been permitted, people were startled to see him, their only alert being the sirens of the escorting motorcycles. Many people looked overwhelmed. But there Papa was the politician again, doffing his hat to those who recognized their president and waved at him.

The next stop was the Boeing aircraft plant with its sprawling assembly lines that were producing a new B-17 Flying Fortress every day. As our motorcade crawled through the long, huge sheds, proceeding at barely five miles an hour, workers stopped, looked, and their jaws dropped. They couldn't believe it. It wasn't until Papa waved that they shouted and waved back.

In many of the defense plants across the country, there had been serious labor unrest due to the strict controls on wages at the same time living costs in the wartime economy were rapidly rising. Boeing's workers were grumbling about this, even mentioning the word "strike," despite the desperate need for Flying Fortresses, which were being shot down every day. We rolled slowly along, stopping when FDR spotted a foreman, or when a shop steward or other union representative came forward.

To help me see better, the Secret Service men had positioned me atop the backseat. I loved it, though I didn't wave or call attention to my glorious vantage point. I probably did grin at the occasional shout of "Buzzie" from the people we passed. But my smile must have looked a little clenched to anyone closely observing.

In truth, I was torn between exhilaration and misery. Something I'd eaten, or maybe a passing bug, had given me an incipient case of the runs. Could I hold out or not? I wasn't sure. There used to be "Sistie and Buzzie stops" when we were little, but it would have been a disgrace to ask for one now that I was twelve. At last we were on our way out of the Boeing plant heading for the floating bridge to Mercer Island. We now traveled rapidly, but it couldn't be quick enough for me. I was in agony. The Secret Service men probably wondered at my increasingly grim expression. All I know is that my toes were curling inside my shoes. The glory had vanished. I had only one thought: hold on.

Finally, we wound slowly down through the trees of our driveway. The car had barely stopped when I vaulted down—no time for thank-yous—and ran into the house to the nearest bathroom. Ensign followed suit.

Papa was carried down the steep lawn and steps into the house where, after refreshing himself, he settled himself onto the living room couch. Having changed clothes, I joined the crowd. Drinks were about to be served. My mother wanted a picture of Sis and me with Papa, so we perched beside him.

In that photo I appear most interested in Ensign, who was on my lap. I was, I'm sure, trying, for once, to be a little studied, less eager. Only on the outside, though. Inside, I was intensely proud to be there with my grandfather.

Soon we kids gave way to all the other people being brought in to meet him. It was the only occasion when Mummy and Popsie would have a chance to put forward people they thought FDR should meet. I watched from the sidelines, observing my grandfather being polite and pleasant, nodding, and occasionally laughing—but clearly, to anyone familiar with him, bored stiff. I wondered how Mummy and Popsie could do this to him, yet I understood why they felt they had to. Partly it was their positions with the *Post-Intelligencer*, but I guess, in the back of their minds, it was also their desire to be identified as Papa's unofficial ambassadors in the Northwest. As president, FDR couldn't escape from anyone, not even his own children.

Later that evening, we said good-bye to Papa as he left to return to the *Ferdinand Magellan*, which had been brought up from Tacoma. He then headed south to the Kaiser shipyards of Portland, and then on to California, before returning home across the country. All along the way, traveling east, he stopped to visit plants and military installations.

In Texas, however, he interrupted his official schedule to stop and see his daughter-in-law, Ruth, Elliott's wife. There he enjoyed the opportunity to play with her three small children, Tony and Chandler—and David, just born. In spite of the war's consuming burdens, President Franklin Roosevelt remained an attentive grandfather.

Soon after Papa's visit, I got word that I was to become a student at a private school again. For years I'd been aware of the reputation of the Lakeside School, considered to be the best school in the region. My mother had characterized it as snobbish, catering to the country club set and thus not where I belonged. But the previous summer, I'd met three friends at camp who went there, and their descriptions of it had made me want to join them. My experience attending public schools since second grade had been a decidedly mixed bag. Moreover, my love of all things related to the navy made the U.S. Naval Academy my goal at the time, and I thought private school would give me better preparation for Annapolis.

And so I was launched into a decidedly different school atmosphere. At Lakeside, we wore shirts and ties with a jacket and gray slacks. Classes were smaller, and teachers challenged students. The quality of the instruction was more thoughtful, more intellectual, more demanding. Since I wanted to make a good impression, I paid somewhat more attention. While this was a strain, disturbing the comfort of my dream world, I began to feel something like a sense of belonging. As one of the gang, I joined in the wisecracking and horse-play at lunch. Like my stepfather, who would have preferred to live near the country club, I felt more at ease with my Lakeside schoolmates. Were he and I both snobs?

Still, I never progressed past the acceptable fringes at Lakeside—it didn't help that none of my classmates lived anywhere near us—and once home, I lost any sense of motivation I'd felt at school. The school station wagon picked me up on the Mercer Island highway at 7:30 in the morning for a pokey hour-and-a-half drive to school each day, picking up one boy after an-other, and it was eleven hours before I got home. I did very little work before going to bed, exhausted, at 8:30.

The real problem, however, was even more fundamental: I simply could not work. Even knowing that I'd be tested the next day failed to light a fire under me. I'd gaze at my books and papers, head in my hands, daydreaming, and then finally nod off. In the process, a few pages might have been looked at, a couple of arithmetic problems attempted—but most times I never even made the effort to tackle the problem.

A blank look became a too-often repeated response to any teacher trying to figure out how I was spending my time. "I don't know," I'd say, as if daring them to dispute the truth of it. But I *didn't* know, and most of the time I sim-ply couldn't surmount my inertia.

To make matters worse, it was not hard for me to hide where and how I was falling short. My mother remained unable to see anything beyond what she perceived as the usual troublesome "growing pains" common to any preadolescent boy. Anything beyond that was "looking under the bed," an ex-ploration both Grandmère and Mummy were deeply suspicious of.

Back in 1939, a camp counselor had told my mother that I didn't socialize very well. I wasn't readily "one of the boys." On his recommendation, Mummy enlisted an undergraduate psychology student at the University of Washing-ton to spend time with me and then report back to her on our conversations. A trusting ten-year-old, I was thrilled to have an older friend to hang out with. The student, who was about twenty years old, began to spend some Saturdays with me. He would take me on excursions, such as a museum or a concert. This was great fun, and I looked forward to each Saturday. We even got to play catch with the new baseball mitt and ball I had recently been given by Popsie for my birthday.

One Saturday we had nothing scheduled. My young keeper asked about a sandbox he'd seen in the basement. The box was big, 6 by 8 feet, and I had placed my army and navy figurines inside, pushing the sand this way and that, adding small boxes for buildings. I stationed the soldiers on land and had the warships sailing by in formation. Placing myself in these fantasies wasn't a central part of my play; I simply loved organizing these little armies and creating narratives for them.

Since the debacle of my grand show in the playroom of the Lawtonwood house, I was secretive about my fantasies. I didn't use my sandbox in the new house very often, and I certainly did not share with anyone the elaborate stories I could create by arranging and rearranging my ships and soldiers inside the box. But I freely explained all of this to my Saturday companion. He was friendly; he drew me out and I gave forth. I was happy to share the landscape of my dream world with a confidant. He seemed to understand.

Early the following week, my mother asked me to talk with her and Popsie after they had settled into their cocktails. To my great astonishment— and to her great annoyance—my sister was told to go upstairs, get on with her homework, and to shut the door of her room. In this ominous atmosphere my mother recounted, in a measured and deliberate way, what my Saturday companion had reported to her and Popsie. She detailed what I had revealed to him, all the fantasies played through the landscape within my sandbox.

My mother's look and tone of voice expressed serious concern. Her disapproval, softened only by a pained expression of regret, and joined by Uncle J.'s frown and nodding of head, was plain. She sternly advised me that we would never again be living in the White House and that I was to put all of that out of my mind. She told me that I must never consider that I could be like Papa.

It wasn't the first time my mother had clearly made this point to me. Once, on an earlier occasion, I had owned that, when I grew up, I wanted to be like Papa. Mummy looked at me very seriously, as if I had said something quite rude and offensive, and then she said with finality, "You can never be like Papa. Who do you think you are?" I was taken aback by her response, but I understood deeply what she was saying—I had committed blasphemy.

In my mother's view, identifying with my grandfather amounted to heresy; it didn't matter that this was not central to my sandbox creations. I don't remember what else she said or what I replied. My "friend" had spied on me. The sense of betrayal I felt when I realized that this young man had been hired by my mother to check me out was sickening. I never saw him again.

The idea that I might be suffering from growing up in the orbits of my grandfather and grandmother, whose powerful auras were double-edged, was untenable. To recognize that my family situation was actually causing harm would have forced my mother and stepfather—and everyone else in the family—to examine truths that struck too close to home. We were all too close to the sun.

My teachers at Lakeside had some idea of what was going on, or at least they saw the effects of it. The first to write home about it was my Latin teacher, who reported to my mother: "It appears that Curtis is not especially interested in Latin. He has a great deal of ability but he does not seem to like the routine procedure which is necessary for the mastery of basic fundamentals. . . ."

I was allowed to drop Latin, and I was glad to be relieved of the burden of the effort I wasn't making—one less conflict to cope with.

The headmaster of the lower school spoke several times to my mother about my poor performance. Individual teachers continued to write her concerned, puzzled notes. I was obviously bright enough, they said, but I didn't perform. No one, however, saw the big picture. My teachers didn't know that on the playing field, during football games, for example, I avoided encounters, did not want to be competitive, didn't engage. When the head football coach asked me into his office to discuss my unsatisfactory participation, I choked up with tears. After that, he left me alone.

My mother chalked up these reports to "adolescent laziness" and wrote courteous replies to faculty and administrators at Lakeside. "I sincerely hope that he will begin now to develop a greater sense of responsibility. . . . In the meantime I hope you will let me know at any and all times if there is anything I can do to help in this situation." These polite notes fulfilled her responsibility, and that was that.

Children are expected to grow out of their fantasy world. I did not. "I can't do it" was my out whenever I was asked to concentrate on something. I didn't want to be tested, and I became adept at avoiding challenges. Within my dream world I could achieve anything, belong anywhere, have all the recognition I wanted, be whatever and whomever I wanted to be. The identity that my dream world lent me was sufficient, even satisfying. What started as an indulgence at age seven became gradually entrenched in my psyche, and as I grew older, there was no breaking it.

Uncles Elliott and Franklin with FDR at the Casablanca meeting with Winston Churchill, December 17, 1943. Said my stepfather to his father-in-law: "I'd give my eye teeth. . . ."

CHAPTER 23

M y world—my real one, that is—turned upside down the following spring, 1943. Our stepfather had decided to enlist in the army. All of FDR's sons were already in the armed services. John Boettiger, at forty-three, was well beyond the draft age. He was performing an important civilian job at the helm of a daily newspaper in a major city. But the pressure was on for all able-bodied men to serve their country. According to my mother, Popsie was beginning to feel left behind—although no one had questioned his patriotism.

I was almost thirteen and fascinated by the war, and I closely followed my uncles' involvement. But it did seem odd that Popsie was enlisting in the army. I could tell that my mother wasn't too thrilled with his choice. What I was not able to see at the time were the forces that impelled him to don a uniform. I now realize he was caught in the heightened dramatic mood of wartime urgency. At the heart of the decision were his fantasies of being engaged in the White House inner circle, especially accompanying FDR to any rendezvous of the Big Three.

In a letter to my mother, Popsie recorded the moment that had convinced him to enlist. Papa had just returned from meeting

Winston Churchill at Casablanca in January. My grandfather had summoned his sons Elliott and Franklin Jr. to join him at this groundbreaking North African meeting, and Randolph Churchill, son of the British prime minister, had attended as well. When Popsie saw FDR upon his return, he'd exclaimed, "I'd give my eye teeth to go on a trip like that!" My grandfather had replied that it wasn't possible. This must have stung. Not satisfied with that answer, and perhaps feeling he was being put off, Popsie had pressed him. Papa then had replied, "Well, John, you are not in uniform," assuming that that would end the matter.

FDR's remark set into motion events that ultimately proved ill fated for my stepfather. I feel quite sure that my grandfather, unprepared for being pursued on the issue, had simply been attempting to end the discussion. But Popsie took it for a straightforward reply. As a matter of principle, FDR never intervened on his sons' behalf during their military service, and he wasn't going to intervene for his son-in-law. In fact, all my uncles complained throughout the war of being held in grade a bit longer than usual because of their accident of birth. They'd been handed privilege all their lives, but in wartime being sons of the president worked against them.

While all this was common gossip within the family, my stepfather seemed blind to it, and he gave up his prestigious, and useful, newspaper job to join the army. He may have felt some qualms about his decision, but once everyone in Seattle had heard that Popsie planned to go into uniform, changing his mind was impossible.

As soon as he enlisted, whatever expectations John Boettiger had were quickly quashed. Sensitive to congressional criticism—nepotism being a prime target—the senior brass went out of their way to appear uninfluenced by White House "suggestions" or any sort of favoritism when it came to appointments and posting. So John Boettiger was given a captaincy, in my opinion a rank below what his age and experience deserved.

In fact, my stepfather was highly qualified as a writer and seasoned newspaperman. He had executive experience as the publisher of a well-known daily paper. He was good company, urbane, and savvy about politics, and he fit in easily with a variety of people. Such capabilities would have rendered him useful, surely, as a staffer to any number of senior military or civilian wartime officials.

But that is not the way the U.S. Army looked at the desire of the president's son-in-law to serve in the armed forces. They'd already been raked over the coals by the press and assorted enemies of Papa when they'd commissioned Uncle Elliott a captain in the air force. It didn't matter that Elliott's credentials—he was a qualified pilot—were sound. He was the president's son. The Republicans even went so far as to make it an issue in the 1940 election, coming up with the campaign slogan, "I want to be a captain, too!"

Popsie went first to the University of Virginia for training in "military government" and then to North Africa, where he faced the boring daily grind of army life, often with nothing to do, finding his company in the junior officers' mess distasteful. His superiors concerned themselves more with making sure the president's son-in-law didn't create problems than they did with trying to make the best use of his talents. They regarded him, above all else, as a potential liability, and faced with such an unreceptive environment, he quickly grew bitter.

John Boettiger looking jaunty in his new uniform.

It now seems clear that the army, right from the time he volunteered, went out of its way to bury the president's son-in-law where he couldn't flap his wings. Of course, it is also true that a lot of people who had quite useful skills found their talents wasted as a result of the army's shortsightedness when it came to assignments. But many men, particularly those as distinguished and well connected as my stepfather, managed to negotiate their jobs with the army or navy before signing on the dotted line.

There were virtually no bright spots to Popsie's military stint, although FDR did request that he join his staff for the Cairo and Tehran conferences in late 1943—in the first of which he met with Churchill and Generalissimo Chiang Kai-shek and in the second with the British Prime Minister and Marshall Josef Stalin. Yet even during these momentous back-to-back meetings, Major John Boettiger could not completely savor the triumph because he ranked far beneath his brother-in-law Elliott, ten years his junior, who was a full colonel and commander of a large air force unit. Popsie wrote to my mother: "I am brutally truthful when I say to you: it is not worth the candle!" Unhappy as she might have been, my mother tried valiantly to shore up Popsie's vulnerable ego in her sympathetic letters to him.

Finally, my stepfather attempted to pull strings in order get posted stateside. My mother talked directly with Grandmère about what they were going through. Reporting on the conversation, she wrote to Popsie, "She [my grandmother] is a bit cynical about our whole situation—feels you should have thought *beforehand* of all the hardships for 'US' and made the remark that, of course, you were trying for your no. 2 plan [to be assigned to the Pentagon and hence live at the White House] because you just wanted to be in on all the excitement!"

<hr />

My mother and Johnnie had followed Popsie to Virginia to be with him during training before he shipped out. Sis was now off at a boarding school, and with Ensign as my only companion in Seattle, I felt completely lost in our rambling house. Though I was always a loner, I still liked having other people in the background. Pretty much the only choice I had for human companionship was Mrs. Williams, the cook. I spent hours playing gin rummy with her, or with George, a new Secret Service agent. Those were the bright spots at the end of my day and during the long weekends.

Once Popsie was sent overseas, my mother and Johnny finally returned to Mercer Island. She tried to pick up where she'd left off at her *Post-Intelligencer* job, but after a few months, the new publisher made it clear to her that her contributions could just as well be made by others—in effect, freezing her out. She tried to stick it out but finally quit.

While this was happening, Mummy and I began talking in a way we never had before. I guess Sis, when she'd been around, had been the chosen confidante. Now my mother badly needed someone to confide in, someone who wouldn't gossip or embarrass her by repeating something indiscreetly, and I was more than ready to assume my new role. More and more she saw John Boettiger's enlisting as a disaster, for her, for them. We went over the details many times, but the theme was the same; Popsie had been totally unrealistic.

Yet, however satisfying this sea change in our relationship was, it didn't have much of an effect on my dream world. When I sat and talked with my mother, I felt my self-confidence being palpably strengthened, but it didn't translate to other areas of my life. In school I continued to perform poorly and avoid challenges.

Came the summer and I was off to the same camp as the year before, on an island on Lake Coeur d'Alene in Idaho. Reported Mummy to Grandmère: "Buzz is not happy at camp this year, but I'm making him stay for six weeks. . . . I think it's just that he is starting on the lazy period of adolescence and prefers to lie around home rather than to have to get up at the sound of a bugle and carry out a fairly military routine all day."

My teachers made similar observations about my lack of energy when I entered my second year at Lakeside, during the month that Italy surrendered. Sis was away at the Sarah Dix Hamlin School in San Francisco. In Seattle, schoolwork was the last thing on my mind. In my eighth grade classrooms, an ample amount of homework was regularly assigned, but as far as I was concerned, such demands existed in a parallel universe.

Again, my mother received letters from nearly all my teachers noting how tired I seemed and that I was unable to meet the challenge of concentrated study. (They are painful for me to read.) Although exhaustion is a fairly reliable sign of depression, what I sensed was that my energy was being sapped by the demands of living in two worlds. Having to venture out of the one I preferred, in order to deal with the other, was a continual drag.

Unexpectedly, that winter I was chosen for the first string of my class basketball team. I was thrilled and very proud. My mother, however, took in only that I seemed tired much of the time and therefore came to the conclusion that participating in anything so strenuous wouldn't be good for me.

I objected, but not for long. Like a lighthouse beacon signaling rescue, the White House now loomed on the horizon. We were scheduled to go there for Christmas, for the first time since 1939. Popsie wouldn't be joining us. But his letters home were finally showing some feeling of satisfaction in his role. He had been with U.S. troops when they invaded Sicily in July and when they landed in Salerno in September, and he had been awarded a medal for his "meritorious service." As for me, I was giddy with anticipation of another White House Christmas. Plus, I'd miss six whole weeks of school—which didn't bother me at all.

CHAPTER 24

Christmas 1943. Now, going on fourteen, I thought myself quite the adult. At nearly seventeen, my sister really was mature, and proves it by playfully admonishing one of my younger cousins.

The White House! The only thing spoiling my pleasure at returning home was the fact that Ensign had to stay behind. With my mother, Johnny, and me in the train compartment, it would be crowded enough already. Sis was taking a train from San Francisco and would meet up with us in Chicago. From there, we'd all board the *Capitol Limited* for Washington.

Johnny was almost four years old now. But Sis and I were so much older and in our own orbits that it was almost as if we were growing up in separate households. Johnny had been born when I was nine and Sis was twelve. After the novelty of our new baby brother wore off—we had liked playing with his fingers and toes—we went on about our lives. We might have been a little jealous of Mummy's intense focus on him, but, mostly, we paid scant attention.

The previous summer had been difficult. Marion, the nurse who had been hired in Seattle to care for him, was so young that she could practically have been my sister's chum. Johnny had his meals with her in the kitchen, and we didn't see a lot of him, even when we were home. And with Popsie absent, Mummy ate with Sis and me, which simplified life for the cook, who now had housekeeping chores as well. So Johnny, at this stage in his life, was virtually an only child and had the disposition to prove it. With his sullen moods, he often seemed a first-class pain to Sis and me.

Thank God for Hazen, who adored Johnny and seemed to know how to manage him better than anyone else. Mummy frequently took advantage of Hazen's soft spot for him to give herself free time on the weekends. Even Mrs. Hazen got into the act. She'd come to assist the nurse if there were weekends when my mother, Sis, and I were invited to stay with friends—four-year-olds not being everyone's idea of the perfect houseguest.

As we sped eastward on the train toward Chicago, the Pullman porter kindly baby-sat Johnny, so my mother and I had time to sit in the dining car and talk. I found myself a captive audience—a very willing one—to my mother's confidences, mostly family gossip. Though she didn't talk about it, I could sense her loneliness.

One of the burdens on Mummy's mind was worry over money. Sis's and my schools were expensive, she reminded me, and so was the Mercer Island house, now too big for our needs. She had even written Popsie, pointing out that selling it might be a good idea and noting the kind of price it could easily fetch. I wondered, was it possible that we would not be living in Seattle when the war ended?

We arrived in Washington the first week in December, just as Papa returned from the meetings in Tehran and Cairo. Upon entering the White House, Sis and I immediately sought out Tommy. She was just where we knew she'd be, under the stairwell next to the elevator—in her usual cramped space, the desk piled high with papers. She was delighted to see us, and we wanted to linger, but Mummy intervened: "Don't bother Tommy! Look at all the work she has to do! Just say hello!"

No longer the right size for bounding off to Papa's bedroom first thing in the morning to play on his bed, we now more sedately had breakfast with our mother and grandmother and whatever other guests were at the table. My mother described one such scene to Popsie: "Then the four of us [Johnny, Sis, and me with our mother] had breakfast with LL [Lovely Lady, my stepfather's name for Grandmère] in the West Hall. Hick and assorted guests were present—but we four were in dressing gowns!"

Accompanying either Grandmère or our mother, Sis and I always said a brief good morning to Papa. Even in wartime he always could adroitly maneuver back and forth between his family and his work—and always, no matter how busy, made time for us.

His wartime routine didn't seem all that different to us, with the staff still crowding around his bed as he ate breakfast. Always there was someone important in the corridor outside his bedroom who had to be squeezed in for "just a brief word." When we'd be introduced to these VIPs, usually old Washington hands, as "Sistie-and-Buzzie," you could see from their faces they expected us to look just as we had in the mid-1930s. Politely, we'd say hello and excuse ourselves. Taking our cue from Mummy, we strode ahead purposefully, just as she did, no more galloping down the corridors.

After we'd said good morning, Papa was out of bounds for the rest of the day. This was a wartime White House. But his still-regular cocktail hour, which we were welcome to join, was a highlight of each evening for me. I couldn't get enough of the political chat, as Papa mixed drinks while freely entering into all the talk surrounding him, wisecracking, poking fun, laughing, obviously having fun. Of course, the talk centered on the Washington crowd geared up for war, just as it had been focused on the New Deal previously, but I don't remember any serious subject quieting the room. What I remember was the style, the way everyone strove to make the conversation amusing, creating smiles and giggles.

My grandfather, in the middle of it, was relaxed. If he found himself distracted by a particularly clever riposte or provocative statement and lost track of the proper ratio of gin to vermouth for the martini pitcher in front of him, he'd simply add a dash more gin. Then, using the dropper attached to the top of a small medicine bottle he'd add a couple of drops of absinthe—"for taste," he'd say with a grin. Connoisseurs of martinis did not appreciate FDR's casual concoction. But they drank them without a murmur of complaint.

As she always had, my grandmother chose to tend her correspondence during cocktail hour. It was a good excuse to avoid a scene in which, generally, she didn't feel at ease. The casual, joking atmosphere was not her scene. To her way of thinking, such banter was often amusing but nearly always at the expense of someone else. With her built-in empathy for the underdog, she couldn't help identifying with the object of the fun. If she was seriously concerned, FDR took her side.

While my grandfather loved to tease, he was protective of his wife. Yet on some occasions his kidding did get under her skin, which she recounted in her autobiographies. What she seemed not to appreciate was the difference between good-humored gossip—with perhaps just the slightest hint of malice—and the crueler remarks that left a lasting sting, the sort that our cousin Alice Roosevelt Longworth was well known for. Such nastiness, however, did not feature in the conversation around my grandfather; he would not have approved.

Earnest as she was, my grandmother could see the humor in much of the clichéd and cartoonish criticism *of her* political and social activities, even when it mocked her. She and Papa, separately and together, had many enemies, after all, and they were often caricatured. So after years of being made fun of, she was able to make knowing fun of herself and her foibles. It was when it was closer to home—private, not public, faultfinding—that it occasionally stung. She reacted by retreating within herself, even if the criticism was only mild or just implied.

When Grandmère did arrive for the cocktail hour, the room's atmosphere became more subdued. When she saw one of the company laughing too loudly or slightly slurring his words, her face might register concern, tinged with a note of sadness. The alcoholism in her family had left its permanent bruise.

Since I was the youngest dinner guest, I would be the last out on the way to the family dining room. I found that, since no one was watching me, I could stealthily empty the dregs from a martini or two, especially if someone had been foolish enough to leave a marinated green olive. Then I quickly followed the others, glancing at the seating chart as I went past the second-floor usher's desk so I could identify my dinner companions. Today, among my most treasured belongings are one of FDR's martini pitchers and six of the small silver-plated goblets he often used.

By the time I arrived in the hallway, the old elevator would already be full, with my grandfather in his wheelchair and the others packed in tightly around him. Showing its age, it often bobbed up and down, emitting fearful little screeches of protest. The capacity listed was at best an estimate. "No more! Too many already!" shouted those inside. So Sis and I ran down the nearby stairs, usually beating them to the first floor. Grandmère wouldn't think of having the elevator replaced during wartime, and, indeed, all repairs in the White House, including keeping its legendary exterior white, were put off "for the duration."

Only when the guest list for supper was dominated by strangers—and that was rare—did all of us, including me, leave his study first, allowing Papa privacy to slip from his chair behind the desk into the wheelchair held firmly in place by his valet. My grandmother, in the meantime, would be leading the group to the grand staircase at the east end of the hall, making sure to employ a leisurely pace as we descended. She might also walk us through the reception rooms, discussing the portraits hanging there—anything to give him those extra minutes.

By the time we'd reach the family dining room, my grandfather would be in his seat, and the wheelchair would have disappeared. My grandmother now sat down opposite him, and the conversation that had begun upstairs resumed but in a more decorous tone.

With several weeks in Washington before Christmas and time on my hands, my favorite destination was the Smithsonian, where I admired the wonderful model ships on display and stared at a huge case housing a three-dimensional exhibit showing how minesweepers cleared the North Sea of mines in World War I.* I also visited the Jefferson Memorial, which had been officially dedicated by Papa that April. The plaster statue of Thomas Jefferson was a temporary one, painted to look like bronze, because of the shortage of metal in wartime—another one of those odd bits of information Papa would pass on to me.

When I turned thirteen the previous April, I stopped having Secret Service protection—at least, so far as I know. If agents were following me discreetly at a distance, I wasn't aware of it. Therefore, I often walked around Washington alone, admiring the many ornate government buildings. On one very cold day, I boarded a bus back to 1600 Pennsylvania Avenue and sat down in the back. The bus driver stopped, walked back to where I was sitting, and said, "Sonny, you have to sit in the front." Those sitting around me had a good giggle. I'd forgotten the nation's capital was still a "Jim Crow" town, and indeed it remained so until after the war.

When Grandmère was traveling, as she frequently did, my mother would take her place as White House hostess. Over dinner, I'd watch my grandfather and notice how relaxed he seemed sitting opposite my mother. Mummy usually made sure that only friends whose company FDR truly enjoyed were invited to join them.

As Christmas approached, more family members arrived, including Uncle Franklin and Uncle John, with their wives and children. Conversation during meals soon centered on family gossip—often quite uninhibited. My grandmother looked on somewhat disapprovingly. My ears flapped.

———— ∞ ————

During this trip east, Sis and I learned that our father wanted us to visit him and his new wife, Katherine. We had met Katherine before she and Dad were married, not long after Sis and I moved to Seattle. They now had two children, whom Sis and I had never met. Many years later I found a letter from

---

*When in Washington in the 1960s, I asked about this fantastic work, but nobody remembered it.

my mother to Dad offering congratulations and best wishes when his first child with Katherine was born and he'd sent a telegram announcing the event. But Sis and I never heard about it.

The connection between Dad and us had become even more frayed over the past few years. My father sent us presents for our birthdays and at Christmas, but we rarely replied with a thank-you note; indeed we never made any effort to keep in touch. Dad once wrote to my mother to complain that he hadn't heard a word from either my sister or me. He suggested that we each write him one letter a month, noting that "small attentions" such as letter writing are "unusually appreciated" in wartime.

My mother may not have encouraged us to correspond with Dad, but the truth was that after three years of not seeing him, I had a hard time even conjuring up his face. A picture of my father in my bedroom would have been heresy. My once deeply affectionate re-

Katherine Leas, about to become our stepmother, with Sis and me in 1938.

gard for him, and the sense I'd had of keeping that feeling alive, was hard to maintain. With Popsie overseas in the war and Mummy newly dependent upon me, I had changed.

My father had begun laying the groundwork for a reunion back in June, wanting to know if we'd be coming to Washington or New York during the summer. He had been temporarily assigned to the Pentagon in anticipation of going overseas, so he had proposed that we visit him in Washington. But as it turned out, we remained on the West Coast, and our mother had never mentioned this overture.

I would later learn that when Dad first got word that he was to be sent overseas, he'd asked for an appointment at the White House to say good-bye to Papa. He'd wanted to see his former father-in-law to discuss Sis's and my future in case he didn't come back. In an exchange of letters between my grandmother and mother, Dad was derided for seeking a visit to the White House just so he could boast about it. Undoubtedly, his brief meeting with FDR made good telling when he went to his Pentagon office the next day, but Papa was our legal guardian, and in my view, Dad's visit was entirely appropriate.

Knowing nothing of all this, Sis and I were surprised at Dad's request for a visit that Christmas. We were unaware of his meeting with Papa, and now, at Christmastime, we were worried that we'd be missing something at the White House if we left to spend time with him. We also felt awkward—and perhaps a little guilty. Sis and I had now been using the Boettiger name for three years, and although no one had officially, or even informally, notified Dad, we knew he must have had some inkling. Being caught out, confronted with our duplicity, worried us.

Our father was then living in Chevy Chase with his new wife and family. We could have no reasonable excuse now, Mummy told us, not to visit when he lived so close by. Besides, she said, we hadn't spent any time with him since the summer of 1940, when he'd taken us to British Columbia for a few days. It was odd to have her arguing his case suddenly, but she knew Dad would make a fuss if she made more excuses. And she too was fearful of a confrontation, especially if Dad brought up the matter of the Boettiger name.

I joined my sister in moaning and groaning about the fact that we had to see him. But off we went, sulkily, to meet Dad at the Chevy Chase Country Club. We immediately received a warm welcome from both him and Katherine. We watched Dad play a tennis match, but we were too shy to join in a game of doubles. As my father introduced us to their friends—"my children," he would say—his pride in us was obvious.

Leaving the club, we drove to their house to meet our half-brother and sister, Stephen, three, and Katrina, five. They were talkative and fun, delightful, really, and they entertained us as we played with them. Dad, a pre-dinner whiskey in hand, watched with pleasure. We soon sat down, all six of us, to

The Dall family—including Sis and me—gathered in front of Dad's house in Chevy Chase in 1943. Mingo, no longer working at the White House, joined us at my father's request.

enjoy Katherine's home cooking, taking second helpings. In spite of ourselves, we were warming to the household.

Over supper, Dad told stories and made jokes. I found myself laughing until the tears rolled down my cheeks, and Sis, too, was smiling. After dinner we kissed Katrina and Stephen goodnight. Katherine took them up to bed, while Dad, Sis, and I talked briefly in the living room.

He didn't chide us about our neglect of him, but he did remind us how important letters were in relationships, how much keeping in touch meant. Then he drove us back to the White House, dropping us at the guard's gate, as he'd been instructed by our mother. I quickly integrated myself back into the White House scene with a callousness that saddens me today, as I look back.

———

Soon after our visit with my father, we left the White House for Hyde Park. Papa had decided not to remain in Washington for Christmas Day. There were so many of us—family, children, guests—that it was a kind of jolly Roosevelt bedlam. Sis and I ate with the grown-ups while our younger cousins ate together in the servants' dining room. Yet the fact of Granny's absence left a very large hole. While my grandmother sat at the head of the dining table, with FDR at the other end, she never took Granny's chair in front of the fireplace in the library, opposite Papa. And, in fact, no one sat in it, even with Grandmère's urging.

On Christmas Day my grandfather gave me an elegant model of a Breton sailing ship, beautifully rigged and mounted on a wooden stand. Undoubtedly, he'd received the model as a gift, and I was flattered to have it passed on to me. After that, opening the other gifts was anticlimactic.

Snow had fallen and covered the ground. Since we didn't have sleds, I convinced Sis to go with me to the pantry where we borrowed large round metal serving trays from the White House brought to Hyde Park by the servants. Several hours later we returned them, shamefacedly, rather dented. Drinks were served to the adults on our sleds for the remainder of our stay.

Two days after Christmas, Sis and I went down to New York with Grandmère and Mummy and saw my first-ever Broadway play, Moss Hart's *Winged Victory*, a patriotic smash hit. It had been commissioned by the U.S. Army Air Forces as a morale booster—Hart crisscrossed the country to research it— and it paid stirring musical tribute to America's pilots, their crews, and support staff. Nearly three hundred actors performed, and afterward we had the fun of going backstage to meet the cast. Every actor was in the U.S. Army Air Forces and was billed in the program with his actual rank, with the women's roles being performed by the wives of the actors.*

Victory was something on everyone's minds, for in my grandfather's Christmas Eve radio address to the nation, broadcast from Hyde Park, he had announced that the Allies were making plans "for stepping up our attack on our

---

*Many were well known already, or were later to be. Red Buttons, Lee J. Cobb, John Forsythe, Mario Lanza, Karl Malden, Gary Merrill, and Edmond O'Brien were among those in the cast of *Winged Victory*.

enemies as quickly as possible and from many different points of the compass." He had also informed his rapt audience that General Dwight D. Eisenhower had been selected to command the Allied invasion, giving up his post in the Mediterranean.

It was Papa's thirteenth "fireside chat" since we'd been at war, and as usual, it was packed with information—statistics, reports on his meetings in Teheran and Cairo, even ideas for the postwar future. Yet the simple fact of FDR's voice, a wonderful baritone tenor, radiating out across the airwaves, was enough to reassure his listeners that the tide, indeed, was turning.

Fala, FDR's little Scotty who knew quite well "who he was."

CHAPTER 25

During the almost nine months my stepfather was overseas, I didn't appreciate, but know now, what severe pressure my mother was under. With school fees and trips back and forth across the country, she was dealing with a family situation that was greatly strained. Popsie's absence and money worries were placing great pressure on their marriage, and Mummy was finding it difficult to keep up the façade that everything was okay, that their special relationship was still on its pedestal.

My stepfather's entry into the army had been quite traumatic for her, and as my mother wrote plainly to him when he arrived overseas, she felt she'd been left in the lurch by his decision, abandoned both at home and in the professional life they shared. To his credit, he understood what she was telling him and acknowledged the truth of it in his letters.

All along in their relationship, they had mutually fostered an idea of their unique closeness, referring to themselves, coyly, in their correspondence as "US." Mummy, now on her own, was starting to have forebodings about how this partnership would emerge from the bruising effects of war. Their US-ness was certainly harder to sustain when separated. The small to medium-sized resentments my mother felt soon triggered recognition of large dissatisfactions, some of which would continue to cloud their life together even after she and Popsie were reunited and ensconced in the White House.

It didn't help that Johnny was then at a difficult stage. My mother's letters to Popsie during this period are dotted with references to my kid brother's frequent "whoopsing." He chose to throw up "at the most inconvenient times," she said, for example, just as she had joined the cocktail hour, Johnny in tow, to introduce him. He suffered frequent colds, was disagreeable with his nurses, and had a penchant for tantrums, often clinging to her neck while yelling. As I look back, I imagine Johnny was feeling dislocated and perhaps internalizing his mother's anxieties. At the time, however, I was less than sympathetic.

After Christmas, events began to unfold that presaged a momentous change in my family's situation. My first inkling of this came when my mother announced that she would be flying back to Washington after taking me cross-country to Seattle and settling her affairs there. Right after New Year's, my stepfather had returned stateside from Italy to work at the Pentagon, and the two of them, with Johnny, would be staying on at the White House. It was only to be for a while, Mummy told us. Papa was having trouble recovering from a lingering flu and other health problems, and she felt he needed her. (In fact, Papa had proposed in November that she consider assisting him with personal matters in the White House.)

The bottom line, though, was that Papa had indicated he wanted my mother close by, and that was the most impelling call to arms she could hear. My grandfather sorely missed his personal assistant, Missy LeHand, who had suffered a debilitating stroke two years earlier. Missy had always understood, with great sensitivity, just the way Papa wished delicate matters to be handled. Grace Tully, now his secretary, was less able to deal tactfully with things like the many daily favor-seekers. My mother was happy to fill this role. Unlike her brother Jimmy, who'd been their father's assistant a decade earlier, Mummy would have no title, no salary, and no specified duties.

Time magazine reported: "The President's daughter will preside over social engagements and welcome visitors of state any time Eleanor Roosevelt is off on a trip, but she has made it plain that she will not be considered an 'assistant hostess.' She has reiterated her old instructions to the State Department's protocol office: at White House guest dinners, 'Put me anywhere, I'm not official.'"

The truth was that my mother had her own fantasies of her father needing her, and like all of us, she found the glory associated with the president and the White House hard to resist, though she would fiercely deny such tendencies. She loved acting as his hostess, loved just being around him. What began as the simple assignment of being there for whatever task he might deem best performed by someone who had his complete confidence soon turned into a position of serious influence—one quickly noted by Washington insiders. Among other duties, she monitored who did and who did not get to see the president. (She was protecting her father's health, she said.) That in itself made her someone to be reckoned with. She was smart enough to play down her part, but it was a substantial one.

After it was decided that Mummy would return to Washington, three of us "Boettigers" headed west—Sis to her boarding school and Mummy and me to Seattle. Popsie and Marion, my brother's nurse, were looking after Johnny at the White House. Soon, the telephone and telegraph wires started burning up, as efforts got underway to rent the house and to turn me into a boarder, not a day student, at Lakeside.

Once back on Mercer Island, my mother worked hard to get the house ready, hiring carpenters and roofers, and so on, and overseeing their efforts. To her dismay, a pending rental contract fell through at the last minute, forcing her to fly back to Washington without having secured a tenant. The challenge of finding a suitable occupant now fell to the family lawyer. Soon, he turned up a dozen SPAR officers willing to pay $350 a month, and so, back east, Mummy could rest easier.*

---

*SPAR was the name given to the U.S. Coast Guard Women's Reserve. The acronym was taken from the Coast Guard's motto, *Semper paratus*, Always ready.

Suddenly, it was time for me to take up residence at Lakeside. Skeptical as I was about boarding, the arrangement that had been made for me was quite special. I would live with the headmaster, James Adams, and his family. And an extraordinary exception was made: I was allowed to bring my dog. After helping load all the heavy suitcases—I'd been firmly instructed to leave nothing behind—the Secret Service transported me and Ensign to the Adams's antique-filled house on the sprawling campus ten miles north of downtown Seattle.

While I experienced a great deal of kindness from the sensitive Mary Adams and took my meals with the other boarders in the school refectory, I continued to be terribly lonely. I had never been so entirely on my own before and simply was not up to it. The only solution I could manage was to retreat even more to my dream world. Ensign proved to be the sole saving grace. Dogs require attention, and taking care of him kept me anchored to the real world, at least enough to be sure he was okay. When I finished classes, always my first thought was to find him. My free time was usually spent taking him out for a run. Indeed, Ensign was my closest friend. On weekends, especially, it was he and I against the world.

After the Easter holidays, Mr. Adams told me I'd be moving the following weekend to the dormitory, to bunk in with the twenty or so boarders there. Having previously been a day student, I'd never really made friends among them, and they considered me an outsider. Ensign, naturally, moved with me, sharing a rather small room with me and two other boys. They, not surprisingly, sneered at my devotion to—and dependence upon—my dog.

It was around this time that I came down with a high fever and was sent to the infirmary. For three days I was held captive there. Once I started to recover, I learned that Ensign was nowhere to be found. He must have run away, I was told by one of my roommates.

I was beside myself. Rallying instantly, I fled the infirmary to head off in search of him. After covering a great deal of ground, and whistling and calling for hours, I finally found Ensign hiding in the woods next to the school grounds.

The rest of my time at Lakeside passed with painful slowness. Every bit of my being was focused on the moment school would be officially out. I already knew the plan was for Hazen, accompanied by his wife and niece, to drive Ensign and me in my family's car from Seattle across the country to the White House.

Even with escape in the offing, my continuing poor academic work worried me. Would I fail and not receive a diploma? This quite justifiable fear moved me to apply myself, if only enough to squeak by. As it was, the lower school principal wrote my mother, "Buzz's work at Lakeside has been more or less irregular." Nonetheless, I did manage to graduate. Acceding to a special request from my mother, and to my great joy, I was permitted to leave school the day after the last exam, skipping the final ceremonies.

The automobile trip across America, from one Washington to the other, gave me a new appreciation for just how long three thousand miles is. The roads were two-lane all the way, and even slower going than the train had been. Hazen's thirty-something niece, Jean, was our navigator, and she had a map on her lap the entire way. We stayed at motels or, if stopping in a city, a small hotel—providing, of course, that they accepted dogs. We ate at nondescript cafeterias, having been given a strict budget by my mother. After such a tedious drive it was with great relief that we finally reached 1600 Pennsylvania Avenue, pulling up to the guard's kiosk at the White House front gate.

As we stopped, the fellow on duty peered in the car windows at four weary people and a large dog. Tourists probably looking for a hotel, he thought. Hazen produced his Secret Service identification and explained who I was. With a laugh, the guard waved us in and then went back into his little booth to telephone, announcing our arrival.

With Ensign in tow, I made my way straight to the usher's office to check with Mr. Crim. He told me that my mother and Johnny had gone to meet my sister at the airport but would be back soon. He suggested that the Hazens wait in the

After many years of acid bickering, Sis and I had finally become good friends.

sitting area of the entrance hall. After taking Ensign out for a few minutes to christen the north portico, I left him with the Hazens. I ran up the stairs, taking the steps two at a time, and dashed into Tommy's office to tell her we'd arrived.

Shortly, my mother returned with Sis and Johnny. We said good-bye to the Hazens, and my mother, Sis, and I took the elevator upstairs. It was Ensign's first ride on one, and he couldn't wait to get off. Freed of his leash, he ran up and down the long hall, exulting in his freedom. The three of us made ourselves comfortable in my mother's big sitting room and talked and talked. We had a lot to catch up on after months apart. Returning from his office at the Pentagon, Popsie joined us.

Later, as we walked down the hall to Papa's cocktail hour, Mummy explained that Grandmère wasn't returning to the White House until the next day and that she'd been the one to select the guests for this evening's dinner. There were to be just ten of us.

We waited for my grandfather to be wheeled into his study from his adjacent bedroom. As always, he had changed his shirt and suit for the evening. Even if no one changed into evening clothes anymore, men of his era and upbringing still liked to mark the end of the work day by putting on clothes that wouldn't be considered business garb.

Fala, my grandfather's Scotty, was escorted in by Papa's valet. He had been an early Christmas gift offered to Papa in 1940 by my cousin Margaret "Daisy" Suckley, and the Scotty was now a celebrity in his own right. Although Margaret Suckley's status as "cousin" had never been firmly established, genealogically speaking, that is how we referred to her. She was a person of great importance to Papa. She lived alone a short drive north of Hyde Park, in Rhinebeck at her family's estate, Wilderstein. She never married, and the affectionate intimacy she enjoyed with Papa seemed to arouse no jealousy on the part of Grandmère—she seemed glad to have someone around to function as Papa's "gopher." Yet after Cousin Margaret's death in 1991 when she was nearly one hundred, the actual depth of their friendship and the extraordinary rapport she and FDR had enjoyed became clear from their exchange of letters, found in a suitcase beneath her bed.*

Cousin Margaret had taught Fala a number of parlor tricks and I knew what was coming. The valet held aloft Fala's supper dish to hand to Papa, and I moved Ensign out of view. Even though Ensign had eaten his supper, I wasn't sure he could handle it. First, Papa asked Fala to sit up; next he commanded him to roll over—and only then did he lean down to reward him with his food bowl.

Everyone laughed and applauded. Fala was used to it. He was quite the dog of the world, accustomed to adulation and always ready to show off. The president's constant companion, he was catered to and spoiled by everyone. In fact, after Fala's first weeks in the White House, he appeared to be ill. The vet figured out that Fala was suffering from overfeeding. In the wake of this diagnosis, FDR insisted that no one but he *ever* give his dog "even a crumb."

Among the guests at the table were such regulars as Henry Morgenthau and Bill Hassett, two of the men Papa felt most comfortable around. Bill, a

---

*Geoffrey Ward subsequently edited a book of Papa's and Cousin Margaret's letters titled *Closest Companion* (Boston: Houghton Mifflin, 1995).

New Englander and lovely man who'd spent his entire career employed in the corridors of power in Washington, had earlier in the year been elevated to full presidential secretary. Henry Morgenthau, Secretary of the Treasury from early on in Papa's administration, had been one of my grandfather's closest friends for over thirty years. A neighbor at Hyde Park, he'd always been "Uncle Henry" to me.

Listening to them, feeling the exciting atmosphere, it was hard to believe I'd so recently been cooped up in a car watching so many farms and small towns roll by. After supper, Sis and I took the two dogs out together; it was very clear which one had the alpha disposition. Though twice his size, Ensign fell in line and quickly followed his new friend's lead. I watched as the two of them set off to chase the squirrels that abundantly populated the big trees on the South Lawn. Ensign was as happy to be there as I was, it seemed.

CHAPTER 26

FDRL

Lt. Com. Franklin D. Roosevelt Jr.—
once my adored idol.

A thrilling invitation was relayed to me by my mother at the start of that summer in Washington. It couldn't have been more unexpected. Uncle Franklin was offering to take me with him on the shakedown cruise of the destroyer escort newly under his command. A week at sea on a U.S. Navy warship! I could think of hardly anything else; in my imagination I was already exploring every inch of the vessel. I couldn't help wondering if, while on board, I might actually see its guns fired or a depth charge dropped.

The plan, I was told, was for me to come down from Hyde Park to New York and then go to the Brooklyn Navy Yard, where I'd meet up with Lt. Commander Franklin D. Roosevelt Jr. This rendezvous was to happen sometime around the middle of July.

Since we were only stopping briefly in Washington en route to Hyde Park, my father, still living in the Washington suburbs with his wife and children, was told we wouldn't have time to see him. The usual lies were employed— ones that made me cringe when, in later life, I first read the letter my mother wrote to him at the time. Saying we had to see the dentist, along with a whole host of other fabricated obligations, she put him off until we would return to the White House at the end of the summer.

Upon arriving at Hyde Park, I was pleased to find myself sleeping in the traditional "eldest boy room," the one that had once been Papa's and then Uncle Jimmy's. Sis and I, Johnny and his nurse, Jean, "rattled around" in that large mansion that June. We weren't exactly alone. There was still the butler, a cook, a maid to clean house, and Mrs. De Pew taking care of the laundry as usual, so you could hardly say we were roughing it. But I was again aware of how empty the Big House felt without Granny.

To Sis's disappointment, the army no longer brought horses to Hyde Park for the summer. At the age of almost sixty, Grandmère had given up riding, but she didn't come out and say so, preferring to give the excuse of wartime privation.

At Hyde Park, she still preferred her own quarters at Val Kill, but mindful of her responsibilities, as ever, she drove over early each morning to join us after breakfast. If for some reason she couldn't do this, she would come for lunch. Though Sis and I were seventeen and fourteen, we understood that our grandmother still had a need to keep close track of us. We didn't mind. Grandmère often brought guests to lunch whom she thought might interest us. On one occasion, our guest was none other than the celebrated African American opera singer, Marian Anderson. Accompanied by Granny's old and out-of-tune piano, she sang "Comin' Through the Rye" for us after lunch.*

---

*Though I think many people have forgotten this now, in 1939 my grandmother had resigned from the Daughters of the American Revolution in protest when Miss Anderson was prevented from presenting a concert at the DAR's Constitution Hall in Washington.

We also took ourselves over to Val Kill for a swim at least once a day. If we lunched at the Big House, Grandmère had formed the habit of reading to us after we'd finished. That summer, her choice was Stephen Vincent Benét's *John Brown's Body*, the Civil War epic poem, which has as its narrator a young boy. I remember clearly the sounds of its cadences as she spoke them, but whether it was the book or the satisfying meal, hearing my grandmother read this invariably put me to sleep. Sprawled out on the mat in the large screened porch off the library, I would doze until Sis decided to nudge me with her foot.

In the evenings we liked to wander outside to look at the river and stroll among the huge trees, which gave off a mysterious air in the waning light. We even fell back—as if we were little kids again—into the habit of playing hide-and-seek there. But a stop was soon put to this pastime. The reason: we were sharing the trees with U.S. Army sentries posted to guard the Big House. There was an MP battalion billeted on the Roger's property that adjoined Springwood. Though technically a training unit, the men assigned to it were responsible for guarding the president's estate. They were understandably uncomfortable at the notion of Sis and me hiding behind trees! I can only imagine how Granny would have reacted to the presence of armed men, their rifles at the ready, every hundred feet or so.

Once it turned too dark to enjoy the outdoors anymore, we'd go inside, and Sis would read in her room while I went up to the third floor to hang out with Jean. After riding herd on Johnny all day, she welcomed me as the closest thing to adult company. We'd play cards—she'd taught me cribbage as we'd gotten bored with gin rummy—and make each other laugh until quite late. My sister disapproved and sternly informed me, "It is past your bedtime."

During the summer, for a few hours each day, I was expected to work on the family farm across the road. Every morning I'd walk over and join the farmer's sons in their odd jobs, mostly haying at that time of year. When we'd brought the hay in we'd switch over to working in the barn, going aloft to distribute it. It came in loose, freshly cut from the fields, with a horse pulling the wagon. Compared with the highly mechanized farm in eastern Oregon where Sis and I'd spent two weeks three years earlier, the Springwood farm seemed quaintly old fashioned, even primitive. Granny had not invested in what she had referred to as "newfangled things."

The air in the hayloft would be thick with hay dust, the work arduous—at least for a spoiled kid like me who was not used to sustained physical effort. One morning, I saw spots before my eyes, turned white, and started to faint, and I was quickly helped down the ladder to recover. I was able to walk back to the Big House, yet I couldn't help but feel shaken. Nothing like that had ever happened to me before.

After this incident, I was sent to lend a hand in the greenhouse or in the vegetable patch behind the hemlock-enclosed rose garden. Thinking I could get away with it, I padded the number of hours I worked, but I was soon caught. At twenty-five cents an hour, there was not a lot of money involved in my dishonesty, but the principle of the matter was made plain to me.

When I was still haying on the farm, Ensign once decided to follow me across Route 9 and turned up in the farmyard unannounced. Immediately, the farm dogs were on top of him. I raced forward, right into the melee of fighting dogs, yelling at the top of my voice. Miraculously, I extracted Ensign from the pack without getting bitten. I then took him home using my belt as a lead. We were both pretty upset. Until then I hadn't made much of an impression on the farmhands, but now the story of the bravery I'd exhibited spread through the estate. Even my sister, working during the day at Val Kill, cataloging our grandmother's library, quickly heard of it. In a small place that's a world unto itself, news travels fast.

I enjoyed visiting the newly completed FDR Library, where I roamed the stacks freely. I was fascinated by the variety of objects stored there for exhibits—some valuable, and many not—that my grandfather had collected over several decades. Fred Shipman, the director of the library, and his staff were never bothered by my wandering about, but my grandfather's habit of "borrowing" back books and papers and unconcernedly carrying them off to the Big House or farther afield to the White House made Mr. Shipman grind his teeth. FDR had formally made the National Archives the repository of his effects, and that meant they held themselves responsible for safeguarding the material.

Papa was amused when Grandmère brought this concern to his attention; he listened politely and then carried on as usual.

As the summer progressed, I was on tenterhooks. I kept expecting to hear about my promised rendezvous with Uncle Franklin. Each day passed and no word came. Even Grandmère got into the act, but Franklin put her off.

In the middle of July, Mummy accompanied Papa to Hyde Park for a brief visit. My grandfather, who was on his way to the West Coast, stayed only briefly at the Big House. During the two days he was there, the somnolent atmosphere disappeared and the air positively buzzed with the electricity of his presence. Looking back, it is amazing that FDR was able to make so many visits to Hyde Park; between May and September 1944, he came eight times. For him, the Big House would always be home.

Time, meanwhile, was passing, and there was still no word from my favorite uncle. My mother assured me that she'd been reminding him, adding that it had done no good. She was trying not to let me

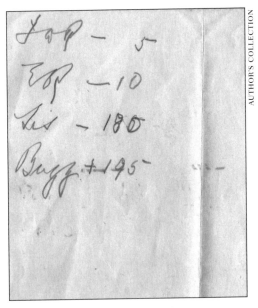

FDR had won! Or was it me?

see her own annoyance, but, of course, I did. And she could see that I had my heart utterly set on it.

Before she returned to Washington, I pleaded with Mummy to try again for a commitment from Uncle Franklin. After all, it had been his idea in the first place! As the summer days began to grow shorter, serious doubts crept up on me. My anticipation was now replaced by anxiety. My mother reminded me that this particular brother of hers had always been known for conveniently forgetting promises he made. This bit of information didn't help.

While Papa was with us, he played cards with Grandmère, Sis, and me on the screened porch after lunch. Recently, my sister sent me a copy of the penciled score of one of those games (in my grandmother's hand), probably gin rummy. Predictably, it shows that my grandfather won. Never cautious, he took the most risks, and it paid off.

Always, I looked forward to the cocktail hour with its fast-paced conversation. In the Big House it would be held in Papa's small study, which had been used as the schoolroom for my mother and her brothers when they were growing up. Papa had turned it into his office after he contracted polio and his children were away at boarding schools. A dozen or more people would cram into this room, no more than ten by twelve feet, all of them jostling around, drinks in hand, engaging one another with gossip laced with quips. Just as in the White House, FDR sat behind his desk with the cocktail tray in front of him, having fun being in the center of it all.

⁂

July had come and gone with no word from Uncle Franklin. My anxiety was so great that I was losing weight while he was keeping me in suspense. Finally, my mother took the bull by the horns and phoned him directly at the navy yard to let him know this. He explained that after he'd made the offer, he'd been told that taking me on the shakedown cruise was in violation of navy regulations—something he must have known for some time but hadn't bothered to tell us. My uncle had seemingly little idea what effect his casual and well-intentioned offer had had on me. For him, the navy's ruling had simply meant the end of the matter.

His offhanded explanation was not good enough for my mother, who exasperatedly dismissed her brother as "callous" and then urged him to now try to make it up to me in some way. Thanks to the pressure she exerted on my behalf, Uncle Franklin invited me to come aboard one day for an engine testing that was to take place off the coast of Long Island. We'd be returning to Brooklyn later that afternoon. It's hard to describe the letdown I felt. Still, something was better than nothing. I was going to go to sea, after all, even if only for a few hours.

When I arrived at the navy yard on the appointed August morning, I found a half-dozen other guests were also along to witness this particular trial run of the USS *Ulvert M. Moore*. As it drew close to noon, we shoved off with the help of a tug and headed past, first, Governor's Island, then Staten Island, and next the Statue of Liberty, and then, finally, we moved out to open sea. Although a destroyer escort is relatively small in terms of navy ships, it seemed huge to me. We civilians were put out of the way in the back of the bridge, while our host, Lt. Commander Roosevelt, was otherwise occupied with his duties.

After lunch we were all taken on a tour of the ship by one of the junior officers. Meanwhile, various speeds were being tested. Eventually, when this had been accomplished to my uncle's satisfaction, we turned around and headed toward the harbor.

As we made our way back into the waters of the navy yard, we took onboard a pilot. It was standard procedure—the captain would turn over the conning of his ship to a pilot, whose job it was to dock the vessel. As the pilot slowly maneuvered the ship toward the dock, I could see my uncle fidgeting and fuming at the man's method of bringing the ship in to its berth. Finally, Franklin couldn't stand it any longer and loudly announced "I'm taking over."

Everyone grew very quiet. Such behavior was the equivalent of a hard professional slap at the pilot. My uncle then reversed engines and warped his ship handily into the small space between two others. I was impressed but also keenly aware of the pilot's humiliation. When I described the scene to my mother, she dismissed Franklin's behavior as "showing off." For me, the incident revealed something more; I now saw my uncle, whom I'd utterly adored, in a more realistic light.

I had been excused before the photographers came to record the luncheon for the now and future presidents.

CHAPTER 27

A t the beginning of September, just before leaving Washington, I was invited to participate in a traditional White House ritual, the stag dinner to honor a visiting head of state. More intimate than a formal diplomatic reception, these evenings were occasions when the president, cabinet members, and other administration officials gathered to fete a foreign bigwig. (Secretary of Labor Frances Perkins was, of course, not invited.) The night I'd be going, the invitees were gathering to meet Rafael Trujillo. I would later understand that Trujillo had been a dictator who brutally ruled the Dominican Republic for over thirty years until he was assassinated in 1961. I also learned that the derisive nickname given to him by his compatriots was *"Chapitas,"* meaning "bottle caps," a reference to his fondness for wearing rows of medals. I saw them in their full glory that night.

Truth be told, it did not matter to me who it was, or where he was from. Just having the chance to participate in the drama was all I wanted. My sister tried to feign indifference once she learned it was a "men only" affair, but I knew she was jealous. I was going to a grown-up White House evening and *she* was not, an unusual upending of our normal balance of power.

As the appointed time drew near, I dressed carefully in my best suit—in fact, my only suit, because Mummy said I wouldn't need such clothes once I was in military school, which was where I soon was headed—and joined the other guests in the East Room. After a quick glass of champagne, ginger ale for me, the assembled gentlemen followed my grandfather in his wheelchair down the long hallway to the State Dining Room. We processed to music from the Marine Corps band.

The military aides, resplendent in their full dress uniforms, made sure we proceeded properly, in order of rank. I, naturally, brought up the rear. Knowing my place card would be at one or the other end of the long table with junior military and naval aides sitting on each side of me, I didn't have to check the seating chart. The young lieutenants and I actually had something in common; they, too, were accustomed to being seen and not heard!

After Papa offered his welcome, we were served several courses along with accompanying wines—which, sadly, the waiters were not about to pour for me. Avid as I was, the raising of glasses, the toasting across the table, went on a little too long, and I confess to feeling relieved when Secretary of State Cordell Hull rose to signal the meal's conclusion. I had had a good time, especially conversing with the military aides. But these events did drag on, and I could see why my grandfather complained that they were tiresome.

In those crowded early September days of 1944, as I was packing to go to boarding school, I received another important invitation: lunch with my grandfather and his vice-presidential running mate, the junior senator from Missouri, Harry S. Truman. The three of us were served a salad, then sandwiches, and then vanilla ice cream (my favorite) at a table in the garden outside the Oval Office. Papa was enjoying himself as he always did when he got the chance to talk politics with another pro—and as usual, he did most of the talking.

They mostly swapped stories, and I could tell that my grandfather was listening alertly. When the Democratic convention was considering vice-presidential candidates, Harry Truman was one on the short list FDR had agreed to, but in fact, he didn't know Truman well at all and had never before had a serious talk with him. It was clear at lunch that Papa was drawing from the visitor his reactions, his opinions, his personal compass points. FDR was looking for character traits—hoping to confirm that Truman was the kind of person who might continue his liberal policies, his way of governing.

I knew from my mother, very confidentially, that my grandfather was considering the possibility of stepping down from the presidency after Germany and Japan were defeated. While Truman didn't know this, he was very aware of FDR's fragile health; friends in the Senate had told him he might well end up becoming president during the next four years.

To me, observing the two of them together, the contrast was striking. One was the very embodiment of the confident country squire, while the other was a son of the mid-West, the product of a small-town life that informed much of his outlook. Now in his second term in the Senate, Captain Truman had led troops, an artillery battery, at the front in France during World War I and had won his first electoral victory as a county judge. More recently—and this is how he'd made a reputation on Capitol Hill—Senator Truman had chaired a committee that investigated corruption related to war contracts. The integrity with which he carried this out was, I think, the major reason Papa had selected him as his running mate. Our guest seemed a reserved man, measured in statement, and carefully deferential towards "Mr. President."

After we'd finished dessert, my grandfather excused me from the table, saying that he and his visitor now needed to discuss confidential campaign strategy. Seeing how reluctant I was to leave, Papa tried to make it up to me by suggesting we meet later that afternoon for a swim.

It wasn't until long after the day itself that I learned what happened when I left that table there in the sunny, peaceful garden. It had been the moment

FDR had chosen to inform his running mate—swearing him to the strictest confidence—about the top-secret development of the atomic bomb, then in its last stages of production at Los Alamos. (The first test of the bomb was expected within the coming year, and in fact, the first mushroom cloud arose in the New Mexico desert on July 16, 1945.)

I don't believe that Papa was able to reveal very much to Senator Truman, probably only that a weapon was being developed, one with the potential to shorten the war against Japan by several years. However, bringing him into this loop was a gesture of trust, one being extended to a person my grandfather knew little about.*

Strangely, this was also the day when, talking with my mother, I became fully aware of the increasingly alarming health problems dogging my grandfather. The careless habits developed during the demanding and stressful war years—no regular rest, inattention to his diet, on top of continuing to smoke two packs of Camels a day—were catching up with him. He had always seemed so invulnerable to me that I never thought about the day when he wouldn't be president.

Papa did nap when he could, often once a day during that last year, but his job as commander in chief was paramount, above all other concerns. Generally, he intervened in military operations only when decisions impinged on the political side, but he was fully informed on a day-to-day basis through regular telephone contact with General Marshall and Admiral King. Admiral Leahy, Chief of Staff, was in an office close by. In addition, he was scrupulous about reviewing the daily intelligence reports. (FDR had found the intelligence reports of both the army and navy insensitive to factors he mastered intuitively.) As historians have judged, Franklin Roosevelt considered himself in wartime harness, just as the captain of a ship in a war zone would.

My mother, always concerned with Papa's health, was pleased I was getting him into the pool, but she worried about his ebbing stamina. Once we

---

*The following August, it would be President Truman who would have to make the decision to drop the bombs on Hiroshima and Nagasaki.

My grandfather waiting for me to throw the ball to him.

were together in the pool, I forgot all about her concerns. We splashed about and threw the volleyball vigorously, and at first, he seemed his usual ebullient self, happy to be in the water where he was always in his element. I demonstrated for him how Grandmère had taught me to do the backstroke that summer. But soon, after only about ten minutes, he asked to be pulled out and then, as usual, got a massage. Seeing his shrunken legs and thighs—they were as thin as sticks—I realized that my mother's anxiety was rooted in reality.

Taking the elevator upstairs from the basement after swimming was my normal routine. I never gave an instant's thought to the possible impropriety of a distinguished guest entering on the first floor and finding a skinny fourteen-year-old in a wet bathing suit on the lift. On this occasion, though, I was caught out. Coming up from the basement, the elevator stopped on the first floor, and on walked Marian Anderson, en route to see my grandmother. Shyly, I reminded her that Sis and I had had lunch with her and Grandmère the previous summer at the Big House and that afterward she'd sung for us.

She smiled and politely chose not to notice the small pool of water my dripping bathing suit was making on the elevator floor. When the door opened on the second floor, Miss Anderson was greeted warmly by the headwaiter before he escorted her to my grandmother in the West Hall. I scooted down the long hall to where my bedroom was and hurried to get dressed and join them for tea.

As I continued to prepare to leave for school, my mother got it into her head that my stepfather should have "a talk" with me. Both Popsie and I wished to be elsewhere, I know, when the moment came. We had never talked about sex, though earlier that summer when I had just arrived in Washington, I inadvertently walked into the bathroom shared by him, my mother, and Johnny. There I was startled to see him washing his private parts with extraordinary vigor. Instantly, I began to back out, stammering apologies, but he turned and said to me, "*Afterward,* you must always wash yourself *thoroughly*." The incident stuck in my mind a long while. I knew the basics—I'd already read the *Boy Scout Handbook* on the subject—but what did washing yourself "afterward" have to do with anything? The *Boy Scout Handbook* didn't cover that.

After that incident, the official conversation was rather harmless. Still, my jaw dropped when my stepfather suggested that masturbation could lead to insanity. Popsie backed off a bit, thankfully, and we parted with a vague promise of further discussions. I suppose one generation talking to another about "it" is always awkward. With my stepfather, it was further complicated by my not having any real rapport with him, nothing shared, no common interests, no way to laugh together. An easy but wary politeness was all that bridged the gap.

CHAPTER 28

AUTHOR'S COLLECTION

Northwestern Military and Naval Academy, where I was to spend four years, was an impressive place—from the outside.

O ne day in the early summer of 1944, when I had been browsing the back pages of *National Geographic*, my eye was caught by a directory listing of various prep schools, each trying to be distinctive in twenty-five words or less. Only one mentioned the magic word "naval," and that was Northwestern Military and Naval Academy, located in the resort town of Lake Geneva, where families from Chicago and Milwaukee had long vacationed.*

Intrigued, I sent away for their brochure. Soon after, I received the school's hardcover—and rather impressive, I admit—promotional

---

*It amused me to learn recently that Lake Geneva, once known as the "Newport of the West," had been repositioned as the "Hamptons of the Midwest."

book and shared it with my mother. The illustrations showed lots of fancy uniforms and parading. My mother had never heard of the school nor had anyone else she asked among our small circle. We did receive a nice—but not very informative—letter from the superintendent, the Reverend James Howard Jacobson. Nowhere was anything said about the school's academic standing, nor could we tell whether either Annapolis or West Point had ever heard of it. The "naval" training that had attracted me in the first place was not mentioned. The only letter we received that indicated that someone had objectively explored the school was from the regional Secret Service office. And all it did was confirm that there didn't seem to be any particularly thorny security problems if I were to board there.

Despite this deficit of information, we decided that I should go. When my father wrote, asking to be brought up to date about my plans for a prep school, Mummy delayed replying until all the arrangements were in place. She then explained, "Buzz begged to be allowed to go to a military academy with an excellent record for preparing its students for the U.S. Naval Academy."

She was full of praise for this paragon among educational institutions in her letter to him: "I finally agreed that Buzz's own choice was the best bet. It has an extremely high academic scholastic standing, both with colleges and the Academies. Also, it is small enough so that Buzz will get plenty of individual attention and supervision, physically as well as scholastically. Being a military school it puts great emphasis on the physical well-being of its students. . . . When Buzz sees you he can show you the school catalogue and descriptive book, which has been sent to us."

In fact, the decision to go to NMNA had little to do with anything that might have informed a sensible choice or with anything Mummy had written about in her letter to Dad. I could just as well have stabbed a pin in a map. What it basically came down to is that I wanted to be in uniform.

Anybody in the school business could have told my mother or me, if we'd listened, that generally speaking, military schools are not known for their academic programs, that they are often used by wealthy families to exile boys with serious behavioral problems at home, and lastly, that they are not considered especially useful for gaining access to either West Point or Annapolis. But we never sought any such guidance, and so I was to spend my four high school years at the Northwestern Military and Naval Academy.

During the time that these arrangements for me were being made, Papa indicated his awareness of my plans. We were all gathered at the table, when he said, casually, that he'd heard I wasn't going to Groton, where I'd been "registered since birth." Groton was the elite New England school he and all my uncles had attended. I don't know what got into me, except that I'd already painted myself into this particular corner, but I replied, "Groton is too snobbish."

The expression that passed across my grandfather's face as he heard me say this made me think that he actually knew why I said what I did. He seemed to understand that I was trying to earn points with my maternal overseers. But I regretted it, and not just because my grandmother looked at me with a troubled expression and changed the subject.

After supper, Mummy scolded me: "You shouldn't have said that to Papa!" I'd realized that myself as soon as the words left my mouth; she didn't need to rub it in. What I could not admit—*would not* admit—to anyone was that I wanted to be in uniform, just like all my uncles.

※

Feeling somewhat under a cloud, I set off for New York, accompanied by a Secret Service man. We changed at Pennsylvania Station for the overnight train to Chicago. Upon arriving there in the morning, we went directly to the Palmer House, the hotel where all the new NMNA boys were assembling in the lobby before taking a local line to Walworth, Wisconsin. Overcome with fear and suddenly aware of my impending isolation, I said an abrupt good-bye to my temporary guardian.

On the train, a few of the boys were excited. I supposed they knew each other, since they came from the greater Chicago area. I sat silently. I was on my own, more so than I'd ever been before, and already felt homesick. After we arrived at the little station at Walworth, a bus took us around Lake Geneva to the school.

Founded in 1888 in Highland Park, Illinois, Northwestern moved to Lake Geneva in 1915. It had been established by a veteran military school instructor, Harlan Page Davidson, who oversaw it as superintendent for twenty-two years before passing the reins to his son. But by the time I arrived there, the Episcopal Church had taken over the running of it, and a priest, Father Jacobsen—the man who had written us the letter—was at the head. Perhaps because the Wisconsin National Guard loaned him the imposing rank of colonel, our superintendent was always in uniform.

The stately stone school entrance, with its portico supported by Grecian columns, opened onto hilly grounds that were dotted with huge trees. The large main building, which housed all the school's major facilities, was as impressive as in the pictures. I entered into a grand central hall that rose two floors high, right up to the roof. On both sides of this immense space were balconies, off of which were small bedrooms, each housing two cadets.

There was a large study room at the center of the main building, a skylight above, and classrooms extending on all sides. The dining room was on the ground floor, with half windows at ground level. A gymnasium was buried on the other side. Off the main floor were offices and quarters for the teachers. Except for outdoor activities, everything that would occur in the days of my future life here would happen within this building. As I looked up and around, it seemed like a lot of space for not much more than a hundred boys.

"Plebes," as we freshmen were known, just like at West Point, could expect hazing from our betters, meaning any third, second, or first classman. We were expected to salute all first-class cadets until the Thanksgiving break and to respond "Yes, sir!" to everyone. We were to perform personal services for the first-class men—shining their shoes, and so forth. We were not to speak unless spoken to in the dining room, and we were to sit bolt upright on our chairs with our backs six inches away from the back of the chair, our caps placed behind us to ensure compliance. We were each given a napkin ring with our cadet number. I still have mine and use it daily.

"Let Fall!" And so we did, with a clatter!

When the bugle called us to the study hall, we were to sit at our desks at attention—which meant arms folded just so, elbows extended out at a right angle to the body, a fairly tiring position after a few minutes. It was your usual disciplinary rigmarole—nothing too extreme but enough to keep us on our toes.

Arriving two weeks before the rest of the cadets were due, we plebes spent nights in leaky tents just below the parade ground, close to the shore of Lake Geneva, and we learned to march in formation in "close order drills." And as it turned out, there *were* exercises to justify the naval part of the school's name. These consisted of rowing great World War I cutters, heavy boats made for the rough ocean that had five oars on each side. There were ten crew members in all. A senior classman was the coxswain, shouting orders while attempting to steer the cumbersome boat.

What a hapless bunch we were! With all of us around fourteen, and not all having had our growth spurts yet, we found the enormous oars impossible to handle smoothly. Getting the oars aloft vertically was a huge effort. "Let fall" was the next command. Down they came, and why someone wasn't conked on the head I didn't know. I vividly remember ducking as the sound of oars crashing into one another brought cries of outrage from our coxswain. It was so absurd that some of us laughed—demerits for them!

During these first couple of cold, wet weeks I was pretty miserable; I'd acquired a bad cold and longed for home. Then we moved inside, and military school began in earnest. Never before in my life had I been subjected to such a strict regime, and it lasted from morning to night. Each day we would respond to bugle calls six to ten times—for getting up, mess call, starting classes, assembling in the rotunda, parading, taps, and lights out. I was always exhausted by the day's end.

In the morning we dashed out of bed upon the first notes of reveille and ran down to the washroom. The last plebes to arrive got the worst clean-up chores assigned to them. Some new boys had a terrible time making their bed, but at least I knew how from summer camp. After we'd gone to class, there would be inspection, and demerits were given if the room wasn't one-hundred percent shipshape. My roommate was a kid who couldn't get it right, and we both suffered on account of his failings. Luckily, my company commander's room was at the end of our hall, and he proved sympathetic to the situation, arranging for me to room with someone else.

Demerits meant extra duty or extra study hall time—or, if sufficiently accumulated, a paddling in an impromptu kangaroo court run by the senior cadets. Names would be called out, and the summoned boy would go forward, bend over, and receive one or several whacks—strong blows meant to hurt. Some boys cried. We were ordered to watch and dreaded being called next. It was not a pleasant scene, and it revealed plainly to us which upperclassmen were to be avoided at all costs. My own years of training as a "good boy" paid off. I was never called forward.

I enjoyed the ceremonies of raising and lowering the flag, morning and evening. I liked learning to do all the things with a rifle that I'd seen so often performed by the honor guards on the South Lawn of the White House. Every Sunday there was a parade, at least until the snow became too deep on the parade ground. Accompanying our marching—as they often did when we marched to the mess hall for supper—were bagpipes and drums, long a school tradition. Although we had only a couple of pipers and the drumming was mediocre, I liked marching in formation.

Somehow, out of this exhausting activity and stress, I emerged from the fog of my homesickness and felt accepted. I liked NMNA, even if I was only a plebe there. I liked the routine, I knew what was expected of me in each situation, and I could respond well. I belonged.

Although when I first got there, there was the odd remark about "Buzzie from the White House," it wasn't the same as it had been at the public schools back in Seattle, where I'd felt singled out and isolated. Once the presidential election kicked into high gear, I found myself in an enclave of Dewey partisans, since most of the boys' parents were Republicans. New York Governor Thomas E. Dewey was running against my grandfather on the Republican ticket. But election day came and went, and nobody minded when I smiled modestly and acknowledged that I was pleased my grandfather had won. Though I knew not to show it, I was thrilled to be guaranteed another four years of returning to the White House.

In spite of what my mother had written my father, I found the academic work at NMNA hardly demanding at all, and for this I was grateful. It was far easier for me to get by in my studies than it had been at Lakeside. My test grades were upper-middle level without any major effort on my part. I still had the same difficulty paying attention, and I'd get sleepy during the evening study period, my mind wandering off to my dream world. I became adept at posing with my head in a textbook or my pencil poised on paper—my mind engaged totally in my fantasies.

My mother wrote to me regularly, and I enjoyed getting all the family news. At the end of November, a letter arrived that knocked me for a loop. It was from my father. Here are a few excerpts from his page-long typed letter:

Dear Buz,

Today is Thanksgiving day and I've been thinking about you and wondering how you are getting along in school. I would be much interested to know how

Finally feeling at home in military school, now the battalion adjutant, first on the left.

you like the school and what courses you are taking. . . . Have you gained any weight?

. . . You are just nearing the age when I can help you, perhaps, by some friendly advice now and then, solely offered to help you develop into a fine useful man, one of real value. . . .

He then recounted his ten years in the military, including stories from World War I. "The best military advice that I can give you now . . . would be as follows," he wrote.

1. Be absolutely honest always, and always "shoot straight."
2. Be absolutely loyal to your country, and to your friends.
3. Honor your father and your mother.

Then followed some useful advice about taking an extra year to prepare for one of the "Government Service Schools." Dad closed by asking what I might like for Christmas.

I didn't know how to reply. Torn between loyalty to my mother and this expression of support and affection from Dad—I'd never received anything like it—I put the letter carefully aside. I treasured what it said but felt immobilized by the conflict within me. It wasn't until at least fifteen years later, when I'd again made contact with my father, that I told him how much I'd appreciated that letter, how deeply I was moved by his willingness to treat with such care a son who didn't even use his own name.

While letting the dogs run and chase squirrels on the White House lawn, my mother, sister, and I enjoyed our reunion.

s Christmas approached and I prepared to return to Washington for two weeks, we plebes were fitted out with new full dress uniforms. I couldn't wait to show off my finery at the White House. More important, I was proud that I had found a niche for myself in school life.

At my mother's request, I was allowed to leave school a day early. A Secret Service agent was to meet me in Chicago and escort me on the long journey to Washington. Of course, there was no way I could know that once we arrived at the White House, I'd be unpacking for my last stay there.

Despite being on holiday, I wore my uniform almost all the time. I now had the luxury of not being sent off to bed at a regular hour in the evenings, and it seemed to me I was quite the young man. At least, that was the image I aimed to present—and everyone obliged by commenting, "Buzzie's very adult for his age!" It was true in some ways, but in others, I remained woefully immature. I had a sophisticated shell, but underneath it was a different story.

Christmastime brought with it the usual official White House seasonal schedule and frantic pace, with one crowded reception followed by another. Then the family was to go to Hyde Park to gather at the Big House, as we had the previous year. Once the holidays were over, we would return to Washington to await my grandfather's fourth inauguration.

Because that would take place on January 20th, Sis and I were to have a five-week break from school. As my grandmother knew well, this being her fourth to cope with, inaugurations were huge undertakings. There would be thousands of details to plan and coordinate—even if, in wartime, the pomp and circumstance would be muted. Adding to her responsibilities was the fact that Papa wanted all of their grandchildren to be present at the ceremony— and there would be thirteen of us attending, ranging from a couple of three-year-olds to the eldest, Sis and me. Where was she to find beds for everyone? Every stage of the arrangements was an organizational challenge, with the overseeing of all the details falling to my mother.

Practically never off the telephone, Mummy sat at the small desk in her bed-sitting room, with a card table piled with notes at her side. She had to co-ordinate with my uncles' numerous ex-wives as well as the present ones, making detailed schedules for each offspring's transportation—no small task since they were traveling during wartime and coming from around the country.

There was little that Sis and I could do to help her, so we did our bit by joining Grandmère at the Christmas receptions, helping her welcome guests, nodding, smiling, and making small talk. We had the drill down pat.

During the cocktail hour, my grandfather, in addition to relaying the latest developments on the war fronts, would ask for the latest developments relating to the family gathering. He wanted to be kept up to date on who was coming when, and he seemed to keep all the complicated details in his mind quite effortlessly. My grandmother seemed to be relishing the hubbub, throwing herself into the spirit of the upcoming reunion.

We all understood that it was the last inauguration we would witness this way. The very confidential information Sis and I had from Mummy— that Papa might choose to retire before his term was up, once the Axis was defeated—was never far from our minds. Daily, my mother expressed her worry about Papa.

How much did my grandfather understand about his diminishing strength? Did he have some premonition of his imminent death, just three months away? I cannot be sure, nor could my grandmother or my mother at the time. But over the years, talking with each of them, certain things became obvious, starting with the fact that he insisted on gathering us all together that Christmas. His desire to have the entire family in attendance at the inauguration must have had to do with more than the simple fact that it would be his last term as president.

On the surface, everything seemed the same, though it was clear he was tiring more easily. What he was truly feeling is impossible to know. Even with my mother he did not talk about his health.

Just before we went to Hyde Park, about a dozen of us were in the family dining room, with my grandparents in their usual places at the center of the table opposite each other. The usher bustled in to announce that "Mr. Elliott and his bride" had arrived. Grandmère rose immediately to greet them in the entrance hall and show them to their room. When she returned to our supper, smiling broadly, she said that "Bunny" (my grandparents' nickname for Elliott) and Faye would soon join us. Without direction, the butlers had come in to set two more places, with Papa indicating that they be placed on either side of him. We all shifted around.

In a few minutes, Uncle Elliott and my new Aunt Faye appeared. He made a grand entrance, she following demurely behind. Papa pushed back his chair and put his arms around both of them. We were a kissing family. It was the custom—and always expected, not only by Papa, Grandmère, and Granny but by all my uncles and aunts. It didn't matter if you were male or female, old or young; everyone kissed everybody in greeting, and this practice extended even to close friends such as Louis Howe, Missy LeHand, and Lorena Hickok. So they embraced and then went around the table, with my grandmother introducing the few guests Elliott might not know.

After they sat down, Elliott described their marriage ceremony overlooking the Grand Canyon the day before and their struggles with the press for privacy. (Their wedding ceremony so quickly followed their decision to get married that no family members were present.) The intense media interest was not simply because he was the president's son but also because the bride, Faye Emerson, was a movie star (mostly in grade B films, my mother cattily noted when she'd heard).

Faye and my uncle had met at a Hollywood party, and she was now his third wife. She had recently been in Arizona filming her latest vehicle, *Hotel Berlin*. I hadn't seen Uncle Elliott for some time. Before enlisting in the air force, he'd been living in Texas, having long ago made a point of turning his back on what he dismissed as the "East Coast crowd." He had acquired a Texas drawl, which his brothers mocked, and sounded quite different from my other uncles. In good form that evening as a honeymooning newlywed, he kept Papa and the rest of us entertained with one boisterous story after another.

After supper, while Sis and I took Fala and Ensign out, my mother and Popsie took Faye on a tour of the White House, while Papa had a few minutes in his study alone with his son. The next day my mother remarked to me how much she'd liked Faye, though she couldn't resist adding, "She's a bit broad in the beam." (My mother's own figure had changed little since she was a lanky, newly married twenty-year-old.)

FDR clearly found my attractive new aunt good company. My grandmother, while cordial, remained reserved. That evening she wrote to Hick: "Elliott's new wife (his third) is pretty, quiet and hard, I guess. She seems capable but I don't think she is more than a passing house guest! I hope I've behaved well!" By now she'd seen too many wives come and go. Still, within a year, Faye, who was a very bright, charming, independent-minded woman, would become Grandmère's favorite daughter-in-law.

To my mother's long list of organizing duties was added another chore—this one dumped on her unexpectedly by her just-married brother. "But she likes dogs," responded Uncle Elliott innocently when my grandmother questioned his assumption that Mummy would not mind fetching his bull mastiffs, Blaze and Dutchess, from the nearby air force base. My uncle's blithe excuse was that he and Faye had things to do in New York when the dogs were scheduled to arrive.

AUTHOR'S COLLECTION

Christmas 1944, at the Big House. My new Aunt Faye and Uncle Elliott shine. My grandfather looks tired. I am in the back, barely visible, next to my sister.

My own concern in this canine matter was for Ensign, who was an old softie. Both of the mastiffs were, I expected, bigger than he was, and together they could easily make mincemeat of him. At the same time, Grandmère worried about Fala. As it turned out, Dutchess, the bitch, proved to be fine company and loved romping with Ensign and me. (Fala chose to keep his distance.) Blaze, the male, on the other hand, had to be kept in the White House kennel most of the time—and for good reason. He once attacked Fala, sending him to the vet for emergency stitches. He obviously hadn't gotten word just *who* the little dog was.

Over the holiday at Hyde Park, Papa seemed to be husbanding his strength, and when it came to opening presents on Christmas Day, he told us he'd rather wait and open a few gifts each day the following week. I was delighted to receive ship models, including two large wooden boxes of "recognition models," a collection of current U.S. Navy ships that had been FDR's Christmas gift from the staff of the White House Map Room. My grandmother's practical gifts included socks knit by the Women's Volunteer Service in Britain and, especially important to me, initialed dress white shirts from Brooks Brothers, the same ones my uncles always got. I had arrived.

Duchess and Ensign become chums.

The matter of my name, though, continued to confront me. Grandmère was insisting on the Boettiger name through the initials on my shirts ("CR<u>B</u>"), while at the same time my grandfather was inscribing a book to me as Curtis Roosevelt Dall. Though I was regularly using my stepfather's name, I was secretly pleased that Papa had chosen my real name for the inscription.

While we were at Hyde Park, Cousin Margaret Suckley came to visit each day, wheeling Papa to his office in the new FDR Library, which was now functioning as both presidential archive and museum. Daisy, as she was known to us, sat with my grandfather while he worked, fetching for him and responding in kind to FDR's occasional droll remark. Papa liked his office there, my mother said, adding that it would be a marvelous place for him to work when he retired.

Before the New Year, we headed back to the White House, where Papa became invisible to us, toiling in the Oval Office in the West Wing from morning to night. We'd say good morning and see him at cocktails and supper every evening, but, without fail, he would return to his study to work. Mummy was now totally engaged helping Grandmère with inauguration arrangements.

Although our mother didn't tell us about it until after Christmas, it appears that just before Sis and I'd arrived at the White House there'd been an upsetting episode that was still troubling her. Grandmère's habit was to place any papers she wanted Papa to read on his bedside table, but on this occasion, she had taken a large batch in to him during the cocktail hour, which was quite unusual, and unfortunate timing. My grandfather, increasingly exhausted, was less able to deal patiently with many of the demands placed on him. (In fact, by this point, he'd taken to limiting the number of papers that could be placed in his bedside in-tray.) He had regarded the large sheaf of documents with exasperation and then tossed them over to my mother, peremptorily instructing her, "Sis, you take care of these." My grandmother, insulted, had immediately left the room.

According to Mummy, Papa quickly realized what he had done and regretted it. As they had just been about to go downstairs for supper, she suggested that he immediately wheel himself into my grandmother's room to apologize; Mummy would take the guests downstairs. And that's what he did. Soon, both my grandparents joined everyone at supper in the family dining room, with Grandmère pushing Papa's wheelchair.

The truth is that Mummy was very uncomfortably lodged in the middle of the long-standing friction between her parents. Trying to protect her father, she earned her mother's resentment. Her position at the White House was already awkward; even though she was the eldest child and adored only daughter, she was in the difficult position of residing in her parents' home at her father's request and what amounted to her mother's sufferance. While her work was often fascinating, it had not been an easy year for her. And the assignments Papa handed off to her were ones that were almost always complicated by some sort of personal element that required special delicacy or discretion.

Although Mummy would have denied it, the fact that her power within the inner circle was increasing during this period did not go unnoticed. How could it be otherwise? This was Washington, where political insiders closely tracked any changes in the power structure.

While my grandmother always had her husband's ear, she was less influential during wartime. She must have felt hurt as her husband's attention to her causes diminished. Domestic politics—traveling across America, talking

In the year before her father's death, my mother became an important figure in the White House, although always in the background. Here she is assisting him in welcoming Gen. Charles de Gaulle (and hoping her French is up to it). Left: Secretary of State Cordell Hull.

to people—that was her realm. Defeating Germany and Japan was now the president's absolute priority. (In contrast to the New Deal days "Dr. Win the War" was how he described himself in one of his fireside chats.) Domestic politics and legislation took second place, except as they affected the war effort. This left my grandmother on the outside.

She may well have resented my mother's growing prestige. Grandmère occasionally overstated my mother's influence in remarks that came off sounding rather double-edged. For example, she might tell someone, "Anna is the only one who would know about that," or "I'll have to ask Anna." My source for these quotes is Joseph Lash, who in 1971 published them in his memoir, *Eleanor and Franklin*. Most likely he heard them from his wife, Trude, a close

During the war years my grandmother was often reduced to playing the normal role of a First Lady, here welcoming troops on the White House South Lawn.

friend of my grandmother. Lash's conclusion is telling, if a bit exaggerated: "Whatever mother and daughter's intentions, the relationship was shaped by the President—his needs, his weariness, his desire to be shielded from the one person who knew him beyond all masquerade and stratagem." I doubt the validity of the last phrase. My grandfather had neither the time nor the energy to get into the thick of domestic affairs, especially issues close to my grandmother's heart, such as racial discrimination.

There is absolutely no doubt, however, that Papa appreciated the usefulness of his wife's firsthand observations as well as her assessments of a wide variety of social and political problems. Indeed he often trusted her observations more than those coming from government departments. Occasionally he'd ask Grandmère to speak to this or that person and obtain a reaction, but these were casual requests, never formally structured. Grandmère and Papa had the deep mutuality of two people whose working relationship was one of long standing. But in wartime this rapport was stretched.

Everyone who knew my grandparents recognized the unique qualities of their four decades of marriage. The inevitable question is, how much influence did my grandmother actually wield with the president? Or how little? It was a matter of ongoing speculation, even within the family. In my judgment, looking back at my grandparents' history, each situation had its own answer, ranging from a great deal of influence to practically none. With the onset of the war, it was more likely the latter. After we'd moved back to Seattle, my mother told me that the year before Papa died, he had asked Grandmère to spend more time with him and not to travel so much. But my grandmother would not alter her schedule.

Of course, it was my grandmother's dedication to her "outside" life that gave her such a devoted following and such influence with the American people. With her extremely busy schedule, she actually *needed* her daughter's help. Here's how my grandmother explained Mummy's coming to the White House in her widely syndicated "My Day" column: "We are going to keep him away from work for certain periods of time, no matter how unpopular we are." Put this way, the two of them were in cahoots, and it implied that it hadn't been Papa's decision to ask my mother to stay and assist him, although it actually was.

Mummy understood her mother's conflicted feelings over the fact that she had become influential in the White House over the course of 1944–1945. Grandmère was human; it had to affect her. Before Mummy accepted her father's invitation to live and work at the White House, she had known all along that she would have to discuss it with Grandmère before accepting.

According to my mother, when the two reviewed the situation, Grandmère said that the one thing she wanted to avoid was the kind of experience she'd had with Louise Hopkins, the wife of my grandfather's confidant and chief wartime diplomatic adviser, Harry Hopkins. Louise was a good-looking socialite, a former editor at *Vogue*, who'd married Harry after the death of his second wife. Grandmère felt that Louise had overstepped her bounds when my grandmother wasn't present and that she made too much of her rapport with my grandfather. She'd experienced the same thing with Aunt Betsey,

Uncle James's equally charming first wife. Both women were attractive and adept at the repartee FDR liked. They held a personal appeal for my grandfather—a situation Grandmère most likely felt was "not good" for Papa!

Despite being her daughter and not a flirtatious outsider, Mummy took her mother's message to heart. And so she instead followed the example of Missy Le-Hand, who'd avoided my grandmother's disapproval by respecting Grandmère's strong sense of identity and prerogatives as First Lady—and as FDR's wife.

Nevertheless, friction between mother and daughter inevitably developed. My mother was unable to hide her concern over what she saw as Grandmère's failure to understand that Papa needed to focus on his wartime duties to the near exclusion of everything else. My grandmother refused to contemplate the ill effects of the fifteen-hour days he was putting in, seven days a week. Mummy felt that her mother was oblivious to the signs of FDR's diminishing energy. It was my mother who had insisted that the White House physician, Rear Admiral McIntyre, call in a heart specialist to regularly check her father.

Looking back, as difficult as it may seem to accept, Eleanor Roosevelt was indeed one of the last in her husband's intimate circle to recognize how rapidly and steadily her husband's vitality was diminishing. With matters of health Grandmère was, of course, the purest expression of the Roosevelt philosophy that "the vigorous life" was to be carried forward, no matter how one felt. She may have observed but chose to ignore FDR's declining health, plain as it was to see.

My mother once archly observed that Grandmère had always been some-what evangelical in her approach to FDR. She had always acted as a conscience for her husband, and this was even more pronounced once Papa became president. While he was not always keen to be on the receiving end of Grand-mère's devotion to moral ideals, this Calvinistic approach was shared by her husband. Her toughness, never talking about one's illness or disabilities, and her sense of duty, were part of his makeup too.

Topping off her White House "career"—my mother sitting with Sarah Churchill and their fathers aboard the USS *Quincy*, anchored in Malta, on their way to Yalta.

ew Year's Eve, 1945, was a relatively quiet affair, another of those occasions when FDR's coterie mixed with ER's, with each family member having been allowed to invite a few friends. There was much anticipation of the bottles of bubbly that were to be opened just before midnight; amazingly, they were from a case of champagne that Marshal Josef Stalin had sent FDR for Christmas. As explained in the accompanying note, the champagne came from the Soviet leader's home republic of Georgia.

Eagerly, we all awaited a taste. However, as the first drinkers raised their glasses to their lips, there quickly came cries of "Oh my God!" and "How awful!" What message might our Russian comrade be trying to convey?

The stuff was sweet, somewhat like a carbonated soft drink, as unlike Veuve Cliquot or Moët & Chandon as anything one could imagine. Amid the laughter, a consensus was easily reached: "Quite undrinkable." But by then midnight was at hand, and there was no choice. So we all raised our glasses to each other and to the New Year. Then we wryly toasted "Uncle Joe!"

While I stayed on in Washington, awaiting the inauguration, I was pleased to have further grown-up, heart-to-heart conversations with my mother, especially when Popsie wasn't around. During one of these exchanges, she made clear just how anxious she was about their prospects once the war was over. Popsie would be discharged before the end of the year, we expected, and it was surmised that even the war with Japan would end soon after that.

I listened and tried to respond helpfully to Mummy as she worriedly envisioned their postwar domestic and professional scene. She'd been candid with Sis and me about Popsie's moodiness and lack of direction. The whole subject made me a little nervous. I'd pretty much cut my moorings to my father, and my life had been centered on Seattle for almost six years. How much longer we would be coming to the White House was an open question. And my home at Hyde Park might soon be in the hands of the Department of the Interior.

What's more, Mummy's preoccupation with "US" drew a closed circle around her and Popsie. Since getting married they had always wrapped themselves in a private cocoon. Wartime had severely tested this romantic notion. There had been cracks in their solidarity, and for the first time, fault lines had become apparent to both Sis and me. We wondered what kind of family life we might resume. Would we stay in Seattle? I'd come to like our home on Mercer Island.

My mother also spoke to me about their future in journalism. She took it for granted that she would work alongside Popsie again; that's how it had been and how she expected it to be in the future. But I wondered to myself whether he'd be as eager to carry on that aspect of their partnership as she presumed; at least from my observations, he'd always seemed to be of two minds about her sharing a career with him. It had not been difficult to see the occasional tensions between the two of them when they worked together at the *Post-Intelligencer*. As pleasant as it might be to have two salaries, the truth for Popsie was that his wife was not unlike her own mother in providing— when she felt it necessary—a ready-made hair shirt for her husband. And his tolerance for criticism was even less than hers.

There was also the fact that Popsie had made it plain, while they were at the *P.I.*, that he far preferred writing to the business side of a newspaper, meaning the issues of circulation, advertising, operating costs, and so forth that he'd had to concern himself with as publisher. Though he had had almost no experience as a publisher before he took the job, it is to John Boettiger's credit that the *P.I.* did see sizeable increases in circulation and advertising while he was running it. Still, when it came to his job qualifications, it had been more than ten years since he'd been a reporter. And Popsie was well aware that people identified him mainly as the president's son-in-law.

Meanwhile, I could see Papa going out of his way to be supportive of his son-in-law, who so obviously was frustrated and bored in a Pentagon job that offered little scope for his talents. During cocktail hour, FDR would very purposely ask Popsie to mix the drinks. Though Papa's hands had begun to tremble noticeably, making the task difficult for him, that was secondary to acknowledging John Boettiger as family in front of the other guests.

The previous spring, just before the invasion of Normandy, Papa had asked Mummy and Popsie to help him write his D-Day message, which he intended to broadcast to Americans on the day that tide-turning operation was launched. I heard my grandfather give much of the credit for composing it to his son-in-law, whenever the subject came up. Whichever of my relations produced it, it was intensely moving. Now known as the "D-Day Prayer" but originally titled "Let Our Hearts Be Stout," it is still a relevant invocation:

> . . . For these men are lately drawn from the ways of peace. They fight not for the lust of conquest. They fight to end conquest. They fight to liberate. They fight to let justice arise, and tolerance and goodwill among all Thy people. They yearn but for the end of battle, for their return to the haven of home.
>
> Some will never return. Embrace these, Father, and receive them, Thy heroic servants, into Thy Kingdom. . . .

While Papa acknowledged Popsie differently than he did his own sons, his efforts to include and credit him were obvious. Whether this ever mitigated

The fourth and last inauguration of President Roosevelt, taking the oath of office on the South Portico of the White House, with most of his grandchildren gathered on the steps to the left.

for my stepfather his feeling of not being properly treated by the U.S. Army (or, more to the point, of never being posted to FDR's personal staff), I don't know. While he was always on the scene during evenings at the White House throughout 1944 and into 1945, he seemed relegated to the background when any of my uncles arrived for a visit, however brief. The pecking order of Papa's affections was clear.

All of this contributed to the general tension in the air as Inauguration Day approached. Sis and I were given assignments, mainly to shepherd our cousins and their nurses around so they wouldn't get lost. The White House was big, a confusing place if you weren't accustomed to it.

It was the simplest of inaugurations, with no ceremony at the Capitol. We all gathered in the morning for the religious service in the East Room, and then for the actual swearing-in, the grandchildren went out the basement entrance and gathered on the curved steps going up on the right toward the balcony where our grandfather would be sworn in as president of the United States for the last time.

Papa appeared on the balcony, "walking" stiffly, cane in one hand and hanging on to Uncle Jimmy's arm. (My uncle, now a marine colonel, had been awarded both the Navy Cross and the Silver Star for bravery in combat.) Chief Justice Charles E. Hughes was there waiting for them. After repeating the oath, FDR then gave a short address—only six minutes long—in which he reminded his listeners, quoting his old Groton headmaster, Dr. Endicott Peabody: "'Things in life will not always run smoothly. Sometimes we will be rising toward the heights—then all will seem to reverse itself and start downward. The great fact to remember is that the trend of civilization itself is forever upward; that a line drawn through the middle of the peaks and the valleys of the centuries always had an upward trend.'" When he had finished, we all returned inside. I was relieved, as were the other kids, since it was pretty cold, just above freezing, and a light snow had fallen earlier.

Inside the White House, Grandmère and Mummy seemed to be everywhere. My mother told me afterward that Papa had stubbornly, and against their wishes, insisted on appearing without his coat. Now he had to endure the hand-shaking and endless well-wishing. Once lunch was over, Papa wanted all thirteen of us grandchildren upstairs to pose for a picture with him and Grandmère.

Once the inaugural excitement ended, my mother became frantic with the number of things to be done. Two days later she was to leave with Papa for his secret rendezvous with Churchill and Stalin at Yalta. My stepfather, I knew at the time, was making an effort to hide his unhappiness at being left behind, but what I didn't realize, until much later, was that my grandmother had been equally disappointed at her exclusion.

I would learn that behind the scenes—actually in competition with her mother—Mummy had been unusually assertive in maneuvering herself into a position whereby she could accept her father's proposal that his daughter

A much used picture. Everyone can recognize FDR and ER, but who are those thirteen grandchildren? Left to right beginning with my grandmother and me: Sis (Eleanor/Ellie), Bill, Chandler, David, Franklin (now Frank) with Papa in between, Kate, and Sara. In the front row: Christopher, Haven, Nina in front of him, Johnny, and Elliott (Tony).

accompany him. A trip with her father was something she'd desperately wanted ever since the Atlantic Charter meeting in the North Atlantic off the coast of Newfoundland four years earlier, where she saw Elliott and Franklin Jr. at their father's side. Her exclusion at subsequent ministerial meetings had sorely rankled her.

Watching her father summon her brothers to join him as he traveled to meet Churchill, and later Stalin, roused in Mummy the sort of sibling rivalry I'd often seen my uncles exhibit but had thought her immune from. She was even keeping score—her letters to Popsie make this clear—when it came to Churchill's own children, noting when and where his daughters Sara and Mary or son Randolph had accompanied him to high-level meetings. In one angry missive, my mother gave full vent to her sense of grievance: "Why in hell should I be forced to miss all of the actual excitement and interest, and be forced to live the kind of life I now lead?" In the end, we all suffered from our attraction to the president's world and our longing to be part of it.

On January 22, Grandmère, Popsie, Johnny, Sis, and I saw Papa and our mother off in their motorcade at the south entrance under the portico. Mummy's pleasure and excitement were obvious. We waved and waved as they slowly descended the long circular drive. It was the last time I would ever see my grandfather.

Once they were out of sight, Sis and I raced upstairs to get our own belongings together. She was catching a plane to San Francisco, and I had to get the train to Chicago; both of us were long overdue at our respective schools.

When my grandfather came back from Yalta, he addressed a joint session of Congress and apologized for sitting down to give his speech. I saw news photos of this event—my teachers always made sure to clip such items for me—and I was struck by the increased gauntness I saw in Papa's face. A letter from my mother, which arrived shortly after this, upset me even more. Papa was ill, desperately in need of rest, she wrote, and would be going to Warm Springs for a few weeks, just as soon as he could clear the most urgent affairs from his desk.

∞

The date April 12, 1945, rests firmly in my head. Strangely, this is not because of its personal significance to *me*, but because all my life I've met people who say, "I remember exactly where I was and what I was doing on April 12th, the day of your grandfather's death," and then go on to tell me about their experience.

I myself had forgotten where I was and what I was doing until I began writing this book. My friend from NMNA, David Mills, reminded me of the day's events when I interviewed him. He recalled that he and I had been playing tennis during the late afternoon athletic period and that another classmate,

Louis Dehmlow, had suddenly appeared to tell us that the superintendent wanted to see me. "I think FDR died," Louis said softly.

I changed quickly to my uniform and went directly to Colonel Jacobson's office, where he told me that he'd just had a call from my mother. It was true. Papa had been in Warm Springs and suddenly suffered a massive cerebral hemorrhage while sitting and reviewing his papers. He had been unconscious for more than two hours. My grandmother was in Washington, as was my mother, who had decided not to accompany her father to Georgia because Johnny was in Bethesda Hospital with a strep infection. Papa's last words had been, "I have a terrific headache." The official announcement of his death was made by the White House at 5:48 P.M., after my grandmother had been informed.

Colonel Jacobson suggested that I excuse myself from the rest of the day's routine, but I refused, preferring to keep busy. He was kind and solicitous. For my part, I was quite used to hiding everything inside, and I found expressions of concern more irritating than comforting.

My mother had asked that a telephone call be placed to her as soon as possible. The school switchboard put through the call, and I went to the callbox in the hallway. Mummy was brief and to the point: did I wish to come to Papa's funeral at Hyde Park? She made it clear that she and Grandmère would understand if I decided against it, adding that she'd already spoken to Sis in San Francisco, who'd declined. I got the message, and so I also declined.

Even over the phone, I could sense just how stratospheric my mother's anxiety level was. I could almost feel the pressure I knew she had to be experiencing, all the grief she would be able to manage only by staying fully occupied. In front of her, too, lay the inevitable move from the White House. I wondered where she, Popsie, and Johnny would be going to live, but I didn't ask. I knew tradition dictated that the deceased president's family vacate the premises within forty-eight hours so the new chief executive could move in. That it had been home to the Boettigers for more than a year, and that my six-year-old kid brother was still quite ill, did not matter.

I *wanted* to be present at my grandfather's funeral. Even then, I was drawn to the thrill of the rituals and ceremonies that were about to unfold. (My grandmother had declined the honor of having Papa lie in state on the catafalque in the rotunda of the Capitol.) But as we spoke—and Mummy un-reservedly offered to bring me east on the next plane—I could sense how she really was hoping I'd stay put. I would have become an extra responsibility if I showed up. I understood only too well that the right thing to do was to stay where I was. Yet, as the years have passed, I have regretted having done that "right thing." They say funerals are more for the living than for the dead. In my case, I think it would have helped.

Whatever feelings I experienced at the time I've blocked from memory. There were no tears: adults don't cry. My eyes did fill up when I first saw the photos of my grandfather's funeral at the White House and of his interment in the rose garden next to the Big House at Hyde Park. But, as my mother had written in a letter to my grandmother more than five years earlier, "Buzz keeps it all within him and broods." I couldn't even have said to what extent that was true. What I do know is that my grandfather—my Papa—was, and remains, my father image.

Over the next few days, I received a steady stream of condolences at school. I thanked everyone quietly. The only expression of my bottled-up grief came a few days later when the members of my squad were cleaning our guns outside the armory. Our rifles were completely disassembled, and at some point, a boy named Smith teased me, "Well I guess you can't go back to the White House now."

Angry, I turned and walked away, leaving my rifle in pieces. As I left, I could hear my squad mates upbraiding Smith for his thoughtless remark. But I was not even aware of feeling hurt. I just wanted to be alone.

Being in an isolated military school with a lot of other teenage boys, I couldn't, at the time, gauge public reaction to my grandfather's death. Later, though, I did understand that many of my fellow citizens had experienced a deep sense of loss. As columnist Bob Herbert wrote on the sixtieth anniversary of FDR's death, "His hold on the nation was such that most Americans, stunned by the announcement of his death that spring afternoon, reacted as though they had lost a close relative." Someone on whom they relied, who felt like a part of their lives even if they hadn't personally known him, was gone. The sun had set on an era.

I *had* known him—and it would take me decades to come to terms with not just the deprivation of Papa's singular presence but also the indelible impact of having him as my own sun.

My grandfather's simple gravestone in the Rose Garden at Hyde Park.

My life in the White House was over. I would no longer have a home there except in my memories. My dream world would continue to provide a seductive alternative universe, a safe haven for many decades to come. Its hold on me, its lingering effects—robbing me of a will to achieve or to focus on work—dominated my life's course. In the end, however, I place no blame on any other human being. My history—how I grew up, how I developed, what I have been capable of doing, and what I was not capable of achieving—is, for me, a well of lessons. And I have drawn from it throughout my life.

My mother and stepfather divorced in 1949, having made a failed attempt to start a "liberal" newspaper together in Phoenix, Arizona. Tragically, John Boettiger committed suicide the following year, jumping out of a hotel window in New York City.

My mother married again in 1952, this time to James Halsted, a physician with the Veterans Administration in Washington. She died, of cancer, at the age of sixty-nine in 1975.

My sister married Van Seagraves in 1948 and, sixty years later, as I write, is still married to him, living in Washington, D.C. They have three children and six grandchildren. She edited the diaries of one of our distant Delano relatives, Amasa Delano, an excellent book.*

My younger brother Johnny grew up to become an academic and a scholar, teaching at such schools as Amherst, Hampshire College (where he was a founding faculty member), and the California School of Professional Psychology. He has four children and seven grandchildren.

My grandmother, of course, survived her husband and prospered, carrying on a full and active life for another seventeen years. As her passion continued unabated for the service of humankind—using her daily and monthly columns, television, and radio as a bully pulpit—she solidified her position, for a considerable epoch, as the most famous woman, and certainly one of the most recognizable faces, on the planet. Serving as a United States delegate to the United Nations for seven years, she is best known for being the driving force behind the passage in 1948 of the Universal Declaration for Human Rights. Knowing how she felt about her home at Val Kill, I thank God that my grandmother was able to remain there until her death in 1962. It is now, like my grandfather's house, a National Historic Site.

My uncles prospered, or didn't, variously. They had large appetites, whetted by being, just as I was, too close to the sun—and the course of their lives was closely linked to their family identity. Their stories have been much told, often in the tabloid press and occasionally by themselves. James died in 1991, Elliott in 1990, Franklin Jr. in 1988, and John in 1981.

As for myself, I was drafted into the U.S. Army and served the usual two years, received an M.A. from Columbia University's School of Public Law and Government, and worked in advertising and public relations and at such institutions as the New School for Social Research in New York in the early part of my career. In 1964, I joined the Secretariat of the United Nations where my stint lasted nearly eighteen years, the most interesting time as Chief of the Non-Governmental Organization Section. Before I finally "re-

---

*Eleanor Roosevelt Seagraves, ed. *Delano's Voyages of Commerce and Discovery: Amasa Delano in China, the Pacific Islands, Australia, and South America, 1789–1807* (Stockbridge, Mass.: Berkshire House Publishers, 1994).

The three grandsons of the Big Three—Roosevelt, Churchill, and Stalin—at the University of Maastricht for a seminar on Yalta (2005). I sit between Jevgeni Dzjoegasjvili (left) and Winston Churchill.

tired" for good, I served as principal of the Dartington College of Arts in Devon, England, for three years.

Preparing for retirement, I attended Greenwich House's pottery school, and for a few years I exhibited my work regularly. It is now just a hobby, but it continues to give me great satisfaction.

I should add, also, that I married in the family tradition—four times—but this last marriage, to Marina, is still going strong, still satisfying after nearly twenty-five years. I have one child, a daughter, Julianna, and one grandson, Nicholas.

Apart from any "success" I may or may not have achieved, I have prospered immensely—in the sense that I have learned from my experiences. Looking back, I have no regrets.

ACKNOWLEDGMENTS

I have spent more than fifteen years talking with many people about my memoirs, some in interviews, but most in casual conversations, as I constantly checked perceptions, recollections, and opinions against my own memories. I apologize to anyone that I am about to overlook.

First, I want to thank the members of my family who assisted in this effort. I am indebted to my sister, Eleanor Seagraves, my half brother John R. Boettiger, my stepmother Katherine Dall, and my half sisters Mary and Katrina. I thank my godmother, Betsey Cushing Whitney, and my aunt, Mary Roosevelt. I am also grateful to my first cousins who are old enough to remember my grandmother and grandfather: Kate Roosevelt Whitney, Nina Roosevelt, Bill Roosevelt, Frank Roosevelt, Chandler Lindsay, Haven Roosevelt, James Roosevelt, Chris Roosevelt, David Roosevelt, and Laura Silberstein. Finally I thank my distant cousins for their input: Anna Eleanor Roosevelt (Ellie), Janet Katten, Edith Williams, Dick Williams, Nora Stark, Dorothy Kidder, Alice Roosevelt Longworth, and P. James Roosevelt.

For the time and attention they have given to me over the years special thanks go to: Maureen Corr, Jane Field, Pat Baillargeon, Edna Gurewitsch, Rivington Winant, John Gable, Geoffrey Ward, James MacGregor Burns, Susan Dunn, Estelle Linzer, Jeanette

Roosevelt, Christine Totten, Eliot Werner, Louise and Peter Cochrane, Edith and Larry Malkin (Larry provided the name for my book), David Adams, William Emerson, Leslie Scott, Georgia and William Delano, Allida Black, Warren Kimball (by e-mail), Gerhardt Reigner, Alena Lurie, Margaret Marquez, Alan and Ellen Isler, Matthew Stevenson, Diana Hopkins, Robert Hopkins, Robert Edgars, and Mary Soames.

Other interviews and conversations have been very useful, very special. I am grateful to: Ben Cohen, Jane Plakias, Doris Kearns Goodwin, Blanche Cook, Eric Roussel, Joe Persico, Trude Lash, Winthrop Aldrich, Gillian Mackilligin, Mary Ann Glendon, Diana Eck, Lila Doss, Lane Kirkland, Claude Meyer-Levy, Mireille and Jacques Cazotte, Sir Harold Bealey, John Longrigg, Sir James Adams, Hans Ashbourne, Peter Urbach, Brian Holden-Reid, Roger Lewis, Hermione Hobhouse, Margaret Spurr, Sir Percy Cradock, Homai Mehta, Raymond Aubrach, James Mingo, Covington Hardee, Granville Fletcher, Dallas Pratt, Edward McBride, Elizabeth Bumiller, Celestine Bohlen, Steven Aronson, Michael Popovic, Constance Parvey, Arthur Shepps, Joyce Ghee, John Hunt, James Ayers, Ruth Reed, Steven Garmey, Sir John Keegan, Gwen Sears, Grania Gurewitsch, Margaret Shannon, Edward Luck, Carol Lubin, Jean LeConte, Margaret Bruce, Robin Winks, Robert K. Straus, Helen Bergen, Raymond Seitz, Patty Doar, Liz Jobey, Gita Sereny, Flora Lewis, Robert Morgenthau, Henry Morgenthau, Margaret Quass, Michael Straight, Page Putnam Miller, William vanden Heuvel, Trude Peterson, Mrs. Lewis Dehmlow, Anne Cox Chambers, and Jo Ritzen. And my classmates from Seattle: Eddie Fischer, Bill Baillargeon, Bill Baines, Howarth Meadowcroft (Tacoma), and family friend, Ann Donough Stone.

For anyone writing on the Roosevelts, the Roosevelt Library at Hyde Park is indispensable. Beginning with the director, Cynthia Koch, and the deputy director, Lynn Bassanese, I am grateful to the incomparable archival staff headed by Robert Clark (and Ray Teichman, his predecessor). Of particular help to me were Alycia Vivona, Mark Renovitch, Virginia Lewick, Karen Anson, and Bob Parks. Although retired from the staff, Beth Denier did much research for me in the early stages of my manuscript, as more recently did

Ken Moody. On the curator's staff Michelle Fraunberger helped me with pictures. My life was much eased by the help of my friend Cynthia, her husband Eliot, and her staff, Joanne Tammaro and JoAnn Morse.

Institutions are wonderful resources, but it is the people within them that make them come alive. The librarian at the Reform Club, Simon Blundel, was a great help to me; equally so, the director of Columbia University's Oral History program, Mary Marshall Clark.

I am indebted to the early readers of my book, those few people whom one trusts to look at what one has written. Leslie Scott, my friend at the Reform Club, first did this for me and was very encouraging, giving me the push I needed at the moment. Later, Odette Livingston-Smith read my manuscript and gave me comments for improving it. And John and Angela Bennett. Luc Venet was my computer expert.

Without substantial editing I would have been lost. I am grateful to the first person to point out to me the problems of writing a book, Carl Brandt. After much slogging away on my part, Michele Slung helped to make my manuscript, a thousand pages written for archival purposes, into a trade book. It was an awesome task, and she did a remarkable job; she is a superb editor.

My agent John Silbersack has been a pleasure to work with. At PublicAffairs I am grateful to Clive Priddle, Susan Weinberg, and Peter Osnos for embracing the book. My editor, Lindsay Jones, and I have worked closely and effectively these past months—exhausting us both, but I like the results—thanks to Lindsay's attention to detail. For their help with the production of this book, I thank Annie Lenth, Melissa Raymond, and Allison Rizzolo. Vincent Virga is extraordinary, a real "pro," working with me to identify pictures and place them properly in the book.

Finally, I want to acknowledge the foot soldiers without whom no war is won nor book written. Miko Burfit typed the first complete draft of the manuscript. Louise Ferrante typed the edited manuscript, a real rush job. Thanks go to both of them.

For fifteen years my wife, Marina, has put up with my struggling to learn to write, shaping my writing into a book, and then learning to edit. She is a dear!

A NOTE ON SOURCES

I have read hundreds of books, articles, pamphlets, and personal letters over the past fifteen years, and it would be impossible to list all of them here. This is a memoir, not a history, not even an autobiography, and thus I haven't included endnotes in the text. However, I would like to acknowledge a number of authors whose books have been essential reading for me.

Asbell, Bernard, ed. *Mother & Daughter: The Letters of Eleanor and Anna Roosevelt*. New York: Coward, McCann & Geoghegan, 1982.

Beschloss, Michael R. *The Conquerors: Roosevelt, Truman, and the Destruction of Hitler's Germany, 1941–1945*. New York: Simon & Schuster, 2002.

Black, Allida M. *Casting Her Own Shadow*. New York: Columbia University Press, 1996.

Boettiger, John R. *A Love in Shadow*. New York: Norton, 1978.

Bohlen, Charles. *Witness to History, 1929–1969*. New York: Norton, 1973.

Brinkley, Alan. *The End of Reform: New Deal Liberalism in Recession and War*. New York: Knopf, 1995.

Brinkley, David. *Washington Goes To War*. New York, Knopf, 1988.

Burns, James MacGregor. *Roosevelt: The Lion and the Fox*. New York: Harcourt, Brace, 1956.

_____. *Roosevelt: The Soldier of Freedom*. New York: Harcourt Brace Jovanovich, 1970.

Burns, James MacGregor, and Susan Dunn. *The Three Roosevelts: Partician Leaders Who Transformed America*. New York: Grove Press, 2001.

Caro, Robert A. *The Power Broker: Robert Moses and the Fall of New York*. New York: Knopf, 1974.

Churchill, Winston S., and Franklin D. Roosevelt. *Churchill and Roosevelt: The Complete Correspondence.* Warren F. Kimball, ed. 3 vols. Princeton, N.J.: Princeton University Press, 1984.

Cook, Blanche Wiesen. *Eleanor Roosevelt, 1884–1933.* New York: Viking Press, 1992.
———. *Eleanor Roosevelt, 1933–1938.* New York: Viking Press, 1999.

Dallek, Robert. *Franklin D. Roosevelt and American Foreign Policy, 1932–1945.* New York: Oxford University Press, 1979.

Davis, Kenneth S. *Invincible Summer: An Intimate Portrait of the Roosevelts, Based on the Recollections of Marion Dickerman.* New York: Atheneum, 1974.

Dows, Olin. *Franklin Roosevelt at Hyde Park: Documented Drawings and Text.* New York: American Artists Group, 1949.

Edmonds, Robin. *The Big Three: Churchill, Roosevelt, and Stalin in Peace and War.* New York: Norton, 1991.

Freidel, Frank. *Franklin D. Roosevelt: The Apprenticeship.* Boston: Little, Brown, 1952.

———. *Franklin D. Roosevelt: A Rendevous with Destiny.* Boston: Little, Brown, 1990.

Gallagher, Hugh Gregory. *FDR's Splendid Deception.* New York: Dodd, Mead, 1985.

Goodwin, Doris Kearns. *No Ordinary Time: Franklin and Eleanor Roosevelt: The Home Front in World War II.* New York: Simon & Schuster, 1994.

Gurewitsch, Edna P. *Kindred Souls: The Devoted Friendship of Eleanor Roosevelt and Dr. David Gurewitsch.* New York: Plume, 2002.

Jackson, Robert H. *That Man: An Insider's Portrait of Franklin D. Roosevelt.* John Q. Barrett, ed. New York: Oxford University Press, 2003.

Kennedy, David M. *Freedom from Fear: The American People in Depression and War, 1929–1945.* New York: Oxford University Press, 1999.

Kimball, Warren F. *The Juggler: Franklin Roosevelt as Wartime Statesman.* Princeton, N.J.: Princeton University Press, 1991.

Kleeman, Rita Halle. *Gracious Lady: The Life of Sarah Delano Roosevelt.* New York: D. Appleton-Century, 1935.

Lash, Joseph P. *Eleanor and Franklin: The Story of Their Relationship.* New York: Norton, 1971.

———. *Eleanor: The Years Alone.* New York: Norton, 1972.
———. *Love, Eleanor: Eleanor Roosevelt and Her Friends.* New York: Doubleday, 1982.
———. *Roosevelt and Churchill, 1939–1941: The Partnership That Saved the West.* New York: Norton, 1976.
———. *A World of Love: Eleanor Roosevelt and Her Friends.* New York: Doubleday, 1984.

Leuchtenburg, William E. *Franklin D Roosevelt and the New Deal, 1932–1940*. New York: Harper & Row, 1963.

McCullough, David. *Mornings on Horseback*. New York: Simon & Schuster, 1981.

Meacham, Jon. *Franklin and Winston: An Intimate Portrait of an Epic Friendship*. New York: Random House, 2003.

Miller, Nathan. *F.D.R.: An Intimate History*. New York: Doubleday, 1983.

Morgan, Ted. *FDR: A Bibliography*. New York: Simon & Schuster, 1985.

Perkins, Frances. *The Roosevelt I Knew*. New York: Viking Press, 1946.

Persico, Joseph E. *Roosevelt's Secret War: FDR and World War II Espionage*. New York: Random House, 2001.

Rauch, Basil. *From Munich to Pearl Harbour*. New York: Creative Age Press, 1950.

Rollins, Alfred B., Jr. *Roosevelt and Howe*. New York: Knopf, 1962.

Roosevelt, Eleanor. *The Autobiography of Eleanor Roosevelt*. New York: Harper & Brothers, 1961.

_____. *Christmas, 1940*. New York: St. Martin's Press, 1986.

_____. *Roosevelt and Frankfurter: Their Correspondence 1928–1945*. Annotated by Max Freedman. London, Sydney, Toronto: The Bodley Head, 1967.

_____. *This I Remember*. New York: Harper & Brothers, 1949.

_____. *This Is My Story*. New York: Harper & Brothers, 1937.

_____. *You Learn By Living*. New York: Harper & Brothers, 1960.

_____, ed. *Hunting Big Game in the Eighties: The Letters of Elliott Roosevelt, Sportsman*. New York: Charles Scribner's Sons, 1932.

Roosevelt, Hall, with Samuel Duff McCoy. *Odyssey of an American Family: An Account of the Roosevelts and Their Kin as Travellers from 1613–1938*. New York: Harper & Brothers, 1939.

Roosevelt, Mrs. James (Sara Delano). As told by Isabel Leighton and Gabrielle Forbush. *My Boy Franklin*. New York: R. Long & R. R. Smith, 1933.

Schlesinger, Arthur M., Jr. *The Crisis of the Old Order, 1919–1933*. Boston: Houghton Mifflin, 1957.

_____. *The New Deal in Action, 1933–1939*. New York: Macmillan, 1940.

_____. *The Politics of Upheaval*. Boston: Houghton Mifflin, 1960.

Sherwood, Robert E. *Roosevelt and Hopkins: An Intimate History*. New York: Harper & Brothers, 1948.

Smith, Jean Edward. *FDR*. New York: Random House, 2007.

Soames, Mary, ed. *Winston and Clementine: The Personal Letters of the Churchills*. Boston: Houghton Mifflin, 1999.

Stafford, David. *Roosevelt and Churchill: Men of Secrets*. Woodstock, N.Y.: Overlook Press, 2000.

Stettinius, Edward R. *Roosevelt and the Russians: The Yalta Conference*. New York: Doubleday, 1949.

Stiles, Lela. *The Man Behind Roosevelt: The Story of Louis McHenry Howe*. Cleveland: World, 1954.

Tully, Grace. *F.D.R.: My Boss*. New York: Charles Scribner's Sons, 1949.

Van Minnen, Cornelius A., and John F. Sears, eds. *FDR and His Contemporaries: Foreign Perceptions of an American President*. New York: St. Martin's Press, in association with the Roosevelt Study Centre, 1992.

Ward, Geoffrey C. *Before the Trumpet: Young Franklin Roosevelt, 1882–1905*. New York: Harper & Row, 1985.

———. *A First-Class Temperament: The Emergence of Franklin Roosevelt, 1882–1905*. New York: Harper & Row, 1989.

———, ed. *Closest Companion: The Unknown Story of the Intimate Friendship Between Franklin Roosevelt and Margaret Suckley*. Boston: Houghton Mifflin, 1995.

CAST OF CHARACTERS

As a child, I was often confused by the many personalities and places that made up the Roosevelt universe, so I am providing a guide, beginning with my immediate family.

Franklin Delano Roosevelt: my grandfather, "Papa," was known to everyone, then and now, as "FDR."

Eleanor Roosevelt: my grandmother, "Grandmère," was always known when I grew up as "Mrs. Roosevelt" to friends, staff, and servants. My aunts often complained that when they identified themselves as "Mrs. Roosevelt" they were told there was "only one Mrs. Roosevelt."

Anna Roosevelt: their eldest child and only daughter, my mother, "Mummy."

My uncles: James (Jimmy), Elliott (Bunny), Franklin Jr. (Frankie or F. Jr.), and John (Johnny).

My sister: Eleanor Roosevelt Dall. She became, when married, Eleanor Seagraves, but she always was, and remains, "Sis" to me. (My grandmother, mother, sister, and her daughter alternatively used "Anna" and "Eleanor.")

My brother: John Roosevelt Boettiger, "Johnny."

Sara Delano Roosevelt: mother of FDR, my great grandmother was known as "Granny" for both my mother's and my generations and as "Mrs. James" to her Springwood staff.

Theodore Roosevelt: my great, great uncle, cousin to FDR, and uncle to my grandmother. He "gave Eleanor away" at their wedding and, having just been sworn in as president, stole the show at their reception.

Elliott Roosevelt: Grandmère's father, younger brother of Theodore, a sad man driven by his many demons.

My father: Curtis Bean Dall, "Dad," later reduced to "Mr. D" and then "The Man from New York."

Dad's mother: Mary Bean Dall, my other grandmother, whom Sis and I did not know well.

My stepfather: John Boettiger, my mother's second husband, whose name my sister and I used for several years. We first called him "Uncle J" and later "Popsie."

Of course, my own name, **Curtis**, caused the most confusion of all. For most of my childhood, I went by the nickname Buzzy or Buzzie (or Buz/Buzz for that matter)—it was rarely spelled the same way twice.

More People

Admiral Ross McIntyre: chief of the Navy's Bureau of Medicine during World War II, but just a Lt. Commander and the White House physician when he sewed up my forehead when I was four years old.

Anna Hall Roosevelt: my grandmother's mother.

Beebee: my nurse.

Betsey Whitney: Uncle Jimmy's first wife, my godmother, and mother of my cousins Sara and Kate.

Betty Donner: Uncle Elliott's first wife and mother of my cousin Bill.

Bill Hassett: Appointments Secretary to FDR during World War II.

Mr. De Pew: my great grandmother's chauffer.

Dora Delano Forbes: Aunt Doe, my great grandmother's sister.

Edith Helm: my grandmother's Social Secretary.

Elizabeth McDuffie: "Duffy," alternate nurse and factotum among the White House servants. A lovely lady whose husband was for a long while my grandfather's valet.

Elizabeth Riley Roosevelt: widow of FDR's half brother, "Rosie," James Roosevelt Roosevelt (so named to avoid using Junior).

Faye Emerson: third wife of my Uncle Elliott.

Grace Tully: number two secretary to FDR, later replacing "Missy" LeHand.

Gus Gennerich: FDR's body guard who unexpectedly died, to be replaced by "Tommy" Qualters.

Harry Hopkins: first my grandmother's confidante and then—to Grandmère's annoyance—confidante to FDR. Best known for his leadership of the Works Progress Administration and his wartime diplomatic missions of behalf of FDR.

Mrs. Henrietta Nesbitt: housekeeper at the White House whom we all blamed for the mediocre meals we ate. (Amusingly, the café at the new Wallace Center at the Roosevelt Library is named the Nesbitt Café.)

Henry and Elinor Morgenthau: family friends with an estate in Fishkill, known to me as "Uncle Henry" and "Aunt Elinor." He was FDR's Secretary of the Treasury as well as a good friend. She was a close friend of my grandmother.

Henry Parish: my godfather and the husband of Susan Parish, cousins of my grandmother and influential in her early life.

Henry Wallace: FDR's Secretary of Agriculture and later Vice President, but knocked off the ticket of FDR's last term to be replaced by Sen. Harry Truman.

Ivan and Katie Holness: the couple who worked for us in New York City and then in Seattle.

James M. Cox: the Democrats' presidential candidate in 1920 who chose FDR as his running mate.

James Mingo: "GoGo," another factotum among the White House servants, one of my sister's and my favorites.

Joseph Lash: close friend of my grandmother and later, after her death, her authorized biographer. His wife Trude was also a close friend of Grandmère.

Katherine Delano Robbins: Aunt Kassie, sister of my great grandmother.

Lillian Calder: organized the staff at Campobello for Granny as her mother had done before her.

Lorena Hickok: close friend of my grandmother, one not appreciated by her other friends.

Malvina Thompson: "Tommy" to all of us. My grandmother's personal secretary and *the* second grandmother for me.

Margaret Suckley: "Cousin Margaret" to Sis and me but Cousin "Daisy" to the rest of the family, probably one of the most intimate friends my grandfather had.

Marguerite "Missy" LeHand: FDR's personal secretary and confidante, one of my "second grandmothers."

Mademoiselle Margueritte Deschamps: my sister's and my Belgian governess.

Marion Dickerman: "Aunt Marion," and her partner, Nancy Cook, "Aunt Nancy," close friends of my grandmothers.

Mary Livingston Ludlow Hall: Grandmère's grandmother with whom she went to live at age nine, after her mother's death. Her husband was the priggish Valentine Hall.

Mike Reilly: head of FDR's Secret Service detail.

Ruth Goggins: second wife of Elliott Roosevelt, mother of my cousins "Tony," Chandler, and David.

Tom Carmody: "Mody," one of the Secret Service men in Seattle who, along with Hazen, provided company, conversation, and advice.

William Randolph Hearst: newspaper tycoon and for several years my mother and stepfather's boss as publisher of the *Seattle Post-Intelligencer*.

Places

"Algonac": The Delano family homestead, near Newburgh.

"The Big House": The name our family used for our home at Hyde Park. It is formally known as "Springwood," a name FDR didn't like, but the U.S. Park Service has chosen to use. Generally, the family referred to our place simply as "Hyde Park," the name of the nearby village (now quite a big place).

"Campobello": The Roosevelt property on a small island of that name in Canada, just across the Maine border. In the late nineteenth century it was the family's escape from the malaria threat along the Hudson River. The first house built was my great-grandmother's house, which later burned down when Elliott owned it after the war. Granny also built an adjacent house for my grandmother and grandfather when they began to have children. That house is now open to the public, supervised by a joint commission of the U.S. and Canadian governments.

"Oak Terrace": The Hall Family place in Tivoli, where my grandmother lived for many years with her grandmother and aunts and uncles, much in fear of the latter.

"The 65th Street house": Though it has no special name, this was the location of our family's townhouse in New York City, between Madison and Park Avenues. A double house, half was designated for Granny and half for Papa and Grandmère. It was sold by FDR to Hunter College after Granny died.

"The Top Cottage": The house my grandfather built for his retirement. Papa frequently drove us there to observe its construction. In 1944 he used it for visits, but he died before spending a night under its roof. After World War II it became a home for my Uncle Elliott, who then sold it. Years later the Park Service acquired it as a National Historic Site, the same designation for Val Kill and Springwood.

"Val Kill" and "The Stone Cottage": The latter was the first house built at Val Kill for my grandmother and her friends Aunt Marion and Aunt Nancy. Later my grandmother used two of the Val Kill industry buildings to make a separate home for herself. We always referred to it as "Val Kill" to differentiate it from the Stone Cottage, which my grandmother came to own exclusively late in her life. It became the home of my Uncle John and Aunt Ann and their children, my cousins Haven, Nina, Sally, and Joan.

ABOUT THE AUTHOR

Curtis Roosevelt is the oldest grandson of President Franklin Delano Roosevelt and Eleanor Roosevelt. After a long career in the United Nations Secretariat and in university administration he is now retired and lives in France with his wife, Marina.